Michael Oakeshott

Michael Oakeshott

An Introduction

Paul Franco

Yale University Press
New Haven and London

For information about this and other Yale University Press publications, please contact:
U.S. Office: sales.press@yale.edu yalebooks.com
Europe Office: sales@yaleup.co.uk www.yalebooks.co.uk

Designed by Sandy Chapman

Printed in Great Britain by St Edmundsbury Press Ltd, Bury St Edmunds

Library of Congress Cataloging-in-Publication Data

Franco, Paul, 1956-
  Michael Oakeshott : an introduction / Paul Franco.
      p. cm.
  Includes bibliographical references and index.
  ISBN 0-300-10404-9 (alk. paper)
  1. Oakeshott, Michael Joseph, 1901---Contributions in political science. 2. Oakeshott, Michael Joseph, 1901- I. Title.
  JC257.O244F72 2004
  320'.092--dc22   2004009252

A catalogue record for this book is available from the British Library

To the memory of Esther

Contents

Preface

Since 1990, when I published my first book on Michael Oakeshott, interest in his thought has grown steadily. Several books have been devoted to his philosophy, as well as many dissertations and a vast number of articles. In Britain, of course, Oakeshott has long been known outside of academic circles as an important conservative thinker and was even credited (wrongly) as being the philosophical *éminence grise* behind Thatcherism. But even in the United States his name has begun to appear with greater frequency in nonacademic contexts. During the American presidential race of 1996, for example, the *New Yorker* published an article showing how Oakeshott's antirationalist philosophy could be used to justify the absence of vision in both Clinton's and Dole's political campaigns.[1] And a 1999 article in the *New Republic* discussed Oakeshott, along with Leo Strauss, as one of the great Europeans who have shaped modern American conservatism.[2] Of course, during the recent war with Iraq it was Strauss and his neoconservative followers in Washington who got most of the press. But conservative pundit David Brooks ingeniously managed to redress this imbalance by summoning Oakeshott from the dead to hold an imaginary debate over Iraq on the editorial pages of the *New York Times.* While acknowledging that Oakeshott might have had some problems with the effort to impose democracy on a country with a wholly undemocratic tradition, Brooks nevertheless insisted that there was something profoundly Oakeshottian in the planless way the Americans went about the reconstruction of Iraq: like good Oakeshottians, they were "muddling though" and learning from "bumbling experience."[3]

Though none of this is very edifying, it suggests that a general introduction to Oakeshott's thought indicating its continuing relevance into the twenty-first century might be a useful and timely contribution to contemporary political reflection and debate. This is what I have tried to provide in this volume. I focus on Oakeshott's political philosophy, showing how it articulates not only a conservatism that is more compelling and appropriate to our circumstances than other conservatisms but also a theory of liberalism (in the broadest sense) that surpasses other contemporary theories in its philosophical depth, sophistication, and imagination. I do not, however, confine myself to Oakeshott's political philosophy but also examine his important and highly original views on philosophy, history, art, morality, religion, and education. Insofar as

Oakeshott elaborates a political philosophy in which politics is not the highest thing but only a necessary condition for the more substantial fulfillment of human beings in the realm of culture—what he calls the "conversation of mankind"—it is absolutely crucial to explore his reflections on these nonpolitical departments of human experience. In the first chapter of the book, I provide a brief overview of Oakeshott's life with a view to bringing out the character and, above all, the style of the man.

Because I have tried to write a book that will be accessible and interesting to a nonspecialist audience, I have eschewed as much as possible unnecessary references to the growing scholarly literature on Oakeshott. This is not to suggest that such scholarly literature is not worthwhile or that I haven't learned a great deal from it. In general, Oakeshott has been very fortunate in his interpreters. At the end of the book, therefore, I provide a guide to further reading for those interested in pursuing some of the scholarly debates surrounding Oakeshott's philosophy.

I have accrued many debts over the course of writing this book. First and foremost to my editor, Robert Baldock, who several years ago suggested that I write this book and waited patiently for me to get around to it. The Earhart Foundation, Bowdoin College, and the Fletcher Family Fund generously provided grants to support the research and writing of the book. My old teacher Timothy Fuller has remained a constant source of stimulation through his own scholarship on Oakeshott, his work as Oakeshott's literary executor, and his organization of innumerable symposia and conferences on Oakeshott's thought. Ken Minogue shared his reminiscences of Oakeshott with me over a delightful lunch at the London School of Economics. Noel O'Sullivan and his wife, Margot, generously entertained me at their home in Hull and regaled me with stories about Oakeshott as well as with their insights into his philosophy. Noel was also kind enough to show me his collection of personal letters from Oakeshott, from which I have drawn in a couple of places. Leslie Marsh, who started the Michael Oakeshott Association and set up its invaluable website, has been a constant source of useful information. Anna Towlson and her staff were extremely helpful in making available to me the collection of Oakeshott's unpublished manuscripts, notebooks, and letters in the archive of the British Library of Political and Economic Science. My colleagues at Bowdoin, especially Eddie Glaude (alas, now of Princeton), gently forced me to explain from time to time what I was doing and why. My children, Clare and Sam, have given me joy every day of their lives. Sam's friend George kept me honest by continually asking where I was in the book and when I would be done. My wife, Jill, as always, has been *sine qua non*. Finally, my sister Esther, to whose memory this book is dedicated, offered lifelong love, encouragement, and an example of courage that I will never forget.

Abbreviations

References to Oakeshott's works appear in the text with the following abbreviations. BLPES refers to the archives at the British Library of Political and Economic Science at the London School of Economics, where there is a significant collection of unpublished materials (manuscripts, lectures, notebooks, letters, etc.) by and about Oakeshott. Some of these materials have recently been published—alas, too late for me to make use of—in a volume entitled *What is History? and Other Essays*, ed. Luke O'Sullivan (Exeter: Imprint Academic, 2004).

"CBP" "Contemporary British Politics," *Cambridge Journal* 1 (1947–48): 474–90.

"CPJ" "The Concept of a Philosophical Jurisprudence," *Politica* 3 (1938): 203–22, 345–60.

"CS" "The Cambridge School of Political Science," BLPES, File 1/1/2.

"DSM" "A Discussion of Some Matters Preliminary to the Study of Political Philosophy," BLPES, File 1/1/3.

EM *Experience and Its Modes* (Cambridge: Cambridge University Press, 1933).

HCA *Hobbes on Civil Association* (Indianapolis: Liberty Fund, 2000).

"JL" "John Locke," *Cambridge Review* 54 (1932–33): 72–73.

MPME *Morality and Politics in Modern Europe: The Harvard Lectures*, ed. Shirley Letwin (New Haven and London: Yale University Press, 1993).

OH *On History and Other Essays* (Oxford: Basil Blackwell, 1983).

OHC *On Human Conduct* (Oxford: Clarendon Press, 1975).

PFPS *The Politics of Faith and the Politics of Scepticism*, ed. Timothy Fuller (New Haven and London: Yale University Press, 1996).

RP *Rationalism in Politics and Other Essays,* new and expanded edition, ed. Timothy Fuller (Indianapolis: Liberty Fund, 1990).

RPML *Religion, Politics and the Moral Life*, ed. Timothy Fuller (New Haven and London: Yale University Press, 1993).

SPD *The Social and Political Doctrines of Contemporary Europe* (Cambridge: Cambridge University Press, 1939).

"TH" "Thomas Hobbes," *Scrutiny* 4 (1935–36): 263–77.

VLL *The Voice of Liberal Learning: Michael Oakeshott on Education*, ed. Timothy Fuller (New Haven and London: Yale University Press, 1989).

1 The Oakeshottian Voice

> Not to detect a man's style is to have missed three-quarters of the meaning of his actions and utterances.
>
> —Oakeshott, "Learning and Teaching" (*VLL*, 56)

Michael Oakeshott received the best reviews of his career in the obituaries that followed on his death on 18 December 1990. *The Times* of London declared that "Oakeshott was one of the few outstanding political philosophers of the 20th century." The *Guardian* went further and called Oakeshott "perhaps the most original academic political philosopher of this century." The *Independent* chimed in, claiming Oakeshott had provided "the most eloquent and profound philosophical defence of conservative politics that the present century has produced." And, not to be outdone, the *Daily Telegraph* announced flatly that Oakeshott "was the greatest political philosopher in the Anglo-Saxon tradition since Mill—or even Burke." Not bad for a thinker who during his lifetime had frequently been dismissed as a cynical reactionary and a "Tory Dandy."

In the small village on the coast of Dorset in which Oakeshott lived for the last two decades of his life, the impressive obituaries took the villagers quite by surprise. They had known Oakeshott only as a cheerful, if slightly reclusive, man, remarkably youthful for his years, who lived with his artist wife on the outskirts of town in a rustic quarryman's cottage. No one knew that he was a famous philosopher. To the few dozen people who attended the funeral, a somewhat perplexed village pastor announced, "It appears that we have had a very great man living amongst us."[1] It was a fitting epitaph to Oakeshott's legendary self-effacement. Almost all the memoirs following on his death speak of Oakeshott's modesty and unpretentiousness. He eschewed public honors and even declined the Companion of Honour when offered it by Margaret Thatcher. When the Beatles received an MBE, Oakeshott is said to have remarked sardonically, "Perfectly appropriate. Honors go to those who want them."

This last comment points to one of Oakeshott's most salient intellectual traits: his iconoclasm. Unlike his contemporary, Sir Isaiah Berlin, Oakeshott never became part of the intellectual or political Establishment in Britain; indeed, he spent most of his career mocking it. Appropriately, Noel Annan classifies Oakeshott—along with Evelyn Waugh and F. R. Leavis—as one of the great "deviants" of the generation of

British intellectuals who came of age between the wars, someone "who repudiated almost all of [Our Age's] beliefs and assumptions."[2] In the 1920s and '30s, he rejected the positivism that was dominant in the social sciences and resisted the analytic tide in philosophy. After the war, he criticized the collectivism and central social planning that marked the policies not only of Attlee but also of conservatives like Macmillan. Finally, throughout his career, Oakeshott was implacably opposed to the powerful trend toward the politicization of knowledge, the dinning claims that history and philosophy should be relevant, engaged, and in the service of practice. It is precisely because he was, in Nietzsche's phrase, "untimely" (*unzeitgemässe*) that Oakeshott remains of interest to us today.

Michael Joseph Oakeshott was born in Chelsfield, Kent, on 11 December 1901, and he died (as already mentioned) on 18 December 1990. To put this in perspective, he was born in the year that Queen Victoria died, and he died one year after the Berlin Wall fell and one year before the Soviet Union followed the same route. He lived through virtually every important event of the twentieth century: both world wars; the rise and fall of fascism; the Cold War; the rise and fall of communism; and, of course, the steady decline of Britain from the most powerful country in the world to a struggling middling power. Based on the death and destruction wrought, it was the darkest of centuries. But for this reason it was not entirely alien to the political philosopher. As Oakeshott once remarked: "it is characteristic of political philosophers that they take a sombre view of the human situation: they deal in darkness" (*HCA*, 6).

Despite this, Oakeshott's early years seem to have been happy ones. His father, a civil servant in the Inland Revenue, was a Fabian socialist, but this does not seem to have had much of an effect on the young Oakeshott, either as a positive influence or as something to react against. According to Oakeshott, his father "never talked politics at home," he "was never a 'party' man," and "his interests were always more literary than political."[3] Unlike so many of his contemporaries who became prominent writers or intellectuals, Oakeshott did not attend one of the great public schools but instead was educated at a progressive coeducational institution, St George's School, Harpenden. His experience there seems to have been free of the regimentation and worship of games that made places like Eton so unbearable to his contemporaries; instead it was open to genuine intellectual exploration and the cultivation of aesthetic and moral sensibility. Oakeshott fondly recalled St George's as "a place surrounded by a thick, firm hedge, and inside this hedge was a world of beckoning activities and interests. . . . There was a great deal of laughter and fun; there was a great deal of seriousness."[4]

In 1920, Oakeshott went up to Gonville and Caius College at Cambridge. He took the Political Science option of the History Tripos—there was, of course, no separate Political Science department—and in 1922 and 1923 respectively, he received first class honors on both parts of the exam. After completing the Tripos, Oakeshott traveled to Germany to study theology at Marburg and Tübingen in 1923–24 and possibly again in 1925. This has led to speculation that he may have heard lectures by Heidegger, who was teaching at Marburg at the time, but there is very little evidence, at least in Oakeshott's writings, to suggest that he did, or, if he did, that it made much of an impact.[5] In 1925, based on a dissertation that no longer survives, Oakeshott won a Fellowship at Gonville and Caius that enabled him to do research and eventually to teach in the College.

Though we do not have his dissertation, there are several unpublished and posthumously published manuscripts that give a clear idea of Oakeshott's thinking at this time. One of the earliest is a 1924 paper entitled "The Cambridge School of Political Science," in which Oakeshott made some rather pointed criticisms of the political science curriculum at Cambridge through which he had just passed. He criticized the Cambridge School for treating political science as a natural science, focusing on the purely empirical classification of political institutions and forms of government instead of on a philosophical understanding of human nature and the essential state. "If the term Political Science is to have any valid meaning at all," he wrote, "it must refer to a *moral* and not a natural science, that is, our subject is more properly named Political Philosophy than anything else" ("CS," 19–20). Accordingly, he suggested that the Political Science syllabus be reformed so that the first part consists of the history of political philosophy and the second part of a philosophical consideration of the nature and end of the state.

A similar critique of positivistic political science can be found in two manuscripts from 1925, "A Discussion of Some Matters Preliminary to the Study of Political Philosophy" and "Some Remarks on the Meaning and Nature of Sociality." In the former—which may, in fact, be the lost fellowship dissertation—Oakeshott distinguished political philosophy from more limited inquiries such as science, history, psychology, and political economy, insisting that "political philosophy is not a science," but "an effort to come at the true meaning and implication of the complex thing we call political life." Nothing has caused greater mis-understanding in the study of political life in recent times, he claims, than the failure to keep the distinction between philosophy and science "clearly before our minds" ("DSM," 52, 56–57). Along the same lines, he complained in "The Nature and Meaning of Sociality" that "the use of false and misleading metaphors" drawn from mechanics and biology have completely distorted our understanding of social life. The true nature of human sociality does not disclose itself in the behavior of ants and prairie dogs. "The essence of society . . . does not submit to purely naturalistic explanation. . . . [S]ociety is a moral fact and not a natural fact" (*RPML*, 47, 49–50).

In addition to being antipositivistic, these early writings of Oakeshott's were also thoroughly informed by philosophical idealism. British idealism—the school of T. H. Green, F. H. Bradley, Bernard Bosanquet, and J. M. E. McTaggart, among others—was, of course, by this time on the ropes at Cambridge, having been undermined by the "refutations" of G. E. Moore and Bertrand Russell. Nevertheless, there remained pockets of idealism in the university, especially among those who studied ethics, political philosophy, or theology. As a student, Oakeshott had taken McTaggart's Introduction to the Study of Philos-ophy, and he was quite close to the idealist historian of ethics W. R. Sorley, who is thanked in the preface to *Experience and Its Modes*.[6] Ernest Barker, the first occupant of the Chair of Political Science at Cambridge from 1927 to 1939 and a close colleague and friend of Oakeshott's, was partially influenced by British idealism.[7]

In his earliest writings, Oakeshott's debt to idealism was chiefly reflected in his understanding of the interdependence of self and society. He criticized utilitarianism, for example, for failing to grasp this inter-dependence and treating society as an aggregate of isolated selves instead of as a genuine social whole. Appealing to Hegel, Bradley, and Bosan-quet (and also to Plato and Aristotle), he denied that the self is some-thing opposed to society; rather, the self requires society for its fullest development. In his rejection of traditional liberal individualism, Oakeshott used the most extravagant idealist language, claiming that a "self not only requires its society, but in the fullest sense *is* its society." And: "The self is the State; the State is the self." And finally: "'Man *versus* the State' is sheer nonsense" ("DSM," 131, 133, 137).

Apart from political philosophy, Oakeshott's other great interest at this time was religion and theology. In the 1920s, he was a regular reviewer for the *Journal of Theological Studies*, he belonged to a group of Cambridge dons who met regularly to discuss and present papers on theology, and he wrote several essays on religion. In many of the reviews and essays, Oakeshott's purpose was apologetic, but not in any orthodox way. He was concerned to defend religion against the criticisms of science and especially history, which he did by arguing that religion was not to be judged by its theoretical truth but by a pragmatic criterion. "Religion is, after all," he wrote in one place, "nothing if not practical."[8] Following Bradley, he saw religion as the "completion" or "consummation" of morality, providing the endless and debilitating "ought" of the latter with an "is" that is both comforting and energizing (*RPML*, 41–42). The promise of religion is not happiness in another world but a more intense way of living in this one. In one of the most interesting essays from this period, "Religion and the World" (1929), Oakeshott argued that the "world" to which religion is opposed does not refer to everything that belongs to earthly life but to a scale of values that prizes success and external achievement above all else and sacrifices everything in the present to future results. Religion rejects this worldly, "careerist ideal" and promotes a wholly "extemporary life" in which each moment contains the meaning of the whole. For Oakeshott, the religious life "is synonymous with life itself at its fullest, there can be no revival of religion which is not a revival of a more daring and sensitive way of living" (*RPML*, 30–35).

By the end of the twenties, Oakeshott was fully engaged in the life of a Cambridge don. He delivered his first course of lectures in the Lent term of 1928 on the subject of The Philosophical Approach to Politics.[9] As the title suggests, he was once again concerned with the methodological issue of what a philosophical approach to politics consists in and how it differs from other, less concrete approaches. In what was clearly a dry run for *Experience and Its Modes*, he examined three types of thinking—scientific, historical, and practical—and showed them all to be abstract in comparison with the concrete thinking of philosophy. By 1931, Oakeshott was lecturing regularly as a member of the History faculty on utilitarianism and idealist political thought, as well as on the core courses for the Political Science option of the Historical Tripos, History of Political Thought and Theory of the Modern State. Under the leadership of Barker, these latter courses had replaced the non-theoretical courses of the older syllabus, more or less along the lines Oakeshott had proposed in 1924.

In 1933, Oakeshott published his first book, *Experience and Its Modes*. It is a bold and unusually precocious book—Oakeshott was only 31 years old when it was published—devoted to working out the implications of the idea of philosophy as "experience without presupposition, reservation, arrest, or modification" (*EM*, 2). As he did in his earlier lectures, he developed this idea of philosophy by examining the forms of experience of science, history, and practice and showing them to be abstract and incomplete in comparison with the concrete standpoint of philosophy. That philosophy is superior to these abstract modes of experience does not mean, however, that it can dictate to them. Oakeshott argued that within its own sphere, every mode is autonomous and immune from the authority of other forms of experience. To use the thinking that belongs to one form of experience to criticize another is to commit the fallacy of irrelevance or *ignoratio elenchi*. Thus history is independent of science and the practical attitude, and practice has nothing to learn or fear from history or science. Most importantly, philosophy has nothing to contribute to practical or political life. "What is farthest from our needs," Oakeshott wrote, "is that kings should be philosophers" (*EM*, 321).

It perhaps seems strange that Oakeshott's first book was devoted wholly to the theory of knowledge, mentioning political philosophy only once—in a footnote. But nothing was clearer in his writings from the 1920s than that such a methodological prolegomenon was necessary before the substantive issues of political philosophy could be taken up. As early as 1925 he had stated clearly that no progress could be made in any area of philosophical inquiry before we had a proper theory of knowledge or "theory of theorizing." "Ethics, the so-called philosophy of religion, politics, aesthetic, all departments of speculation, depend upon a theory of knowledge." A "political philosophy founded upon no metaphysical prolegomenon, or upon one fundamentally in error, is doomed to propagate not truth, but falsehood" ("DSM," 10, 187–88). *Experience and Its Modes* was that metaphysical prolegomenon.

Oakeshott frankly acknowledged in the introduction to his book that his argument "derives all that is valuable in it from its affinity to what is known by the somewhat ambiguous name of Idealism, and that the works from which I am conscious of having learnt most are Hegel's *Phänomenologie des Geistes* and Bradley's *Appearance and Reality*" (*EM*, 6). No statement could have been more perfectly designed to guarantee that the book would not receive a fair hearing in the philosophical atmosphere of the 1930s, dominated as it was by logical positivism. Predictably, Susan Stebbing concluded her review in *Mind* by saying that "those who have not been convinced by Bradley are not likely to be converted by Mr. Oakeshott."[10] But this missed what was fresh in Oakeshott's book. It is true that Oakeshott's outlook was heavily indebted to Bradley, but what was new was the way he applied this outlook to distinctively twentieth-century problems, the most important of which was: What in this age of science and social science is the task of philosophy? In its preoccupation with twentieth-century positivism and the problem of history, Oakeshott's idealism was much closer to that of R. G. Collingwood and Benedetto Croce than to nineteenth-century British idealism.

Not surprisingly, Collingwood gave *Experience and Its Modes* a glowing review, calling the chapter on history "the most penetrating analysis of historical thought that has ever been written."[11] There is a story that he burst into his lectures at Oxford one day waving a copy of *Experience and Its Modes* and announced that it was the greatest philosophical achievement of the twentieth century.[12] Unfortunately, Collingwood's view did not carry the day—at least not immediately—and it took over 30 years for the first thousand copies of *Experience and Its Modes* to sell out. Since 1966, however, as the influence of analytic philosophy (especially in its early, logical-positivistic guise) has waned, the book has been reprinted three times.

One of the things that gives *Experience and Its Modes* its continuing power is its style. Like his mentor, F. H. Bradley, Oakeshott is a marvelous philosophical stylist; indeed, one can hear echoes of Bradley in Oakeshott's polemical dismissal of various philosophical positions as absurd, monstrous, and grotesque. But the style of *Experience and Its Modes* is ultimately not as highly wrought, metaphorical, or idiosyncratic as Bradley's; it is Bradley tamed by Hume. At once elegant and conversational, it is a style that never slips into technical jargon or lifeless abstraction. And though allusive, it is never heavily erudite; "philosophy, more often than not, has foundered in learning" (*EM*, 8). The book is certainly not bereft of argument—indeed, it contains more explicit argumentation than any of Oakeshott's later works; nevertheless, it tends to proceed by building up an overall picture of the universe of knowledge. It is also, as has been observed by others, a young man's book, written with a self-confidence and grandness of design that Oakeshott never quite replicated in his later writings.

Oakeshott spent the rest of the 1930s drawing out the implications of the idea of philosophy defended in *Experience and Its Modes* for political philosophy. In the most important of his methodological writings from this period, "The Concept of a Philosophical Jurisprudence" (1938), he criticized several of the most prominent conceptions of the philosophy of law from the standpoint of his idea of philosophy as "thought and knowledge without reservation or presupposition."

Oakeshott also began to write on the history of political philosophy, with essays on Locke and Bentham and two lengthy reviews of books on Hobbes. To this period also belongs the book that Oakeshott co-authored with Guy Griffith, *A Guide to the Classics* (1936), which, to the disappointment of many an earnest student of political philosophy, turned out to be, not about Plato and Aristotle, but about the fine art of picking a Derby winner.

In addition to writing, Oakeshott kept up a busy teaching schedule at this time, achieving a reputation as a dazzling lecturer. Noel Annan, who attended Oakeshott's lectures on the modern state in 1937–38, says he was bowled over by them: "There was no lecturer in the history faculty who held a candle to him other than Munia Postan." He remembers especially that Oakeshott gave "dazzling metaphors justifying, or at any rate putting up a very strong case for, the Hegelian concept of the state and its relation to society and public opinion."[13]

Outside the academy, the world, of course, was in political and economic crisis. The principal events are familiar: a worldwide economic depression; the rise of Hitler in Germany; the problem of chronic unemployment (dramatized in 1936 by the march of the men of Jarrow to London); the Moscow show trials; the Spanish Civil War; British pacifism/appeasement; and finally, the outbreak of war in 1939. Against this background, artists and intellectuals became increasingly politicized, generally in a Marxist direction. Even Cambridge did not escape the noise of history. Anthony Blunt, Guy Burgess, Donald Maclean, and Kim Philby began their careers as Soviet spies. The distinguished physicist and lifelong Communist, J. D. Bernal, tirelessly organized and propagandized on behalf of his cause. And even Oakeshott's close friend at Caius, the young historian of science Joseph Needham, wrote a wildly sympathetic review of Sidney and Beatrice Webb's unreadable tome, *Soviet Communism: A New Civilization?*, extolling the virtues of Soviet Man.[14]

Where did Oakeshott stand on all of this? It is characteristic (and also somewhat frustrating) that he did not take a stand at all, at least not in his writings. As we know, a cardinal feature of his conception of political philosophy was that it had nothing to contribute to practical or political life. When F. R. Leavis's *Scrutiny* sponsored a symposium on The Claims of Politics in its September 1939 issue, Oakeshott took the opportunity to restate his view on the nonpolitical character of philosophy and of culture in general. Denying that there is an obligation for everyone to take a direct part in political activity, he wrote:

Politics is a highly specialized and abstracted form of communal activity . . . conducted on the surface of the life of a society . . . A limitation of view, which appears so clear and practical, but which amounts to little more than a mental fog, is inseparable from political activity. A mind fixed and callous to all subtle distinctions, emotional and intellectual habits become bogus from repetition and lack of examination, unreal loyalties, delusive aims, false significances are what political action involves. (*RPML*, 93)

This was not an easy—nor perhaps a wise—thing to say in September of 1939. Nevertheless, Oakeshott's position was not without its own ambiguity. For though he denied that literature, art, and philosophy should engage directly in political activity, he ultimately assigned them the far more important role of recreating the values of society and thus protecting it from a "corruption of consciousness" (*RPML*, 95).

It is in this spirit that Oakeshott's own meager contributions to political discourse in the 1930s should be understood. He certainly did engage with the political doctrines that filled his contemporaries with passionate intensity, but he refused to become an ideologue. Thus, in a review of a book on dialectical materialism, he criticized the authors not so much for their Marxist views as for the dogmatic and unphilosophical way in which they defended them. Of Bernal's contributions to the book he wrote, "they might have been written by Engels himself; his exposition is not even fresh in its parts, it is uniformly stale." This is not true of Marx himself, whose philosophy contains "some profound and illuminating *aperçus*."[15] It is interesting to note that no don at Cambridge lectured on Marx until Oakeshott did so in 1938.[16]

Around this time, at the instigation of Barker, Oakeshott put together a volume of primary documents relating to the principal social and political doctrines current in Europe: representative democracy, Catholicism, communism, and fascism. His selections concisely illustrated the main tenets of these doctrines, and his introduction reflected the intellectual detachment demanded by his conception of political philosophy. He refused to simply condemn communism and fascism: the former, he wrote, is, "among the new doctrines, the one from which we have most to learn"; and the "Fascist criticism of Liberal Democracy is far too acute to be merely ignored." He was also quite critical of representative democracy, locating its chief weaknesses in its theoretical individualism and its materialistic ethical ideal. The latter he referred to scornfully— pinching a phrase from D. H. Lawrence—as "the plausible ethics of productivity."[17] Nevertheless, he conceded that representative democracy contains "a more comprehensive expression of our civilization than any of the others." And his own moral conviction peeked through when he asserted that what ultimately separates liberal democracy from communism and fascism is that it regards "the imposition of a universal plan of life on a society [as] at once stupid and immoral" (*SPD*, xviii–xxi).

Oakeshott did not shrink from defending this conviction when war broke out. He enlisted in the army in 1940 and served until 1945 in an intelligence unit called "Phantom," whose mission was to penetrate behind enemy lines and report on the effectiveness of artillery targeting. The conservative journalist Peregrine Worsthorne, who served in the same unit, tells the story that Oakeshott, now in his forties, engaged in all sorts of "unsuitable escapades" with his younger fellow officers and never let on that he was a famous Cambridge don. Returning to Cambridge after the war and attending a lecture by the celebrated M. J. Oakeshott, Worsthorne was shocked to see his old army friend mount the podium.[18] The story perhaps strains credulity. It is hard to believe that Oakeshott's comrades had no idea what he did; and, indeed, one fellow officer recalled that everyone knew that Oakeshott was a don at Cambridge.[19] Nevertheless, the story captures the modesty and unpretentiousness for which Oakeshott was so famous.

After the war, Oakeshott returned to his teaching duties at Cambridge. Barker had wanted him to succeed him in the Chair of Political Science, but the post went instead to D. W. Brogan, a historian of American political thought. Still, Oakeshott had much to keep him busy. He was asked to edit Hobbes's *Leviathan* for the Blackwell's Political Texts series, and from this came his celebrated Introduction to *Leviathan* in 1946. Interestingly, Oakeshott had not originally wanted to work on Hobbes, but when he asked if he could do somebody else, he was told "everything else had been dished out."[20] The unwanted assignment proved to be fortunate, for not only is Oakeshott's Introduction to *Leviathan* one of the most important essays on Hobbes in the twentieth century, it also gave Oakeshott the opportunity to ponder deeply the thinker who was to exert a powerful influence on his own political philosophy. In Hobbes's radical skepticism about the role of reason in politics and his understanding of the interdependence of authority and individuality, Oakeshott found a message that was relevant to his own troubled age. In one of the most revealing passages in the Introduction, he wrote: "it is Reason, not Authority, that is destructive of individuality. . . . Hobbes is not an absolutist precisely because he is an authoritarian. His scepticism about the power of reasoning . . .

together with the rest of his individualism, separate him from the rationalist dictators of his or any age" (*HCA*, 67).

In 1947, Oakeshott took over the editorship of the newly founded
Cambridge Journal and began to write a series of remarkable essays that
trenchantly criticized the collectivist policies of the Attlee government
and the rationalist mentality that lay behind them. These essays—
"Rationalism in Politics" (1947), "Scientific Politics" (1948), "Contem-
porary British Politics" (1948), "The Tower of Babel" (1948), "The
Political Economy of Freedom" (1949), "The Universities" (1949),
"Rational Conduct" (1950), and "The BBC" (1951)—attracted consid-
erable attention and transformed Oakeshott from a well-regarded
Cambridge don into a major public intellectual. Noel Annan recalls:
"When I returned to Cambridge after the war it was not Leavis to whom
one referred when discussing general ideas. It was Oakeshott."[21]

Oakeshott framed his critique of central social planning in postwar
Britain in terms of a larger critique of rationalism. What more than anything else characterized the rationalist mentality for him was its reductive attitude toward experience, its desire to reduce "the tangle and
variety of experience to a set of principles," its "irritable nervousness in
the face of everything topical and transitory" (*RP*, 6, 7). In politics this
reductive mentality translated into a preference for ideological politics
—the simplicity and (illusory) self-containedness of a set of abstract
principles being rated more highly than the complexity and relative
open-endedness of a tradition of behavior. In addition to being ideological, rationalist politics were also the politics of destruction and creation as opposed to the politics of repair and reform. For the rationalist,
"political activity consists in bringing the social, political, legal and institutional inheritance of his society before the tribunal of his intellect,"
the "consciously planned and deliberately executed" being considered
"better than what has grown up and established itself unselfconsciously
over a period of time" (*RP*, 8, 26). There was a distinct echo of Burke
in this critique of rationalist politics, though Oakeshott himself
grounded it in more strictly epistemological considerations deriving
from his idealism.

How did all this relate to the idea of central planning favored by the
postwar Attlee government? Oakeshott argued that a "centrally planned
society is the ideal of all rationalistic politics" ("CBP," 478), radically
simplifying the complexity of society by imposing a single purpose on
it and concentrating power in the hands of the government to execute
that purpose. Such concentration of power inevitably leads to despotism, albeit of a mild, mediocre sort that makes it more difficult to detect

than old-fashioned tyranny: "Our political observation has been educated to detect only the despot who, in Lincoln's words, belongs to 'the family of the lion or the tribe of the eagle.' Suspecting a tyranny, we look for a Strafford and find only a Cripps, we look for a Cromwell and find only Clem Attlee—and we are reassured" ("CBP," 485). Oakeshott believed the recent experience of war had done much to nourish the ideal of central planning, but he rejected the view, common at the time, that society in wartime should be used as a model for society in peacetime:

> In war all that is most superficial in our tradition is encouraged merely because it is useful, even necessary, for victory. . . . There are many who have no other idea of social progress than the extrapolation of the character of society in time of war—the artificial unity, the narrow overmastering purpose, the devotion to a single cause and the subordination of everything to it—all this seems to them inspiring: but the direction of their admiration reveals the emptiness of their souls. (*VLL*, 116)

Oakeshott was not, of course, the only one making these points. Friedrich Hayek had published his own tract against central social planning, *The Road to Serfdom*, in 1944. In that book, he, too, had attacked the fashionable view that the lessons of war, in which everything is subordinated to a single purpose, should be applied in peacetime. Nevertheless, despite the many similarities between Hayek's critique of central social planning and his own, Oakeshott criticized *The Road to Serfdom* for ultimately being too ideological. The main significance of Hayek's book, he wrote, is "not the cogency of the doctrine, but the fact that it is a doctrine. A plan to resist all planning may be better than its opposite, but it belongs to the same style of politics" (*RP*, 26). This may seem a tad ungenerous, but it highlighted a serious philosophical difference between the two thinkers. Hayek's emphasis on the need to formulate a liberal ideology to combat collectivist ideologies[22] was ultimately not compatible with Oakeshott's critique of all ideologies. More generally, Oakeshott always harbored deep reservations about Hayek's instrumental defense of liberty in terms of its propensity to promote economic efficiency and prosperity.

Oakeshott's essays in the *Cambridge Journal* represented a departure from the purely philosophical voice of *Experience and Its Modes*, and their polemical character has led some of his admirers to assign them a subordinate place in his oeuvre. But these essays are nothing to be embarrassed about. Though polemical, they are informed by

Oakeshott's distinctive philosophical perspective. They are also insightful, elegant, and often quite funny. Of the last attribute, I will give but
one example, taken from an essay in which Oakeshott derisively attacked
the BBC in its self-appointed role as improver of public taste and school-
master to the nation. He wrote:

> Consider the News Bulletins broadcast by the B.B.C. . . . The world
> as it appears in the pages of a newspaper is a thing of rags and tatters,
> grim, grotesque, erratic and entertaining, and any sensible man
> chooses his newspaper for the quality of imagination which has gone
> to compose the picture it offers: truth, except in dull detail, nobody
> asks for. With this, of course, a B.B.C. bulletin cannot compete: the
> picture of the world it offers is necessarily selective. But it is selected
> with a gravity which no newspaper would emulate. The world as it
> appears to the B.B.C. has room for trivialities, but their triviality is
> underlined; no listener is left in any doubt that life is earnest. "The
> object," says the Memorandum [submitted to the Broadcasting Com-
> mittee], "is to state the news of the day accurately, fairly, soberly, and
> impersonally," but to complete the catalogue the word "continuously"
> should have been added. No doubt we owe the multiplicity of news
> bulletins to the war, but is it in the public interest, and to what inter-
> pretation of the social purpose does it belong, to keep the listening
> pubic informed, in a continuous situation report, about the dull
> and doubtful detail of the serious nonsense that is taking place all
> over the world? . . . [L]istening to the news is becoming a nervous
> ailment.[23]

In 1950, after a brief stint at Oxford, Oakeshott was offered the Chair
of Political Science at the London School of Economics and Political
Science, which had become vacant on the death of Harold Laski. The
news that the conservative Oakeshott was to succeed to the Chair held
by Laski and Graham Wallas in the home of Fabian socialism was
greeted with dismay on the left. R. H. S. Crossman wrote indignantly
in the *New Statesman* that "a cavalier iconoclast, [Oakeshott] marches
with his pick-axe into the portals of the School, dedicated by the Webbs
to the scientific study of the improvement of human society; and there
he smashes, one by one, the idols with which Laski and Wallas adorned
its walls."[24] Oakeshott himself drew attention to the irony of his assum-
ing the Chair at LSE in the opening remarks of his celebrated inaugural lecture, "Political Education": "it perhaps seems a little ungrateful
that [Laski and Wallas] should be followed by a sceptic; one who would
do better if only he knew how" (*RP*, 44).

In the rest of the lecture, he went on to criticize what he called the ideological style of politics, arguing that it rests on a mistaken understanding of the nature of political activity and of the knowledge necessary to conduct it. A political ideology—like the Declaration of the Rights of Man or Locke's *Second Treatise*—is merely an abridgment of a concrete political tradition and therefore should never be taken as a self-sufficient or self-contained ground of political activity. Politics is necessarily the exploration of what is intimated in a tradition of political behavior, which tradition has no "changeless centre" or "sovereign purpose" (*RP*, 61). Oakeshott summed up his skeptical understanding of politics in a memorable (and to some, nihilistic) image:

> In political activity, then, men sail a boundless and bottomless sea; there is neither harbour for shelter nor floor for anchorage, neither starting-place nor appointed destination. The enterprise is to keep afloat on an even keel; the sea is both friend and enemy; and the seamanship consists in using the resources of a traditional manner of behaviour in order to make a friend of every hostile occasion. (*RP*, 60)

The next few years did not see much writing but were taken up with Oakeshott's teaching duties at the LSE—which included his legendary lectures on the history of political thought—and his administrative duties as head of the Government Department. In the latter capacity, he introduced various speakers passing through the LSE, including on one rather famous occasion Isaiah Berlin, who had been invited to deliver the first Auguste Comte Memorial Lecture in May of 1953. The title of Berlin's lecture was "History as an Alibi," later revised as the essay "Historical Inevitability." Speaking to a capacity crowd in the LSE auditorium, full of luminaries from LSE, Oxford, and Cambridge, Oakeshott began his introduction by remarking that 1953 marked the centenary of Comte's death—Comte actually died in 1857—adding archly: "And what a century it has been for him!" Then he turned his irony on Berlin, who had recently delivered six enormously popular lectures on BBC radio devoted to assorted thinkers from Helvetius to de Maistre: "There is no need for me to introduce, much less recommend, Mr. Isaiah Berlin to you. His learning is notorious, and joined with it is a brilliant turn of dialectic which has dazzled many audiences. Listening to him you may be tempted to think you are in the presence of one of the great intellectual *virtuosos* of our time: a Paganini of ideas."[25] The reference to Paganini suggested that Berlin's intellectual history contained more show than philosophical substance; and apparently

Oakeshott's ironic tone underlined the insult. Berlin was so unnerved by the introduction that he abandoned his usual custom of speaking extemporaneously and ended up giving "the worst lecture of his life."[26]

Reflecting on the incident later in life, Berlin interpreted "the bitchy introduction" as revenge for an innocent remark he had made to Oakeshott several years earlier—most likely in 1949–50—during a lunch at Nuffield College in Oxford.[27] Apparently, Berlin suggested that Oakeshott should write a book on Hegel and exclaimed that "the need for such a book was so great that better one written by a charlatan than by no one at all."[28] Needless to say, Oakeshott was not persuaded to write the book on Hegel (a pity, too). That his later, barbed introduction for Berlin at the LSE was some sort of revenge for this earlier episode, however, seems doubtful. It is more likely that Oakeshott was drawing ironic attention to the difference between Berlin's history-of-ideas approach to political thought and his own more philosophical approach. Whatever the reason was, the two thinkers, despite their shared antipathy to utopian or rationalistic politics and their common devotion to liberal pluralism, had almost nothing to do with one another for the rest of their lives.

Oakeshott's next important piece of writing on politics was the 1956 essay "On Being Conservative." This essay disclosed a subtle shift in his thinking on politics, reflected in his rejection of Burke as a useful guide for modern conservatism.[29] The problem with Burke and his modern followers was that they sought to buttress conservatism with controversial metaphysical or religious beliefs, for example, in natural law or a providential order. Such speculative beliefs, however, were not necessary to defend the conservative disposition in politics, Oakeshott argued. All that was needed was the recognition that in our current circumstances, marked by radical individuality and diversity, the conservative understanding of government as a limited and specific activity was more appropriate than the alternative understanding of government as the imposition of a substantive conception of the common good. "It is not at all inconsistent," he wrote, "to be conservative in respect of government and radical in respect of almost every other activity" (*RP*, 435). For this reason, he suggested that we would do better to listen to a conservative skeptic like Hume than to a cosmic Tory like Burke.

Oakeshott's skeptical conservatism did not appeal to many on the right. The neoconservative intellectual Irving Kristol, for example, relates how he regretfully rejected "On Being Conservative" for publication in *Encounter* in 1956. He found Oakeshott's conservatism "irredeemably secular" and at odds with the ideological, "creedal," mentality of Americans. Precisely because of its ideological character—the very thing Oakeshott had disparaged—Hayek's polemic against socialism struck more of a chord with Americans. And even more resonant were Leo Strauss's writings, which did not seek an accommodation with modernity but defended conservatism on the basis of ancient natural law and metaphysical truth.[30] Oakeshott and Strauss are undoubtedly the two most important conservative theorists of the second half of the twentieth century, but their conservatisms are diametrically opposed. One writer has characterized the difference in terms of "Little Conservatism" (Oakeshott) versus "Big Conservatism" (Strauss).[31] While these labels certainly do not exhaust the issue, they point to what remains a fundamental divide within contemporary conservative thought.

From quite early in his career, as we have seen, Oakeshott was concerned with the despotism of practice over the whole range of human experience and the politicization of history, philosophy, and art. It was not surprising, then, that he became quite interested in the issue of education in the 1950s and wrote more than half a dozen essays on the subject over the next 25 years. Besides his inaugural lecture, "Political Education," these essays included: "The Universities" (1949), "The Idea of a University" (1950), "The Study of Politics in a University" (1961), "Learning and Teaching" (1967), "Education: The Engagement and Its Frustration" (1971), and "A Place of Learning" (1975).[32] Noel Annan does not exaggerate when he claims that these essays composed "the finest evocation of 'the idea of a university' since Newman."[33] Their recurrent theme was the corruption liberal education suffers when it is harnessed to the practical and worldly imperatives of "training," "social purpose," and "relevance," instead of being understood as an initiation into the rich intellectual inheritance that composes our civilization. This inheritance is radically diverse, consisting of a vast variety of intellectual pursuits, and Oakeshott disdained the attempt to integrate it in terms of a unified philosophy of life, a *Weltanschauung*, or "a sticky mess called 'culture.'" Instead, he pictured the unity of the world of liberal learning in terms of the image of "conversation," in which the various modes of knowledge appear, not as competitors, but as complementary voices "whose tone is neither tyrannous nor plangent, but humble and conversable" (*VLL*, 98).

This image of conversation received its definitive articulation in Oakeshott's important and beautiful essay on aesthetics, "The Voice of Poetry in the Conversation of Mankind" (1959). Characterizing the essay as "a belated retraction of a foolish sentence in *Experience and Its Modes*"—where he had treated art as a subset of practice—Oakeshott felt the reconsideration of the voice of poetry to be especially important because "in recent centuries the conversation, both in public and in private, has become boring because it has become engrossed by two voices, the voice of practical activity and the voice of 'science': to know and to contrive are our pre-eminent preoccupations" (*RP*, 493). Poetry is to be sharply distinguished from both these preoccupations; it neither serves a practical purpose nor reveals the truth of things. The images it creates provoke neither theoretical inquiry nor moral approval/disapproval; they provoke only "delight" in or "contemplation" of what they are, as they are. Poetry provides a respite from "curiosity and contrivance"; it "is a sort of truancy, a dream within the dream of life, a wild flower planted among our wheat" (*RP*, 541).

This was a view of *l'art pour l'art* that would have made even Oscar Wilde blanch. It was not, however, the only thing "The Voice of Poetry" was about. In considering the place of poetry on the map of human activity, Oakeshott also engaged in a thorough reconsideration of the great theme of *Experience and Its Modes*: namely, the relationship of the modes of experience to one another and to philosophy. As far as the relationship of the modes to each other was concerned, the idea of conversation did not radically alter the understanding found in *Experience and Its Modes*. The emphasis remained on the ineliminable diversity of the voices or modes and their autonomy with respect to one another. What did change in "The Voice of Poetry" was Oakeshott's conception of philosophy. No longer referring to philosophy as "experience without presupposition, reservation, arrest or modification," Oakeshott now insisted that he did not know "where to place an experience released altogether from modality" (*RP*, 512). Philosophy was no longer to be understood as concrete experience, superior to the abstract modes, but as one voice among other voices in a conversation without hierarchy. Despite this change, however, the task of philosophy remained largely the same as it had been in *Experience and Its Modes*: "to study the quality and style of each voice, and to reflect upon the relationship of one voice to another" (*RP*, 491).

In 1962, Oakeshott gathered together many of the essays he had written between 1947 and 1961 and published them as a book under the title *Rationalism in Politics and Other Essays*. Over the next 13 years, until the publication of *On Human Conduct* in 1975, he published very little. Teaching and administering the Government Department of LSE continued to demand much of his time. In the mid-1960s, he set up a one-year Master's course on the History of Political Thought, which attracted a devoted following of graduate students, many of them American. The approach of the seminar was novel in that it concerned itself more with historiographical issues than with the long march through the whole history of political philosophy (though students were required to spend the year studying one great text—either Plato's *Republic*, Aristotle's *Politics*, Hobbes's *Leviathan*, Rousseau's *Social Contract*, or Hegel's *Philosophy of Right*). The seminar began by considering the nature of history in general; and it was in this context that Oakeshott, returning to the issues he had tackled as a young man in *Experience and Its Modes*, read the papers that would eventually be published in revised form as "Three Essays on History" in *On History and Other Essays* (1983). After this, the seminar went on to consider the nature of intellectual history and eventually narrowed its focus to the nature of the history of political thought, analyzing such figures as Strauss, Popper, Macpherson, Pocock, and Skinner. Oakeshott continued to preside over this seminar even after his retirement, until about 1980.[34]

Retirement came in 1968, and with it the usual honors, which Oakeshott greeted with characteristic modesty. When presented with a festschrift in his honor, he wryly observed that the editors were making a "dreadful mistake," treating him as "some sort of a guru or sage. But I knew I wasn't anything like that. The best I could think of myself as was a rather broken-down tutor who lives vicariously in the brilliance of his pupils. A hack-teacher." He also commented that, though it was gratifying to be honored as a scholar "because it is what I would have liked to have been," he didn't really deserve the title. "I had the temperament, the will and the patience, but I lacked the ability. And that's rather pathetic. I succeeded only in looking like a fat girl in a mini-skirt. The spirit is willing but the flesh is weak."[35] In his retirement speech in June of 1969, he poignantly captured the unworldliness that marked his entire outlook on life: "Some people say the world's the thing; and the rare glimpses of it I have had suggest that they may be right. I, too, have dabbled in it from time to time. But, on the whole, I have found it overrated." And he contrasted his propensity for playfulness with the solemnity and overseriousness of the philosophical tortoise: "And although I too have tried to be a philosopher, happiness kept breaking through."[36]

During these years in which he published little, Oakeshott was not idle. In fact, he was hard at work on his grand opus of political philosophy, *On Human Conduct*. A letter to Ken Minogue in 1967 testifies that the writing was not going as quickly as Oakeshott would have liked: "I am not going to get this [book] finished as quickly as I hoped. Not only have I lost the faculty of rapid writing, but I am finding a vast discontent with a good many of the ideas which used to knock about in my head fairly agreeably."[37] *On Human Conduct* finally came out in 1975. Stylistically, it marked a radical departure from *Rationalism in Politics*. Replete with a Latin vocabulary composed of words like *civitas, cives, lex, respublica, societas,* and *universitas, On Human Conduct* was a dense and highly abstract work of philosophy. Oakeshott himself seemed to be fully aware of this. In the same letter to Minogue quoted above, he confessed, "What I've written seems to me a bit *dry.* I shall have to go through it and put in the light-heartedness." Which he did. The result was a work that at times possessed an austere grandeur, but at other times was wittily epigrammatic, fiercely ironic, poetic, elegiac, and downright polemical. The subtlety and elegance of the writing, however, made it unmistakably Oakeshott.

The central ideas of *On Human Conduct* went all the way back to "On Being Conservative" and the writings immediately following it, "The Masses in Representative Democracy" (1957) and the 1958 Harvard Lectures, *Morality and Politics in Modern Europe.* Especially in the latter writings, Oakeshott had begun to anatomize the modern European political consciousness as a divided consciousness, composed of two opposing moral dispositions, to which corresponded two divergent understandings of the office of government. On the one hand there was the morality of individuality, to which corresponded a juridical under-standing of government as essentially an umpire or referee. On the other, there was the morality of collectivism, formed in reaction to the moral-ity of individuality by those unable to bear its burdens, to which corre-sponded an understanding of government as a manager of an enterprise, a leader, a promoter of substantive purposes, a provider of substantive benefits.[38]

On Human Conduct represented the complete working out of the new approach signaled by "On Being Conservative," "The Masses in Repre-sentative Democracy," and *Morality and Politics in Modern Europe.* Oakeshott once again interpreted the modern European political con-sciousness as a divided consciousness, using the Latin expressions *soci-etas* and *universitas* to designate its poles. The former designated an understanding of the state as a nonpurposive association in which the members are related solely in terms of legal rules. The latter designated an understanding of the state as an enterprise association in which the members are related in terms of a common, substantive purpose, whether it be religious salvation, moral virtue, or economic productiv-ity and redistribution. What was new in *On Human Conduct* was that Oakeshott provided a philosophical account of the former mode of asso-ciation, civil association, laying out its essential postulates. In this regard, he developed an elaborate teaching about human freedom—something missing from his earlier writings—that suggested that civil association was the only appropriate model for the state in our modern, pluralistic circumstances.

There is a sense in which Oakeshott's theory of civil association can be understood as a contribution to liberal theory, perhaps the most profound of the twentieth century. Oakeshott himself did not use the term liberalism to style his political philosophy, finding it too ambiguous and loaded down with meanings that did not convey his own. He once commented, "What may now be meant by the word 'liberal' is anyone's guess" (*RP*, 439–40). Nevertheless, his theory of civil association, in its preeminent concern with liberty, its celebration of individuality, and its defense of the rule of law, clearly evoked liberal themes. Nor was this liberal aspect of Oakeshott's political philosophy at odds with his conservatism or his critique of rationalism. His conservatism, as we have seen, was not opposed to modernity, individuality, and pluralism; rather, it was understood to be their appropriate political counterpart. And he never identified liberalism with rationalism. "Parliamentary government and rationalist politics," he once wrote,

> do not belong to the same tradition and do not, in fact go together.
> . . . The root of so-called "democratic" theory is not rationalist optimism about the perfectibility of human society, but scepticism about the possibility of such perfection and the determination not to allow human life to be perverted by the tyranny of a person or fixed by the tyranny of an idea. (*RPML*, 109)

Liberalism *is*, however, a slippery term, so we would do well to specify Oakeshott's skeptical, conservative version a little more precisely. It is standard to distinguish "classical" liberalism, with its focus on limited government and individual responsibility, and "modern" liberalism, which countenances a much greater role for government in social and economic life. Locke, Smith, Tocqueville, and Hayek are associated with the former; and Mill, Green, Hobhouse, Dewey, and Rawls exemplify the latter.[39] It is clear that Oakeshott has more in common with classical liberalism than he does with the welfarist ideal of modern liberalism, but with some important caveats. In the first place, he rejects the natural rights and atomism that belong to a good deal of classical liberal theory; this is his inheritance from Hegel. Second, he rejects the materialism or economism that runs through both classical and modern liberalism, from Locke and Smith to Hayek and Rawls.

John Gray has recently drawn another distinction between two different types of liberalism: *modus vivendi* liberalism, which sees liberal institutions as a means to peaceful coexistence among different ways of life; and Enlightenment liberalism, which seeks rational consensus on issues of justice. Oakeshott, along with Hobbes, Hume, and Berlin, is seen as an exemplar of the former liberalism; and John Rawls, along with Kant, is seen as an exemplar of the latter.[40] It is true that Oakeshott's skeptical and pluralistic liberalism has very little in common with Rawls's "political liberalism," much less the "deliberative democracy" of Rawls's progeny. He would have regarded Rawls's attempt to find a moral consensus on justice, even a minimalistic "overlapping consensus," as nothing more than a species of rationalism. Such a consensus cannot be achieved in modern, pluralistic circumstances; or it can succeed only in suppressing conflicting points of view and characterizing them as "unreasonable." Gray is right to see Oakeshott as having more in common with Berlin's pluralistic liberalism, though I will argue in the sequel that Oakeshott offers a far more satisfying philosophical account of this liberalism than does Berlin.

As elegant and sophisticated as Oakeshott's theory of civil association in *On Human Conduct* was, its practical implications were not clear; certainly they were not spelled out by Oakeshott himself. When Margaret Thatcher came to power four years after the publication of *On Human Conduct*, in 1979, some claimed that Oakeshott "had articulated the real philosophical foundations of [her] policies."[41] But there was very little of Oakeshott in Thatcher's Hayekian emphasis on economic productivity and prosperity. But if not Thatcherism, what sort of conservative regime or policies did Oakeshott's political philosophy favor? Oakeshott, ever elusive, refused to be pinned down to a particular party program, invoking his sharp distinction between philosophy and political advocacy. His most explicit statement of political affiliation was couched in characteristic irony: "I am a member of no political party. I vote—if I have to vote—for the party which is likely to do the least harm. To that extent, I am a Tory."[42]

Oakeshott's coyness about the political implications of his philosophy has appeared to some a kind of dodge. Thus, Stefan Collini remarks: "I think the appeal of Oakeshott has often been an appeal to a kind of political snobbery . . . an appeal to those who aren't faced with making day-to-day decisions. It's an appeal more to those who like to . . . present themselves as having a longer perspective, who are always somehow the voices of true conservatism which any example of everyday, existing conservatism falls short of."[43] Others have pointed out that Oakeshott's theory of civil association had very little to say about the important question of the distribution of resources and opportunities in society or about modern economic and political inequality.[44] And unlike American neoconservatives, he nowhere reflected very seriously on the corrosive effects of capitalism on liberal institutions or on the problem of "individualism" that Tocqueville saw as one of the most dangerous consequences of liberal democracy. Though Oakeshott was no doubt aware of these problems, his rather pure conception of political philosophy had very little room for such sociological considerations. As a result, though he provided a profound account of the postulates of civil association—or liberal democracy—in *On Human Conduct*, he neglected to investigate the social and cultural preconditions that make such a society possible.

Oakeshott published three more books after *On Human Conduct*, but they consisted for the most part of earlier work. *Hobbes on Civil Association* (1975) gathered together Oakeshott's four most important essays on Hobbes, and the title underlined Oakeshott's philosophical affinity with his great English predecessor. *On History and Other Essays* (1983) contained the "Three Essays on History" that Oakeshott had honed over the years of the History of Political Thought seminar and that represented the final fruit of his career-long preoccupation with the problem of historical knowledge. This volume also contained an important new essay on "The Rule of Law," which clarified Oakeshott's views on the relationship of law and morality. Finally, *The Voice of Liberal Learning* (1989) was a collection of Oakeshott's earlier writings on education.

Around 1980, Oakeshott ceased to participate in the History of Political Thought seminar at the LSE and retired permanently to his cottage in Dorset. There he lived with his third wife, Christel (his first two marriages had ended in divorce, and he had enjoyed many affairs over the years, including one with Iris Murdoch), until his death in 1990. A letter to Patrick Riley from these later years showed that, even in his late eighties, Oakeshott continued to read and think deeply and, indeed, was pondering the theological issues that had occupied him as a young man:

> During the last couple of years since I came to live here [in Dorset], spending much of my time re-reading all the books which I first read 50 or 60 years ago, I have gone back to "theology"—or rather, to reflection upon religion. And I would like, more than anything else, to extend those brief pages in *On Human Conduct* into an essay (you know how I admire and value this literary form) on religion, and par-

ticularly on the Christian religion. This ambition came to me, partly, from the re-reading of all that St. Augustine wrote—St. Augustine and Montaigne, the two most remarkable men who have ever lived. What I would like to write is a new version of Anselm's *Cur Deus Homo*—in which (amongst much else) "salvation," being "saved," is recognized as [having] nothing whatever to do with the *future*. Oh, but I know I can never do it now; I have left it too late.[45]

Oakeshott had little to lament, though. He had left behind a distinguished body of work that made important contributions to the theory of knowledge, the philosophy of history, the philosophy of education, and, above all, political philosophy. What set this body of work apart from much of the academic philosophy of the twentieth century was the imaginative vision of the human condition that it disclosed and the literary art with which it expressed this vision. Perhaps what was most distinctive about Oakeshott's body of work was not the doctrine it articulated but the voice that articulated it—a voice that was skeptical without being cynical, ironic without being nihilistic, modest without being timid, learned without being encyclopedic, and serious without being solemn. It was a supremely civilized voice, not in the trivial sense of a Cambridge don with his sherry (a complaint frequently made against Oakeshott), but in the sense of having a clear perception of current barbarism without feeling compelled to combat it with barbarian weapons.

2 Idealism

It was a strangely bold thing for Oakeshott to say in 1933 that the view he was defending in *Experience and Its Modes* "derives all that is valuable in it from its affinity to what is known by the somewhat ambiguous name of Idealism, and the works from which I am conscious of having learnt most are Hegel's *Phänomenologie des Geistes* and Bradley's *Appearance and Reality*" (*EM*, 6). Nothing seemed deader at this particular moment, especially in Cambridge, than the absolute idealism of Bradley and Hegel, having been demolished by the criticisms of Moore and Russell. The logical atomism of Russell and his protégé Ludwig Wittgenstein had triumphed, and their doctrine was soon to receive its dogmatic statement in A. J. Ayer's gospel of logical positivism, *Language, Truth, and Logic* (1936).

A fair picture of the situation of philosophy at this time can be found in the entry under "Philosophy" in *University Studies: Cambridge, 1933.* Here Russell, Moore, and Wittgenstein are depicted as the dominant influences on philosophy at Cambridge since 1919. Russell is credited with having developed a "scientific method in philosophy," which confines itself to solving particular problems instead of elaborating a general metaphysical system. Moore is said to exemplify this method in "his insistence that the business of philosophy is to accept the propositions of common sense and then to analyse their meanings." And Wittgenstein is hailed for his momentous division of all meaningful propositions into either analytic tautologies or empirically verifiable synthetic propositions—a division which Ayer would soon erect into the totem of logical positivism. The essay concludes by denying that philosophy can provide emotional satisfaction, as it has tried to do from Plato through the grand metaphysical systems of Hegel, Bradley, and the "awful example" of McTaggart: "The aim of philosophy is the clarification of thought."[1]

The reason for recalling this essay is not because it is historically insightful—by the time it was written, Wittgenstein, for example, had already begun to move away from the logical atomism of the *Tractatus* and toward the more holistic and descriptive theory of language of *Philosophical Investigations*[2]—but because it typifies what had become the philosophical orthodoxy not only at Cambridge but also at Oxford in the early 1930s. The essay does not try to refute idealism; it simply assumes that it is dead, useful only for occasional target practice by young logicians. To what extent was this true? To what extent had Russell and Moore succeeded in refuting idealism, especially in its British guise? This is no trivial question to address before approaching Oakeshott's self-proclaimed idealistic argument in *Experience and Its Modes*. In order to answer it, we must first try to recover what British idealism was all about and then consider the criticisms that brought about its eclipse.

British Idealism

The two great founding figures of British idealism were T. H. Green (1836–1882) and F. H. Bradley (1846–1924). In 1874, each published a seminal contribution to the emergent philosophical school: Green, a lengthy and highly critical introduction to Hume's *Treatise of Human Nature*; and Bradley, *The Presuppositions of Critical History*. Though linked in terms of their commitment to philosophical idealism, the personalities and styles of these two thinkers could not have been more different. Green was a charismatic teacher who influenced many young men at Oxford to put the idealist philosophy they had been taught into practice in their public careers as churchmen, politicians, and civil servants. In many ways, he embodied the two animating interests of British idealism: the interest in defending Christianity against the skepticism of post-Darwinian science; and the interest in restoring to philosophy a practical purpose aimed at promoting social reform. Interestingly, Bradley did not share these interests. Though sympathetic to religion, he never identified it with absolute reality, seeing it instead as an essentially practical idea afflicted with all the self-contradictions of practical experience. And he did not think philosophy had anything to contribute to practical life or political reform. He lived a fairly reclusive life in Oxford, never teaching, but occasionally coming out at night to shoot cats in the college precincts.

Bradley was the great metaphysician of the British idealists and he is therefore more relevant to the issues we are concerned with in this chapter. I will have more to say about Green in the next chapter in connection with political philosophy. As an idealist, Bradley was of course heavily influenced by Hegel, an influence he acknowledged in a variety of ways throughout his career, though he disclaimed being a full-fledged Hegelian. The *differentia* of Bradley's idealism—and, indeed, of all British idealism—lay in what it was originally directed against: namely, British empiricism. It was against the empiricist theory of knowledge as it had been formulated by Locke, Hume, and especially John Stuart Mill that Bradley's philosophy first took shape. Specifically, he rejected the notion that knowledge somehow begins with psychical particulars, "ideas" or "impressions," and then proceeds by way of "association" to universals. In knowledge or experience, he argued in *The Principles of Logic* (and here he was simply following Hegel's celebrated attack on immediate sense-certainty), we do not begin with separate and independent particulars, but with meanings, universals: "From the very first beginnings of soul-life universals are used."[3] And it is only on the basis of such universals that inference can take place. The brute and atomistic datum from which the empiricist supposes thought and induction take their start simply does not exist.

The critique of the empiricist belief that knowledge begins from or is founded upon the immediate facts of perception was taken up and extended by Bradley's followers, Bernard Bosanquet (1848–1923) and Harold Joachim (1865–1939)—the latter, incidentally, reviewed the manuscript of *Experience and Its Modes* for Cambridge University Press and is duly thanked in the acknowledgments. Like Bradley, Bosanquet and Joachim rejected the rigid distinction between mediate and immediate experience upon which the whole empiricist theory of knowledge was founded. There is no such thing as immediate experience, they argued, experience of isolated particulars without meaning or relation. All experience is in some way intellectual or infected with thought.[4]

Bradley's critique of the empiricist notion of the "given" was not, of course, a merely negative doctrine. It ultimately involved a completely different positive conception of the nature of knowledge, truth, and even reality. No longer could knowledge, for example, be pictured as a building resting on indubitable and incorrigible "foundations." Bradley characterized this metaphor as "ruinously inapplicable. The foundation in truth is provisional merely. . . . My experience is solid, not so far as it is superstructure but so far as in short it is a system."[5] Nor could truth any longer be conceived of in terms of correspondence to a fixed and solid "datum." In place of correspondence, Bradley put systematic coherence as the criterion of truth (and of reality as well). Individual facts and judgments are true (or real) only insofar as they belong to a larger system or whole. As knowledge grows, these facts and judgments are subject to correction in light of the changing whole. In short, knowledge and truth are hermeneutical.[6]

Bradley's disciple Joachim provided the most thorough defense of the coherence theory of truth in *The Nature of Truth* (1906). There he made the important point that coherence is not to be confused with mere formal consistency. Formal consistency involves the arrangement of already accepted truths, the imposition of a universal form on the fixed materials of knowledge. But such distinctions—between the whole and its parts, between form and materials, between the universal and the particular—are alien to the idealist logic of Bradley and his followers; indeed, they belong to the traditional formal logic against which the idealists were rebelling. Coherence is not something outside the elements that comprise it; it is not a coherence of static units or fixed constituents. And if we have to speak of a "form" or a "universal," it must be understood that this form or universal interpenetrates the material parts, giving them their particular character. In short, we have to do here with the idealist notion of the "concrete universal"—the type of universal which, in contradistinction to the abstract universal of traditional logic, characterizes a complex whole or system.[7]

It is interesting to note that Bradley, like Collingwood and Oakeshott after him, found the most persuasive confirmation of this whole non-empiricist picture of knowledge in historical inquiry. In his first publication, *The Presuppositions of Critical History*, Bradley showed that the naïve empiricist theory of knowledge as the passive reception of unadulterated facts could not account for historical knowledge. There are no unadulterated facts that the historian has access to; instead he is confronted by a welter of conflicting testimony from which he critically has to construct the course of events. The historian does not begin with facts; rather, historical facts are the conclusions of the historian's critical analysis, the products of his inferential reasoning. In history, Bradley wrote, "in every case that which is called the fact is in reality a theory."[8] And the ultimate criterion of historical fact is its consistency with a world composed of other historical facts. Bosanquet drew attention to the hermeneutic dimension of Bradley's account of historical knowledge: "A former work of Mr. Bradley's, 'The Presuppositions of History,' gives the best account known to me of the process by which *all* the parts of a whole can be criticised and adjusted *on the basis of each other*."[9]

Bradley's critique of the empiricist theory of knowledge became the basis of his metaphysics in *Appearance and Reality* (1893). Ultimate reality, the absolute, is there identified with a completely coherent world of experience, a single system of noncontradictory experience. This is Bradley's monism. Reality is one, self-contained and self-complete. Appearance, on the other hand, refers to any form of experience that is not self-contained, that does not carry its conditions within itself, that "involves in its very essence a relation to the outside" and "is thus inwardly affected by externality."[10] Among such appearances Bradley includes natural science, morality, and even religion. All are shown to be abstractions from the whole of reality, self-contradictory when taken on their own terms, and dependent on conditions or presuppositions lying outside their own explicit self-understanding. These appearances, however, are not all equally abstract. A complete metaphysical system— which Bradley does not claim to provide in *Appearance and Reality*— would arrange the various forms of abstract experience in a hierarchy based on their relative harmony and inclusiveness. Bradley acknowledged that this doctrine of the "degrees of truth and reality" was perhaps the most Hegelian aspect of his philosophy. It is also, as we shall see, one of the least Oakeshottian.

More Oakeshottian was what Bradley had to say about the relative autonomy of the abstract modes of experience within their own spheres. Though no mode is perfectly coherent, each has its own sphere of relative supremacy. Each mode "must be allowed to have a relative independence"; within its own sphere it "is in a certain sense supreme, and is justified in resisting dictation from without."[11] Thus, while natural science is based on abstraction and falls short of absolute truth, it constitutes a "working point of view" that is "fully justified by success, and stands high above criticism." So long as "metaphysics and natural science keep each to its own business, a collision is impossible."[12] The same is true of philosophy in relation to morality and religion. Philosophy cannot criticize these forms of experience. Though it will certainly understand them differently than they understand themselves, this does not entail denial of their vital point of view. "Philosophy like other things has a business of its own. . . . Except within its own limits it claims no supremacy."[13]

All of this suggests a view about the irrelevance of theory to practice that was deeply at odds with the reformist outlook of British idealism but was to be embraced enthusiastically by Oakeshott. Bradley encapsulated this view in a famous passage from *Ethical Studies*:

All philosophy has to do is 'understand what is,' and moral philosophy has to understand morals which exist, not to make them or give directions for making them. Such a notion is simply ludicrous. Philosophy in general has not to anticipate the discoveries of the particular sciences nor the evolution of history; the philosophy of religion has not to make a new religion or teach an old one, but simply to understand the religious consciousness; and aesthetic has not to produce works of fine art, but to theorize the beautiful which it finds; political philosophy has not to play tricks with the state, but to understand it; and ethics has not to make the world moral, but to reduce to theory the morality current in the world.[14]

This passage obviously echoes Hegel's even more famous warning about philosophy's "issuing instructions on how the world ought to be" in the Preface to the *Philosophy of Right*. Where Bradley sharply diverged from Hegel, however, was in his understanding of the relation between thought and ultimate reality. Whereas Hegel held that ultimate reality is finally revealed to the philosopher and grasped in philosophical thought, Bradley never accepted the identification of thought with ultimate or absolute reality. For him, discursive thought always remains to some extent relational—"in any truth about Reality the word 'about' is too significant"[15]—and therefore self-contradictory; it never attains the undivided unity that Bradley associated with "immediate feeling" and attributed to reality at its fullest. Thus, though philosophical reflection may lead us to see the necessity of the absolute, it is not itself to be identified with it. Thought can overcome its inherent dualism only by committing suicide.[16]

Bradley expressed his distinctive view on the rift between thought and reality in another famous passage:

Unless thought stands for something that falls beyond mere intelligence, if "thinking" is not used with some strange implication that never was part of the meaning of the word, a lingering scruple still forbids us to believe that reality can ever be purely rational. It may come from a failure in my metaphysics, or from a weakness of the flesh which continues to blind me, but the notion that existence could be the same as understanding strikes as cold and ghost-like as the dreariest materialism. That the glory of this world in the end is appearance leaves the world more glorious, if we feel it is a show of some fuller splendour; but the sensuous curtain is a deception and a cheat, if it hides some colourless movement of atoms, some spectral woof of impalpable abstractions, or unearthly ballet of bloodless categories. Though dragged to such conclusions, we cannot embrace them. Our principles may be true, but they are not reality. They no more *make* that Whole which commands our devotion, than some shredded dissection of human tatters *is* that warm and breathing beauty of flesh which our hearts found delightful.[17]

Though Bradley's rhetoric is irresistible here, it seems to reinscribe the empiricist distinction between immediate and mediate experience which his logic had so effectively demolished. For this reason, neither Bosanquet nor Joachim felt compelled to follow him down this path, maintaining instead the identity of philosophical thought and ultimate reality and thus remaining truer to Hegel's original teaching.[18] We will see that Oakeshott departs from Bradley in this regard as well.

Moore's and Russell's criticisms of Bradley came from the opposite direction. Their efforts were directed at defending empiricism, albeit on logical grounds instead of on the basis of the psychological doctrine of association. They rejected Bradley's counterintuitive claim that reality does not consist of discrete facts but of an interconnected whole, the view (as Russell characterized it) that "every apparently separate piece of reality has, as it were, hooks which grapple it to the next piece; the next piece, in turn, has fresh hooks, and so on, until the whole universe is reconstructed."[19] There really are certain facts that we simply apprehend, and it is out of this immediate knowledge—what Russell called "knowledge by acquaintance"—that all our mediate or derivative knowledge is constructed. Against the holism of Bradley and his followers, Moore and Russell reinstated the empiricist and atomistic understanding of knowledge as an aggregation of static bits; the constituents of knowledge do not change in the light of the changing whole. The quote from Bishop Butler with which Moore prefaced *Principia Ethica* expresses the radically unhermeneutic character of this entire outlook: "Everything is what it is, and not another thing."

When we turn to Moore's and Russell's actual criticisms of idealism, we find that they do not really engage the arguments of the British idealists, much less those of Hegel. The most famous document in this regard is Moore's 1903 article "The Refutation of Idealism." The idealism Moore "refuted" in this article was not that of Hegel or Bradley but the subjective idealism of Berkeley, which holds that *esse* is *percipi*, to be is to be perceived.[20] The British idealists, like Kant and Hegel before them, always distinguished their doctrine from Berkeley's subjective idealism and the solipsism it implied: that reality is experience does not mean that it is merely *my* experience.[21] Moore's later attempts to refute idealism—for example, in "Proof of an External World" (1939), by holding up his two hands and indicating their independent existence— were equally feeble. The everyday examples favored by realists merely concealed through familiarity the role of mind in constructing reality. Had they focused instead on the scientist solving a complex scientific problem or the historian trying to construct the past from surviving evidence—the sort of examples favored by the idealists—they might have come to very different conclusions.

Even within analytic philosophy, the attempts of Moore and Russell to salvage empiricism from the attacks of the British idealists came to be seen as misguided. The three seminal works of the second wave of analytic philosophy—W. V. O. Quine's "Two Dogmas of Empiricism" (1951), Wittgenstein's *Philosophical Investigations* (1954), and Wilfrid Sellars's "Empiricism and the Philosophy of Mind" (1956)—all struck deadly blows at the various myths that formed the basis of the empiricist theory of knowledge defended by Russell and the logical positivists. Sellars's attack on the Myth of the Given is particularly reminiscent of the British idealists' critique of empiricism. Like Bradley and Bosanquet, Sellars rejects the metaphor of a "foundation" for knowledge as highly misleading. In a sentence that could easily have been written by Bradley, he states: "empirical knowledge, like its sophisticated extension, science, is rational, not because it has a *foundation* but because it is a self-correcting enterprise which can put *any* claim in jeopardy, though not *all* at once."[22] It is sentences such as this one that have led Richard Rorty to wonder what, in the end, analytic philosophy has really accomplished: "Since the anti-empiricism and the anti-foundationalism on which analytic philosophers now pride themselves was taken for granted by nineteenth-century anglophone philosophers such as T. H. Green and Bernard Bosanquet, one might be tempted to say that analytic philosophy was a century-long waste of time."[23]

Early Political and Theological Writings

Having satisfied ourselves that Oakeshott's idealist point of view in *Experience and Its Modes* was not, despite its unfashionableness, a philosophical non-starter, we may now turn to the work itself. It is important to realize, though, that Oakeshott's engagement with epistemological and metaphysical questions in this work did not spring out of nowhere but grew out of his preoccupation with certain concrete issues in political philosophy and theology in the 1920s. It is to his early writings on these subjects that we must turn first, then, in order to understand the motivating concerns of his first book.

The dominant theme of Oakeshott's writings from the 1920s—very much in keeping with British idealist concerns—was the need for the recovery of a genuinely moral and philosophical approach to politics over against the dominant positivistic approach. The political science curriculum for the Historical Tripos at Cambridge through which Oakeshott had passed was a good example of this positivistic approach. The syllabus remained mired in the Comparative Method—the comparative study of political institutions and the drawing of inductive generalizations from historical facts—that John Seeley and, to a lesser extent, Henry Sidgwick had imposed on it in the latter part of the nineteenth century.[24] It was this inductive historical approach to political science that Oakeshott ruthlessly attacked in the 1924 manuscript, "The Cambridge School of Political Science."

What is perhaps most striking about this early essay is how antihistorical it is. Oakeshott complains that the Cambridge syllabus is almost wholly taken up with the historical and comparative study of political institutions and forms of government. Occasionally the names of Plato and Aristotle are mentioned, but their actual philosophies remain unexplored. Aristotle is celebrated more for his empirical examination of 150 constitutions than for his philosophical investigation of morality and politics in the *Nicomachean Ethics*. All of this misses what Oakeshott calls the "real thing." Occupying itself with the passing forms of government, the Cambridge syllabus never arrives at the essence of the state, which remains "entirely unchanged amid the metamorphoses of form and outward appearance" ("CS," 16, 19). This is precisely the predicament Socrates points up in the passage from the *Republic* that Oakeshott chooses as the epigraph for his essay: "Just as people at times go about looking for something which they hold in their hands, so we, instead of fixing our eyes upon the thing itself, kept gazing at some point in the distance, and this is probably why it eluded our search" (*Republic*, 432d).

Oakeshott concludes that the empirical and historical approach to political science should be abandoned for a more philosophical approach: "Political Science and Political Philosophy either mean the same thing or the term science has, in this connection, no valuable meaning at all" ("CS," 10). More concretely, he suggests that the two current political science papers for the Historical Tripos should be replaced with one devoted to the history of political philosophy and another devoted to the philosophical investigation of the nature and end of the essential state. Six years later, Oakeshott's friend and senior colleague Ernest Barker reformed the political science syllabus at Cambridge largely along these lines. Oakeshott concludes his essay on a very unOakeshottian note, claiming that the philosophical study of politics he is advocating will contribute to practical life and "avail to guide aright that continuing effort we call social reform. . . . [T]here can be small doubt that were such a school built up as I have indicated a wiser generation of citizens and leaders would issue from our walls" ("CS," 34).

Oakeshott continued his attack on positivism and naturalistic explanations of politics in two manuscripts from 1925: "The Nature and Meaning of Sociality" and "A Discussion of Some Matters Preliminary to the Study of Political Philosophy." In the former essay, he criticizes the use of "false and misleading metaphors" drawn from mechanics and biology to understand the nature of sociality. The sociologists' examples of ants and prairie dogs tell us nothing about the true nature of human sociality. Genuine sociality does not consist in mere sociability or gregariousness but in a complete unity of mind. For this reason, sociality is not necessarily incompatible with solitude; in solitude we often seek a more intense union with our fellow human beings than can be found in mere cohabitation (*RPML*, 47–49, 52–56).

Oakeshott claims that the unity of mind that constitutes true sociality has been most profoundly explored by Plato under the rubric of justice, by Aristotle under the rubric of friendship, and, above all, by St John and St Paul under the rubric of Christian love (*RPML*, 57–59). The last reference goes some way toward explaining the odd comment in "The Cambridge School of Political Science" that St Paul is "perhaps the greatest political philosopher" ("CS," 6). The ultimate expression of the unity of mind that constitutes genuine sociality is to be found in religion, an insight Oakeshott believes is shared by Plato, Aristotle, Rousseau, Bosanquet, and, above all, St Paul and Spinoza: "Just as to Plato it was clear that the measure or depth of the unity of a band of pirates is in exact proportion to their justice, so to us it appears that the depth of our sociality is proportionate to this devotion to the highest good we know, which we call religion. Love and friendship are the essence of sociality, and the life of these is hid in religion" (*RPML*, 59–60).

In the lengthy manuscript "A Discussion of Some Matters Preliminary to the Study of Political Philosophy," Oakeshott develops these ideas on the spiritual unity of the social whole and spends a fair amount of space bringing out the interdependence between self and society. Drawing heavily on Bradley and Bosanquet, he criticizes atomistic notions of the self and argues that the self is to be identified, not with what is separate or isolated from everything else, but with the unity of experience as a whole. It is in this context that he uses the extravagant idealist language evoking the identity of self and society that I alluded to before: "A self not only requires its society, but in the fullest sense *is* its society"; "The self is the State, and the State is the self"; " 'Man versus the State' is sheer nonsense" ("DSM," 131, 135, 137). He puts the same point in terms of the idealist notions of the "real will" of the individual and the "general will" of society: these are not two separate notions but one and the same; the real will of the individual is none other than the general will of society, the latter being understood as distinct from the "will of all" ("DSM," 145–56).

Like the other manuscripts we have discussed so far, "A Discussion of Some Matters Preliminary to the Study of Political Science" is concerned to distinguish the philosophical study of politics from scientific and historical inquiries and to indicate its superiority. Philosophy, unlike science and history, elucidates the complete meaning of things or facts. Disciplines such as psychology, sociology, and political economy provide only limited, incomplete definitions of facts. "Political philosophy is not a science . . . On the contrary, it is an effort to come at the true meaning and implications of the complex thing we call political life, but of which we know very little until we have rethought it from the beginning" ("DSM," 52). There is no greater misunderstanding in the study of political life today, Oakeshott claims, than the confusion of philosophy with science, a confusion promoted by expressions such as "political theory" and "social philosophy" ("DSM," 56–59). In order to protect against such confusion, we need a complete theory of knowledge that establishes true principles of definition: "Nothing emerges with more certainty from the history of human thought . . . than the absolute dependence of speculation on ultimate problems upon a theory of knowledge. To put the point in its most abstract form, the theory of theorizing (i.e. the seeing clearly of how to see clearly) must be the first study of any ambitious coming at a true theory" ("DSM," 10). The program of *Experience and Its Modes* emerges here quite clearly: "a political philosophy founded upon no metaphysical prolegomenon, or upon one fundamentally in error, is doomed to propagate not truth, but error" ("DSM," 187–88).

In Oakeshott's first course of lectures at Cambridge, "The Philosophical Approach to Politics," delivered in the Lent term of 1928, we get much more than the program of *Experience and Its Modes*; we get the actual argument. Once again, Oakeshott is concerned with the metapolitical question of the nature of political philosophy and with differentiating philosophical thinking about politics from other ways of thinking about politics with which it is commonly confused. The most important of these nonphilosophical ways of thinking about politics are scientific thinking about politics (including political science, sociology, economics, and psychology), historical thinking about politics, and practical thinking about politics. Each of these Oakeshott shows to be an abstract way of thinking about politics in contradistinction to the "concrete" reflection of political philosophy. Science confines itself to the measurable or quantitative aspect of things and excludes what is not measurable, individual, or unique. History deals with the individual and the unique, but it is abstract because it postulates an objective series of facts and events wholly independent of the historian and it never arrives at a complete explanation of anything. And practical thinking is condemned to an endless "ought to be" that never finds rest in a stable "is."

The primary conclusion that follows from all this is that scientific, historical, and practical thinking have nothing to contribute to political philosophy, nor can they criticize its conclusions. Oakeshott thus defends political philosophy from the three great reductivisms of our age: scientism, historicism, and pragmatism. The last of these deserves some attention, since only four years earlier Oakeshott had suggested that political philosophy might contribute to political life and serve as a guide to social reform. Now, in what will remain his position for the rest of his career, he dismisses the idea that philosophy can be practical. It is true that no past political philosopher has altogether emancipated himself from the practical point of view. Nevertheless, Oakeshott gives high marks to Plato, Aristotle, Hobbes, Spinoza, Rousseau, and Hegel for achieving a relatively pure philosophical perspective on politics. At the other end of the spectrum, he criticizes L. T. Hobhouse and Harold Laski for failing to observe any distinction between philosophical and practical thinking.

Before going on to the complete statement in *Experience and Its Modes* of the argument rehearsed in the 1928 lectures, we must take notice of the other great theme of Oakeshott's writings in the 1920s: namely, religion. Like almost all the idealists in Britain, the young Oakeshott was intensely interested in religion and theological issues. Among the idealists, opinion was split between those who, like Green, identified religion with the absolute and those who, like Bradley, saw it as an important form of experience but ultimately belonging to appearance. On this question, as on so many others, Oakeshott followed Bradley. Religion was the completion or consummation of practical life, but it fell far short of the concrete experience of philosophy.[25]

Oakeshott defended the view that religion is the completion or consummation of practical experience in a paper that he read at the D Society on 19 October 1927. The D Society consisted of a small group of Cambridge dons who met regularly in the 1920s and 1930s to discuss theological issues. The participants were theological "modernists," committed to understanding Christianity in the light of modern scientific and historical knowledge instead of trying to defend its literal truth.[26]

As Oakeshott candidly acknowledges, his paper is pure Bradley.[27] Morality is self-contradictory in that it confronts the individual with an endless "ought": no sooner do we fulfill our moral duty than a new "ought" springs up to prick us on to further activity. Morality is "a battle with no hope of victory, a battle, in fact, in which a final victory is the only irretrievable defeat." Religion solves the self-contradiction that is morality by providing us with a good that is real and achievable: "What in morality is a mere 'should be' in religion becomes an 'is.'" In this way, religion completes morality and supplies it with an energy and "motive power" that would otherwise be lacking if all we had was the endless and debilitating "ought" of moral endeavor. Oakeshott's view of the relationship between morality and religion is best summed up by Pascal: "It is good to be tired and wearied in the vain search for the true good, so that in the end we may stretch our arms to the Redeemer" (*RPML*, 41–42, 44–45).

As he had been with philosophy, Oakeshott was particularly concerned to defend religion from positivistic attacks coming from science and history. The conflict between science and religion was a hot topic in the early decades of the twentieth century, and in 1925 Oakeshott's friend and colleague at Caius, Joseph Needham, edited an important volume of essays dedicated to it entitled *Science, Religion, and Reality*. Needham himself was an active theological modernist, and the general point of view of the volume was that there is no conflict between science and religion, not because they agree, but because they are ultimately concerned with very different things.[28] Interestingly, Needham acknowledged Oakeshott's assistance in the preface to the book, and Oakeshott himself ended up writing a review of it. The review is generally sympathetic to the overall point of view of the book, but Oakeshott picks out Clement Webb's essay on "Science, Christianity, and Modern Civilization" for criticism because it fails to address "the most pressing feature of our theological thought," namely, "the exact bearing upon Christianity of the modern historical criticism of the New Testament."[29] It is to this pressing issue that Oakeshott turned his own attention in his 1928 essay "The Importance of the Historical Element in Christianity."

This essay shows Oakeshott to be an unorthodox religious thinker, though one with clear affinities with the demythologizing and dehistoricizing tendencies of theologians like Albert Schweitzer and Rudolf Bultmann.[30] He acknowledges that the historicity of Jesus' life and death has been an important element in traditional Christianity, but he denies that it is in any way necessary or essential to Christianity today. The belief in the necessity of the historical element in Christianity rests on one of two false theories of the identity of Christianity: (1) that Christianity is identical to the whole of original Christianity, and therefore anything that departs from that original cannot be Christian; and (2) that Christianity consists of some sort of unchanging core or essence that abides in the midst of circumstantial change. Oakeshott rejects both of these theories of identity as abstract and unhistorical: it is ultimately impossible to separate what is original from what is posterior or what is essential from what is accidental in a historical tradition such as Christianity.[31] Echoing Bradley, he argues that religion is essentially a practical idea, and what does or does not belong to the identity of a religious tradition must ultimately be determined by a pragmatic test. On this pragmatic criterion, the historical element in Christianity is found to be wanting. While it once served to endow Christianity with an intense awareness of the object of belief, it now only entangles Christianity in pointless historical controversy that finally leads to unbelief. Therefore, the historical element must be jettisoned and "the presentation of [Christianity] must . . . change to changing needs, becoming, and not for the first time, a religion in which no servile archaeology inhibits vitality or chills imagination" (*RPML*, 63–73).

The "existentialist" note sounded in the final passage is amplified in one of the most interesting of Oakeshott's essays from this period, "Religion and the World" (1929). What makes this essay so interesting is that, in it, Oakeshott not only provides a compelling interpretation of modern religious sensibility but also gives us a glimpse of his own conception of the *summum bonum*. Taking as his text St James's comment that "pure religion is to keep unspotted from the world," he argues that this idea can no longer command our assent if by "world" is meant the rich array of interests and activities, intellectual and physical, that modern people have learned to value and enjoy. The secularism to which religion is opposed "must mean attachment to some world other than this so desirable world of intellectual and physical interests, if it is to be the enemy of any religion we should be distressed to lose." Oakeshott postulates that it consists in a scale of values that prizes success and external achievement above all. Against the "careerist ideal" and "middle-class passion for safety, regularity and possession" that characterize this worldly scale of values, religion urges us to adopt "a more personal standard" in which the realization of self is prized above external achievement and life carries "in each of its moments its whole meaning and value." Instead of sacrificing our lives to the Moloch of the future, religion bids us to live a wholly contemporary life, an "extemporary life" in which "present insight" and "living sensibility" are the highest values. "*Memento vivere* is the sole precept of religion," Oakeshott writes, and "there can be no revival of religion which is not a revival of a more daring and sensitive way of living" (*RPML*, 27–38).

In this essay, one can clearly discern the noninstrumentalism and critique of purpose that will be a constant feature of Oakeshott's ethical and political outlook. Listen to this wonderful passage on "achievement" from his unpublished notebooks (circa 1964):

> "Achievement" is the "diabolical" element in human life; and the symbol of our vulgarization of human life is our near exclusive concern with achievement. Not scientific thinking, but the "gifts" of "science"; the motor car, the telephone, radar, getting to the moon, anti-biotics, penicillin, telstar, the bomb. Whereas the only human value lies in the adventure and the excitement of discovery. Not standing on the top of Everest, but getting there. Not the "conquests" but the battles; not the "victory" but the "play." It is our non-recognition of this, or our rejection of it, which makes our civilization a non-religious civilization. At least, non-Christian: Christianity is the religion of "non-achievement."[32]

It is an idiosyncratic and poetic understanding of religion and Christianity that finds expression in "Religion and the World." Oakeshott quotes a number of poets in support of his view— Wordsworth, Shelley, Goethe—but perhaps the most revealing quote is from Walter Pater's *Marius the Epicurean*: the religious man seeks "freedom from all embarrassment alike of regret for the past and calculation on the future" (*RPML*, 37). Pater was a favorite author of Oakeshott's,[33] and the emphasis on present sensibility and making the most of every moment in "Religion and the World" is highly reminiscent of Pater's aesthetic philosophy of life. In the famous conclusion to *The Renaissance*, Pater wrote: "The service of philosophy, of speculative culture"—Oakeshott would say of religion—"toward the human spirit"

> is to rouse, to startle it to a life of constant and eager observation. Every moment some form grows perfect in hand or face; some tone on the hills or the sea is choicer than the rest; some mood of passion or insight or intellectual excitement is irresistibly real and attractive to us,—for the moment only. Not the fruit of experience, but experience itself, is the end.[34]

The last line especially sums up Oakeshott's noninstrumentalist ethical-religious ideal—not only at the end of the 1920s, but at the end of his life.

Philosophy and Experience

Experience and Its Modes provides a systematic framework for the defense of the two forms of experience that preoccupied Oakeshott in the 1920s: philosophy and religion. It is his concern with the former that is dominant. In the introduction, he states clearly that the purpose of the book is to discover the implications of a certain conception of philosophy: namely, the idea of philosophy as "experience without presupposition, reservation, arrest or modification" (*EM*, 2). As he did in his 1928 lectures on "The Philosophical Approach to Politics," he elucidates the meaning of this conception of philosophy by differentiating philosophical experience from three of the most important forms of non-philosophical experience: science, history, and practice. The reasons for proceeding in this way should be clear from our consideration of Oakeshott's earlier writings. The chief threat to philosophy in the current positivist and pragmatist climate comes from its confusion with and subordination to science, history, and practice. "It is scarcely to be expected, in these days," Oakeshott writes, "that we should not be tempted to take up with the idea of philosophy as, in some sense, 'the fusion of the sciences,' 'the synthesis of the sciences' or the *scientia scientarum*" (*EM*, 2). Against the three great reductivisms of our age—scientism, historicism, and pragmatism—Oakeshott seeks to vindicate the autonomy, and indeed the superiority, of philosophy.

Experience and Its Modes is not, however, exclusively concerned with philosophy and its relationship to the various forms of non-philosophical experience. It is also concerned with the relationship of these forms of experience to one another—of science to history, of science to practice, and of history to practice. The most serious form of intellectual error, Oakeshott claims, is *ignoratio elenchi*, or the fallacy of irrelevance, which arises from the failure to keep the various modes of experience separate and distinct. Therefore, he devotes considerable space in *Experience and Its Modes* to specifying the logical distinctions between the modes and criticizing some of the more common forms of category mistake. He is particularly concerned—as his early theological writings would lead us to expect—to protect practical life from the irrelevant intrusions of science and history, especially as these latter have been used to criticize the claims of religion. Alongside this, we find a new concern with protecting history from the irrelevant intrusions of science and the practical attitude.

All of this is carried out through an analysis of the nature of human experience, which Oakeshott conceives of in a thoroughly idealist manner. Experience is not something other than reality: it "stands for the concrete whole which analysis divides into 'experiencing' and 'what is experienced'" (*EM*, 9). The objects of experience are not independent of our experiencing of them but are constituted by mind or thought. This does not mean, however, that the subject of experience is the sole reality and the cause of what is experienced. To such subjective idealism Oakeshott, like his idealist predecessors, is unalterably opposed. As we have seen, it was only in the minds of "realist" critics that Hegelian and British idealism were identified with subjective idealism; and it was on this confusion that their "refutations" of idealism ultimately depended. Oakeshott sums up his view of the inseparability of experience and reality, along with the radically idealistic and hermeneutic point of view of his philosophy, by saying that "perhaps the only satisfactory view would be one which grasped, even more thoroughly than Hegel's, the fact that what we have, and all we have, is a world of 'meanings'" (*EM*, 61).

Like his idealist predecessors, Oakeshott also conceives of experience monistically: "experience is a single whole, within which modifications may be distinguished, but which admits of no final or absolute division" (*EM*, 10). Neither experience nor reality is composed of separate parts or departments. There is, in the end, only one experience and one reality, only a single system of experience to which all our experiences belong. Nor is this single system of experience to be thought of as the "sum-total" of our experiences. It is just this notion of experience as an aggregate or collection that Oakeshott wants to avoid by speaking of it as a system or whole. Individual experiences "are not fixed and finished units, merely to be added to, or subtracted from one another. Experiences can destroy one another, amplify one another, coalesce, suffer change, transformation and supersession" (*EM*, 348).

This monistic notion of experience as a single, undivided whole entails a change in the way we usually conceive of forms of experience such as history, science, and practice. No longer can these forms of experience be understood as separate *kinds* of experience corresponding to separate *parts* of reality. Instead, they must be conceived of as modifications of the single whole of experience. But there is an even more fundamental distinction than that between the various forms of experience that Oakeshott's monistic view of experience denies: namely, the empiricist distinction between mediate and immediate experience; the distinction, as it has traditionally been formulated, between thought and perception or thought and sensation. Siding more with Bosanquet and Joachim on this question than with Bradley, Oakeshott argues that there is no absolute or final distinction between thought and more elementary or immediate forms of experience such as sensation, perception, volition, intuition, or feeling. Thought is not simply a particular form of experience; it is ultimately inseparable from experience. Experience everywhere involves thought or judgment (*EM*, 10).

Oakeshott backs up this conclusion with an analysis of sensation, showing that it is never "isolated, simple, exclusive, and wholly unrelated; transient, inexpressible, unsharable and impossible of repetition." Sensation always involves at the very least a something recognized, and such recognition "involves us at once in judgment, in inference, in reflection, in thought" (*EM*, 11–14). Of course, the whole attempt to find a form of immediate experience outside of thought—in sensation or perception, for example—belongs to the foundationalist picture of knowledge that the British idealists consistently rejected. Oakeshott himself believes that this foundationalist picture of knowledge rests on a false and distorting analogy. We must rid ourselves of the notion, he writes, that "thought requires raw material, a datum which is not judgment." "In thought there is nothing analogous to the painter's colours or the builder's bricks—raw material existing apart from the use made of it." Thinking

> begins neither from sense-data, nor from given feelings or perceptions; it begins neither from what is immediate, nor with the manifold, the contradictory and the nonsensical. What is at first given in experience is single and significant, a One and not a Many. The given in thought is the complex situation in which we find ourselves in the first moments of consciousness. There is nothing immediate or "natural" in contrast to what is mediate or sophisticated; there are only degrees of sophistication. (*EM*, 18–20)

This passage points to another aspect of the given, besides the fact that it consists of ideas. The given is also said to be "single and significant, a One and not a Many." What receives expression here is Oakeshott's crucial notion of a "world," by which he means a "complex, integral whole or system" (*EM*, 28). The world given in experience is characterized by unity, albeit implicit and incomplete; nothing is simply separate, unique, isolated, or without significance. Like Joachim, Oakeshott distinguishes the unity that belongs to a world from that which belongs to a class. The unity of a class has its seat in an essence or principle, which is arrived at by abstracting a common element from a collection of particulars. It is, in short, an abstract universal. The unity of a world, on the other hand, is not merely a common element abstracted from the particulars that comprise it; rather, it is nothing other than these particulars in their mutual coherence. The unity that belongs to a world or system is one

> in which every element is indispensable, in which no one is more important than any other and none is immune from change and rearrangement. The unity of a world of ideas lies in its coherence, not in its conformity to or agreement with any one fixed idea. It is neither "in" nor "outside" its constituents, but is the character of its constituents insofar as they are satisfactory in experience. (*EM*, 32–33)

In a world or system, universal and particular are inseparable; the universal is, in short, a "concrete universal." Though Oakeshott does not use the term here, it is quite clear that what he theorizes under the rubric of the "unity of a world" is nothing other than this idealist notion of concrete universality.[35] It is a notion that will play a crucial role in his understanding of the various forms of human knowledge and activity.

That we begin in unity does not mean, of course, that there remains nothing to do or achieve in experience. For the unity with which we begin in experience is only partial and imperfect. For Oakeshott, the process in experience is one in which the partially integrated world of ideas given in experience is transformed into more of a world. This is accomplished by making explicit the unity that is already implicit in a given world of ideas. In "the development of a world of ideas," he writes, "we proceed always by way of implication. We never look *away from* a given world to another world, but always *at* a given world to discover the unity it implies" (*EM*, 29–31). This suggests that the criterion of experience, and of truth, is not correspondence—there is no independent reality or nonmental set of facts for our notions to correspond to—but coherence.

With this understanding of the general character of experience, Oakeshott can now more precisely specify the nature of philosophy. Philosophy is simply the effort to achieve a completely coherent world of ideas in experience: it is "experience without reservation or presupposition, experience which is self-conscious and self-critical throughout, in which the determination to remain unsatisfied with anything short of a completely coherent world of ideas is absolute and unqualified" (*EM*, 82). This completely coherent world of ideas is what previous idealists called the "absolute"; and Oakeshott significantly departs from Bradley—though not from Bosanquet and Joachim—by identifying it with philosophy.

What is the relationship between the absolute thus understood and the various modes of experience, or, as Bradley put it, between reality and its appearances? This is one of the most vexing issues in idealist philosophy. Bradley himself was not entirely clear about it, often merely asserting that appearances were *somehow* contained in the absolute. His most sustained discussion of the issue comes in *Appearance and Reality*, where he argues that appearances are somehow necessary and indispensable to the absolute: "in the Absolute no appearance can be lost. Each one contributes and is essential to the unity of the whole." What, after all, could the absolute possibly be without appearances? "Appearance without reality would be impossible, for what then could appear? And reality without appearance would be nothing, for there is certainly nothing outside of appearances."[36]

Oakeshott rejects this idea that the modes of experience are in any way necessary or contributory to the concrete whole of experience, but it is not clear that his solution to the problem of appearance and reality is any more satisfying than Bradley's. The key to his solution lies in the notion of modality, recalling Spinoza's distinction between substantial (self-dependent) and modal (dependent) being. A mode of experience results when the concrete movement toward an absolutely coherent world of experience is "arrested" and a restricted world of abstract ideas constructed at the point of the arrest. By calling it a "mode" Oakeshott means to indicate that such a world of ideas is not a separate *kind* of experience but the whole of experience arrested—modified—at a certain point. A mode of experience "is not a separable part of reality, but the whole from a limited standpoint. It is not an island in the sea of experience, but a limited view of the totality of experience. It is not partial (in the literal sense), but abstract" (*EM*, 71). Conceived of in this way, a mode of experience cannot possibly contribute toward the creation of an absolutely coherent world of ideas. It is a distraction from the concrete end of experience, an abstraction from the concrete whole.

Oakeshott draws from this a radical and not altogether satisfying conclusion. Since modes of experience such as science, history, and practice contribute nothing to the achievement of an absolutely coherent world of experience—indeed, lead away from it, distract from it, hinder it—they must be avoided or rejected. The "main business" of philosophy is precisely to carry out this critical task of rejection (*EM*, 4, 83) and thus clear the way for . . . what? This is the question that confronts us when we try to flesh out Oakeshott's highly paradoxical conception of philosophy. We come back to Bradley's point that "reality without appearance would be nothing, for there is certainly nothing outside appearances." As one perceptive reviewer of *Experience and Its Modes* put it: it is difficult to see "what precisely philosophy is if art, religion, science, history, and practical experience are all irrelevant to it, and if it comes upon the scene only after they have been destroyed or avoided."[37]

Difficulties also arise when we consider the method by which philosophy criticizes and rejects the modes of experience. For Oakeshott, the critical authority of philosophy vis-à-vis the modes of experience rests on the fact that it satisfies—or at least pursues explicitly—the criterion of coherence that the modes themselves implicitly recognize but fail to satisfy in full. Philosophical criticism here is not external but immanent. Another way Oakeshott puts this point is that every mode "constitutes a self-contradiction": its explicit character as a mode contradicts its implicit character as experience; the explicit aim it pursues contradicts the criterion of coherence it implicitly acknowledges (*EM*, 4, 71, 75, 79–80). But all of this depends on the monistic assumption that there is only one world of experience, with one end or criterion, namely, coherence (*EM*, 81). Part of the confusion seems to lie in the way coherence functions in the argument. It may be that truth within a given mode of experience is grounded in coherence, but that does not imply that the mode implicitly acknowledges or pursues the absolute coherence ascribed to philosophy. Perhaps every mode of experience pursues coherence within its own terms, full stop. There is no self-contradiction because there is no generic coherence that all modes of experience acknowledge but fail to fulfill. Perhaps there is not one world of experience but innumerable perspectives—to use Nietzsche's word—that cannot be reduced to any common denominator. This is the pluralism toward which Oakeshott will eventually move later on in his career.

Along with the idea that the modes are necessary or contributory to the absolute experience of philosophy, Oakeshott rejects the Hegelian attempt to determine the exact degree of defect in each of the modes "and thus determine a logical hierarchy of modes." Here again he differs from Bradley, who argued that a complete metaphysics—which he did not claim to provide—would necessarily involve the hierarchical ordering of the various forms of experience "according to their comparative degrees of reality and truth."[38] Such a project, Oakeshott claims, involves a "misconception of the business of philosophy." Though the modes certainly represent different degrees of abstraction, from the standpoint of philosophy these differences are "irrelevant"; "from that standpoint all that is visible is the fact of abstraction, of defect and shortcoming." Once again, Oakeshott's rather abstemious conception of philosophy rears its head: in order to realize its character, "it is not necessary for philosophy to determine the exact degree of defect belonging to any presented abstract world of ideas, it is necessary only to recognize abstraction and overcome it" (*EM*, 83–84).

Oakeshott's argument here invites comparison with a book that bears a number of striking resemblances to *Experience and Its Modes*: namely R. G. Collingwood's *Speculum Mentis, or The Map of Knowledge*. Though published in 1924, Oakeshott never refers to *Speculum Mentis* and apparently claimed not to have read it until after writing *Experience and Its Modes*. Nevertheless, the similarities between the two books are striking and the differences instructive. Like *Experience and Its Modes*, *Speculum Mentis* is cast in the form of a philosophy of the forms of experience. It, too, draws heavily on the British idealist tradition, though Collingwood is more reluctant than Oakeshott to identify himself with it. Like Oakeshott, Collingwood reflects on the major forms of experience—art, religion, science, and history—and shows that each is incomplete, self-contradictory, and abstract when viewed from the standpoint of absolute knowledge. It is only in philosophy that the absolute knowledge implied in all our experiences is finally and explicitly achieved. Where Collingwood departs from Oakeshott, however, and remains truer to Bradley and Hegel, is in arranging the various forms of experience in a hierarchy of increasing coherence and concreteness and showing how each successive form of experience emerges dialectically out of and resolves the self-contradictions of the previous form.

Another important difference leaps out on the first page of *Speculum Mentis*, where Collingwood writes: "All thought exists for the sake of action. We try to understand ourselves and our world only in order that we may learn how to live. The end of our self-knowledge is not the contemplation by enlightened intellects of their own mysterious nature, but the freer and more effectual self-revelation of that nature in a vigorous practical life."[39] No such union of theory and practice is possible on Oakeshott's understanding of the relationship between the concrete world of philosophy and the abstract world of practice. Philosophy can do nothing to further the aims of any abstract world of experience. This means that philosophy must leave history to the historians, science to the scientists, and practice to the virtuosi of morality, religion, and politics. Philosophy may supersede an abstract form of experience, but it cannot take its place. To pass in argument from what is concrete to what is abstract, or vice versa, is an example of *ignoratio elenchi* (*EM*, 81,

353–54). Oakeshott develops the implications of this view in his specific analyses of history, science, and practice.

History, Science, and Practice

Oakeshott begins his critique of the modes with an analysis of historical knowledge. The chapter on history is by far the most original in *Experience and Its Modes* and attracted the most attention. Collingwood was so struck by this chapter that he wrote in his review of the book that Oakeshott's theory of the modes of experience

> has been arrived at, I suspect, mainly from an intense effort to understand the nature of historical knowledge. Mr. Oakeshott writes of history like an accomplished historian, who, driven into philosophy by the problems of his own work, has found current philosophies impotent to cope with their philosophical implications; and in that sense the chapter on history seems to me the real nucleus of the book.[40]

From what we have seen so far, this does not accurately portray the genesis of Oakeshott's project in *Experience and Its Modes*—though it does describe rather nicely the genesis of Collingwood's own philosophy. In taking up the various modes of experience, including history, Oakeshott's primary concern is to show that none embody the concrete knowledge pursued in philosophy. Indeed, one could say that he is primarily concerned to save philosophy from precisely the historicism that came to characterize Collingwood's own philosophical outlook.

Nevertheless, Oakeshott's nonempiricist account of experience does seem to be more readily applicable to historical knowledge than, say, to natural science. In natural science, the empiricist model of knowledge, with its foundationalist metaphor of the builder and his bricks, seems at least plausible. The natural scientist appears to begin with the immediate facts of perception and to construct her knowledge by building on top of that absolutely certain foundation. In history, on the other hand, there is no purely empirical "datum" to speak of; nothing is simply "given." The facts that the historian tries to ascertain have, unlike the facts of natural science, disappeared; they need to be reconstructed. The ostensible object of history, the past course of events, is simply not "there" for the historian in the same way that nature seems to be "there" for the scientist.

This, indeed, is the first point that Oakeshott seeks to establish. Against a naïve objectivism, he argues that history is experience, a world of ideas, and not simply a world of empirical or "objective" fact; it is a world constructed and not simply discovered by the historian. There is no absolute division between the objective "course of events" and "our interpretation of it," between history and historiography. This point has, of course, become a commonplace among both historians and philosophers; and Oakeshott puts it in characteristically radical terms: "History is experience, the historian's world of experience; it is a world of ideas, the historian's world of ideas." By this, he does not mean to proclaim a radical historical relativism or skepticism. Though history consists of the historian's experience, it is not merely *his* experience. The historian's experience is also relatively true or false, and this makes it more than his psychical state as such (*EM*, 89–96).

Oakeshott next shows that historical experience pursues the process characteristic of all experience, the process by which a given world of ideas is transformed into a more coherent world of ideas. History does not begin with the collection of raw data or isolated facts. Whatever comes before the historian as data or material already belongs to a specific world of meaning determined by the postulates and presuppositions of historical inquiry. In addition to these postulates, the historian also comes to whatever she happens to be studying with a general view of the course of events, a hypothesis to guide her in her inquiry. Of course, the "facts" as they are originally conceived come to be transformed as the historian's inquiry proceeds. The given facts are not fixed and inviolable; they are completely dependent on the whole world to which they belong. Any change in this world necessitates a transformation of the "facts" themselves. Historical knowledge thus exemplifies the logic of the concrete universal in which universal and particular, world and fact, interpretation and text, are inseparable (*EM*, 96–99).[41] Oakeshott elaborates on the concrete, "worldly," systematic—one might also say hermeneutic—character of historical fact in this way:

> The truth of each fact depends upon the truth of the world of facts to which it belongs, and the truth of the world of facts lies in the coherence of the facts which compose it. In historical experience, as in all other experience, there are no absolute data, nothing given which is immune from change; each element rests upon and supports every other element. (*EM*, 113)

So far Oakeshott has been concerned to show, against a naïve objectivism, that history is experience, the historian's present world of experience, and not the past course of events; it is "what the evidence obliges us to believe" and not *was eigentlich geschehen ist.* But his whole thesis is not simply that history is experience, but that it is a *modification* of experience, the whole of experience from a limited standpoint. What are the specific presuppositions in terms of which the historian organizes the whole of experience and reality?

According to Oakeshott, the master-postulate or category of historical experience is the idea of the past. History is experience *sub specie praeteritorum*; it is an attempt to organize the whole of experience in the form of the past. But the past in terms of which the historian organizes his present experience is not just any past; it is a special past, which must be distinguished from other pasts, most notably the practical past. The practical past is the past viewed in relation to the present. Whenever the past is viewed as developing toward, influencing, or justifying the present, it is a practical, not a historical, past. This is the past as it is often used in religion. Indeed, the "historical element" in Christianity, about which Oakeshott wrote in the 1920s, is a perfect example of the practical use of the past, designed to justify and make vivid certain practical beliefs. The historical past, on the other hand, is "the past for its own sake"; it is "a dead past; a past unlike the present" (*EM*, 102–6). Here Oakeshott echoes the views of his former housemate and fellow junior lecturer on the Cambridge History faculty, Herbert Butterfield, who wrote in his 1931 *Whig Interpretation of History* that "the chief aim of the historian is the elucidation of the unlikenesses between the past and the present" and the chief error of Whig history that "it studies the past with reference to the present."[42]

Another feature of the historical past, related to its deadness, is that it is seen as "objective," independent of the historian, "what really happened." It is this feature that ultimately makes historical experience self-contradictory, according to Oakeshott. The historian's belief in the pastness and "objectivity" of the past contradicts the actual character of history as present experience. The historian is guilty of a certain kind of philosophical error, and this error is indispensable to carrying on his activity (*EM*, 106–11, 146–47).

This is a highly dubious criticism. Oakeshott maintains that the historian cannot transcend the presupposition of *was eigentlich geschehen ist* without at the same time ceasing to be a historian: the pastness of the past is what the historian "is accustomed to believe"; it "encourages" him; "it is difficult to see how he could go on did he not believe his task to be the resurrection of what once had been alive" (*EM*, 106–7), But is this true? There is probably no practicing historian who subscribes to the naïve objectivist notion of the past that Oakeshott attributes to history, and yet there is no shortage of historians who continue to find meaning in their activity. It seems to be perfectly possible to be philosophically sophisticated about history without destroying it or transcending it altogether.

Oakeshott points to another characteristic of history that convicts it of being an abstract form of experience: the individual in history is ultimately "designated" and not "defined." This criticism invokes the idealist conception of individuality as what is inclusive and self-complete, not what is merely particular, separate, or isolated. The historical individual—whether it be a historical event, institution, or person—partakes of a certain amount of inclusiveness and continuity with its environment, but this inclusiveness and continuity must ultimately be limited if we are not to end up writing a universal history of the world. For Oakeshott, it is the arbitrariness and merely designated character of the historical individual that convicts historical experience of abstraction and incoherence (*EM*, 43–45, 62–65, 119–24, 147–48).[43]

Here again, though, Oakeshott's criticism fails to convince. Though it is no doubt true that historical identities are always to some extent "designated," picked out and circumscribed from the notional totality of all that has happened, it is not clear that this renders the historian's activity futile or self-contradictory. It would do so only if there were some form of experience that altogether escaped the artificiality, angularity, or perspectival character of all human thought. In *Experience and Its Modes*, Oakeshott still believes that philosophy embodies such presuppositionless experience. He will later change his mind on this fundamental issue. Correspondingly, in his later discussions of history, he will confine himself to understanding the presuppositions of the historian's activity without showing that they involve self-contradiction, incoherence, or philosophical error.

From his criticisms of the notions of the past and of the individual that belong to history, Oakeshott concludes that it is an abstract and defective mode of experience. This means that, from the standpoint of philosophy, it must be avoided, rejected, overcome. History can only serve to hinder and distract from the pursuit of an absolutely coherent world of experience. This implies, among other things, that there is nothing in history of which philosophy can ever make any use. Everything in history is vitiated by abstraction, and what is abstract can make no contribution to the coherence of the concrete whole. Nor, by the same token, may philosophy take upon itself the task of making the world of historical experience more coherent—for example, by drawing connections between historical facts, or by discovering a plot or plan in them. The "philosophy of history" is, for Oakeshott, an example of *ignoratio elenchi* (*EM*, 148–49, 153–56).

The main significance of Oakeshott's analysis of history as an abstract mode of experience is that it repudiates any sort of radical or skeptical historicism. "Historicism" is, of course, a notoriously ambiguous term, but I understand by it here the reduction or assimilation of all knowledge, including philosophical knowledge, to historical knowledge.[44] For Oakeshott, philosophy is in no way reducible to history. The latter is an abstract world of experience that philosophy as concrete experience must avoid or reject. Nor can a philosophy be refuted by tracing it to its historical setting or situation. Place and time are irrelevant to philosophy. Of course, every philosophy has a place and time, a historical setting, but these are irrelevant to it *as a philosophy*. What matters about a philosophy is whether it is true or false, and no amount of historical investigation can answer this philosophical question (*EM*, 349).

It is instructive to compare Collingwood with Oakeshott on this question of historicism. Though there is much that links these two thinkers together, not least their common preoccupation with the problem of historical knowledge, in Collingwood there is a tendency toward historicism that is absent from Oakeshott's thought. As T. M. Knox points out in his preface to *The Idea of History*, Collingwood, like Croce, "came to think that 'philosophy as a separate discipline is liquidated by being converted to history.'"[45] Oakeshott, too, in a review of *The Idea of History*, draws attention to this historicistic tendency in Collingwood's thought: "it must be observed that, almost imperceptibly, Collingwood's philosophy of history turned into a philosophy in which all knowledge is assimilated to historical knowledge, and consequently into a radically sceptical philosophy."[46] In this extreme historicistic direction Oakeshott did not follow Collingwood, though we will see that he did eventually abandon the ahistorical view that time and place are completely irrelevant to political philosophy. Nevertheless, in his later writings as well as in *Experience and Its Modes*, the categorial distinction between philosophy and history is strictly maintained.

Let us now turn to Oakeshott's analysis of science, which we may treat more briefly because it is neither as rich nor as original as his discussion of history. His principal aim is to refute the positivist identification of science with knowledge itself by showing that science is not the concrete whole of experience but only an abstract mode. The scientist often fails to recognize the abstractness of her experience because she believes the methods of science are exactly fitted to a reality that lies outside of scientific thought, namely, nature. Scientific knowledge is thought to rest on the absolutely solid foundation of the facts of nature, facts generally conceived to be immediately given in perception. The theory of science has long been based on some such empiricist or objectivist model of knowledge, and Oakeshott joins a number of other philosophers of science—including Karl Popper, Michael Polanyi, Imre Lakatos, Thomas Kuhn, Paul Feyerabend, and Stephen Toulmin—in rejecting it.[47]

The first thing Oakeshott points out is that science does not begin with anything like the facts of perception. The aim of science is to achieve a world of universal, absolutely communicable experience, and in order to achieve this end it must "leave behind the world of perception." The world with which we begin in science is not the world of which we are aware when we first open our eyes; rather, it is a world arrived at through abstraction from this familiar world of perception and practical interest. Like Edmund Husserl, Oakeshott sees scientific activity as properly beginning only after it has transformed the world given to us in perception into a world of impersonal, absolutely communicable quantitative abstractions.[48] The world of scientific experience is the world *sub specie quantitatis*, the world conceived under the category of quantity (*EM*, 169–72).[49]

Having shown that the world given in scientific experience does not begin with empirical facts independent of scientific thought, Oakeshott goes on to argue that the development of this world is governed throughout by its presupposed, quantitative character. Scientific hypotheses are always framed in terms of the quantitative structural concepts given in scientific experience; and this is true of the observations and experiments used to confirm these hypotheses. Scientific observations are not merely empirical; they are always measurements, never percepts: "The eye of the scientific observer is a measure; scientific perception is itself measurement." Finally, the conclusions of science are consonant with its quantitative character. They are always in the form of statistical generalizations, which can never be disproved by a single empirical observation or counterexample (*EM*, 181–87, 201, 206–7).

From all this, it is clear that science cannot be the concrete whole of experience but only the whole from a limited and abstract standpoint. This is a valuable point and a decisive refutation of the positivist identification of scientific knowledge with knowledge itself. Unfortunately, in keeping with the absolute idealism of *Experience and Its Modes*, Oakeshott also wants to show that scientific experience is ultimately incoherent and self-contradictory. The specific self-contradiction involved in scientific experience stems from the generalized nature of its conclusions. Scientific knowledge is ultimately hypothetical or suppositional knowledge; it never asserts a categorical judgment about reality. As a result, its explicit aim as science contradicts its implicit character as experience. The recognition of this self-contradiction involves the destruction of the world of science as a distinctive world (*EM*, 208–11, 215). One could say that, just as the historian ceases to be a historian once he frees himself from the illusion of *was eigentlich geschehen ist*, so the scientist, once she recognizes the merely hypothetical character of her knowledge, ceases to be a scientist. With the achievement of such self-consciousness, science loses its raison d'être and appears as a merely misguided attempt to achieve a completely coherent world of ideas. Philosophy, Oakeshott concludes, "must begin by rejecting alike the methods and results of the arrest in experience called science" (*EM*, 219).

The difficulties with this argument are the same as those brought out above with respect to history, so we need not belabor them. The implications of Oakeshott's analysis of science, however, are not confined simply to the relationship between philosophy and science; they also entail a complete reassessment of the relationship between history and science. Of course, by the time Oakeshott came to it, a good deal of reflection had already been devoted to the problem of distinguishing history from science, the *Geisteswissenschaften* from the *Naturwissenschaften*. His own contribution to this problem focuses on the modal or categorial differences between history and science. The fundamental difference between history and science does not consist in the ontological distinction between their respective subject-matters, human beings and nature, but, rather, in the diametrically opposed presuppositions in terms of which each organizes the whole of reality. Thus Oakeshott allows for the possibility of a quantitative science of human beings, citing economics, psychology, and even political science as examples (*EM*, 219–43).[50] But he rejects the idea of a science of history as a confusion of genres or *ignoratio elenchi*.

As part of his effort to distinguish history from science, Oakeshott rejects the relevance of causal explanation to history. His position on this score is as radical as it can be—more radical than even Collingwood's—rejecting the notion of cause in any sense as incompatible with the presuppositions of history. In science, causality relates to a world of abstract instances, not of concrete events, and is therefore clearly incompatible with the presuppositions of history. More generally, the idea of causality depends on isolating an event and making it the cause of similarly isolated effects. But this, too, contradicts the character of history, which never isolates an event from its environment or severs it from its relationships to other events. The historian does not seek to explain the connections between events in terms of extrinsic causes or general laws but, like the novelist, "by means of greater and more complete detail." The principle of explanation invoked here is what Oakeshott calls "continuity":

> the only explanation of change relevant or possible in history is simply a complete account of change. History accounts *for* change by means of a full account *of* change. The relation *between* events is always other events, and it is established in history by a full relation *of* the events. The conception of cause is thus replaced by the exhibition of a world of events intrinsically related to one another in which no *lacuna* is tolerated. (*EM*, 126–32, 141–43)

As a number of critics have noticed, it is not clear from this just what the "intrinsic relation" between events consists in for Oakeshott, or how, without encompassing the totality of history, the historian decides what is relevant or irrelevant to her account.[51] Some criterion of inclusion or exclusion, of significance or insignificance, would seem to be required. Oakeshott attempts to fill this gap in his later account of historical explanation in *On History*, published 50 years after *Experience and Its Modes*.

The final mode of experience that Oakeshott takes up is practical experience. Once again, he is primarily concerned to show that practice is an abstract mode of experience, that it does not provide what is finally satisfactory in experience, and that it therefore must be avoided or superseded. This critical examination of practical experience is of the utmost importance because, of all the modes, practice is the most alluring and distracting. Far more frequently than either science or history, practice has been taken to be the concrete whole of experience, what is absolute and satisfactory in experience. Philosophy has always suffered from the despotism of practice, as has history; even "the emancipation of science from the despotism of practice" has been "slow and uncertain." This insistence on the despotic and limiting character of practical life runs though almost all of Oakeshott's writings and distinguishes his anti-positivism from that of many of his contemporaries—not only the pragmatists, but also the existentialists who assert the primacy of practical life or the *Lebenswelt*.

Oakeshott's account of practical experience is highly derivative of Bradley's.[52] He locates the *differentia* of practice in the idea of action or alteration of existence: practice is experience *sub specie voluntatis*. Practical activity involves the alteration of "what is" so as to make it agree with an unrealized idea, a "to be" that is "not yet." It presupposes two discrepant worlds—a world of "what is" and a world of "to be"—and consists essentially in the attempt to reconcile them. The discrepancy between these two worlds, however, can never finally be resolved, and this is what prevents practice from ever achieving a completely satisfactory or coherent world of experience. The resolution of the discrepancy between "what is here and now" and "what ought to be" that practice undertakes can never be definitively accomplished: "No sooner is it realized at one point in the world of practical existence, than a new discord springs up elsewhere, demanding a new resolution." Every success in practical life is partial and contains the seeds of new imperfections and future tasks: "Nowhere in practice is there uninterrupted progress or final achievement" (*EM*, 256–63, 288–91).

Oakeshott repeats here what he argued in his early essay on "Religion and the Moral Life": that the endlessness of practical life is to some extent mitigated in religion. Religion is "practical life in its most concrete mood"; it is the "consummation of practice" (*EM*, 292–95). Nevertheless, practical experience never altogether escapes incompletion, and this constitutes its essential abstractness. To resolve the discrepancy between "is" and "ought" once and for all is impossible because it would involve the destruction of practical experience itself. Like all abstract modes of experience, practice is self-contradictory. It attempts to resolve the discrepancy that is the very condition of its existence (*EM*, 304). It follows from this, at least according to Oakeshott, that practical experience "must be rejected *in toto*." It is a divergence from the concrete purpose in experience and prevents us from achieving an absolutely coherent world of ideas:

> Not until we have become wholly indifferent to the truths of this world of practice, not until we have shaken off the abstractions of practical experience, of morality and religion, good and evil, faith and freedom, body and mind, the practical self and its ambitions and desires, shall we find ourselves once more turned in the direction which leads to what can satisfy the character of experience. (*EM*, 310–11)

An important implication of this analysis is that the conclusions of philosophy cannot be established or disproved by appeal to practical experience. To subject the conclusions of philosophy to the criticism of practice is to commit an *ignoratio elenchi*. But Oakeshott is even more emphatic about the irrelevance of philosophy to the world of practical experience. Philosophy can make no relevant contribution to the coherence of this abstract world. Practice takes place—it must take place—in a kind of "mental fog." Philosophy as self-conscious and self-critical thought can only serve to disperse this "mental fog" on which practical success and satisfaction depend: "It is not the clear-sighted, not those who are fashioned for thought and the ardors of thought, who can lead the world. Great achievements are accomplished in the mental fog of practical experience. What is farthest from our needs is that kings should be philosophers" (*EM*, 319–21, 353–55).

This is perhaps a strange conclusion for someone destined to make his greatest contribution in the area of political philosophy to reach. How Oakeshott takes the idea of philosophy defended in *Experience and Its Modes* and applies it to political philosophy is what we must investigate next.

3 Political Philosophy

Having freed philosophy, in *Experience and Its Modes*, from the dangerous confusions produced by scientism, historicism, and pragmatism, Oakeshott could now begin to address the most pressing issues of political philosophy. He did not, however, leave the epistemological and methodological preoccupations of *Experience and Its Modes* entirely behind. Indeed, what is striking about Oakeshott's writings on political philosophy in the 1930s is how much they continue to be concerned with the metapolitical issue of the nature of political philosophy. And what more than anything he emphasizes about the nature of political philosophy is its "radically subversive" character, its dissolving impact on the categories of ordinary reflection on politics.[1] The corollary of this radically subversive character of political philosophy is that it can never serve as a guide or aid to political activity. The furthest thing from our needs is that philosophers should be kings.

This antipolitical conception of political philosophy was, of course, radically at odds with the intellectual temper of the 1930s in Britain. Many writers and academics of the Auden generation were attracted by the union of theory and practice in communism, and those who weren't became politicized in reaction against the extremist ideologies of communism and fascism. Oakeshott's fellow idealist R. G. Collingwood was typical in this latter regard, writing in his *Autobiography* that the events of the 1930s, especially the policy of appeasement, "broke up my pose of a detached professional thinker."[2] This was not the case with Oakeshott, whose philosophical detachment during this critical time, while possessing an austere integrity, can also appear weirdly out of touch. He rarely commented on the tumultuous events of the decade; and even in his volume on *The Social and Political Doctrines of Contemporary Europe*, published in 1939, he maintained a studiously neutral stance on the respective merits of representative democracy, communism, fascism, National Socialism, and Catholicism, insisting that "this is a book for those interested in ideas" (*SPD*, xiv).

All of this makes it extremely difficult to discern what Oakeshott's considered views on substantive political issues in the 1930s were. It is not even clear that his outlook was particularly conservative, though there was certainly a conservative bias in his sharp distinction between theory and practice. Perry Anderson is way off the mark when he asserts that Oakeshott in the 1930s spoke "with the authentic voice of the radical Right" and compares him to Carl Schmitt.[3] Nevertheless, there are hints of Oakeshott's general political outlook in his writings from this time, and there are glimmers of his substantive political philosophy to come. I pursue these hints and glimmers in the second half of this chapter, but first we must consider his much more thorough discussion of the nature of political philosophy.

What is Political Philosophy?

Though Oakeshott does not explicitly discuss political philosophy in *Experience and Its Modes*, he gives some indication of its nature in the brief discussion of ethical thought toward the end of the book. There he makes two points that recur throughout his discussions of the nature of political philosophy. First, he denies the view, traditional since Aristotle, that ethics is somehow practical or normative. Ethics is the attempt to *define* our moral and practical concepts, and this attempt is completely different from the attempt to construct or make coherent a world of values. Here Oakeshott simply repeats what he has already said about the general relationship between philosophy and practice: the judgments that belong to each are irrelevant to each other, and therefore a truly philosophical ethics will never be able to offer any sort of practical guidance (*EM*, 336–40). He also echoes Bradley's view (quoted more fully above), that the business of ethics is not to prescribe or construct a morality: "All philosophy has to do is 'understand what is,' and moral philosophy has to understand morals which exist, not to make them or give directions for making them. . . . [E]thics has not to make the world moral, but to reduce to theory the morality current in the world."[4]

The second point Oakeshott makes about ethical thought concerns the nature of philosophical definition. In opposition to intuitionist thinkers like G. E. Moore, H. A. Prichard, E. F. Carritt, and W. D. Ross, who held that moral concepts were ultimately irreducible and indefinable—to define moral concepts like right and good in terms of nonmoral ideas was to commit the "naturalistic fallacy"—Oakeshott argues that an adequate definition of any concept can never be achieved in terms of the abstract world or context in which it is first presented to us. Philosophical definition involves relating what is abstract to a world or context that is concrete; it involves making explicit the reference to reality that remains only implicit in our abstract experience. This process of making explicit what is merely implicit, of referring abstract concepts to reality or the totality of experience, is a transformative process; philosophical definition always involves transformation and supersession. For this reason, Oakeshott concludes that it is impossible to philosophically explain or define the abstract concepts of morality and practice "without explaining them, as such, away" (*EM*, 340–44).

This second point expresses what is perhaps the most distinctive feature of Oakeshott's idea of philosophical explanation, the feature that has the greatest consequences for his entire understanding of the nature of political philosophy: I mean the transformative character of philosophical thought. For Oakeshott, what we begin with in experience is never absolute or completely satisfactory; it is simply where we begin. As we concretely reflect on this initial "datum" and try to see it in a wider context, it soon loses those abstract features that initially identified it for us. We leave behind one world and enter another. This does not happen all at once; but at some point in the course of reflection we become aware that the old world and everything in it has been transformed utterly. It is precisely because he sees such a total transformation taking place that Oakeshott denies that we can "apply" the concrete knowledge gained in the process of philosophical reflection to the abstract world from which we began. Philosophy can offer no practical guidance because it has left behind the abstract concepts and categories upon which the practical world depends.

Oakeshott elaborates these ideas about philosophical definition and explanation in relation to political philosophy in his important 1938 essay, "The Concept of a Philosophical Jurisprudence." The object of this essay, he states at the outset, "is to consider the meaning and possibility of a philosophy of law and civil society" ("CPJ," 203). He is particularly concerned to determine the relationship of a philosophical explanation of the nature of law to the various forms of explanation that currently constitute the world of jurisprudence. This task is especially urgent because philosophical jurisprudence is currently conceived of as merely one kind of explanation of law among others, no more valid or comprehensive than any other explanation ("CPJ," 213). From the standpoint of *Experience and Its Modes*, this involves a gross misunderstanding of the nature of philosophy. Philosophy is not one mode of experience among others, it is the concrete whole that the modes imply. And philosophical explanation is not simply one explanation among others, it is the criterion by which all other explanations must be judged.

Oakeshott considers four prominent nonphilosophical approaches to law current in early twentieth-century Britain: analytical jurisprudence (founded by John Austin), historical jurisprudence (associated with Henry Maine, Frederick Maitland, and Paul Vinogradoff), sociological jurisprudence, and economic jurisprudence. He emphasizes that these are not "complementary methods of inquiry" but "mutually exclusive types of explanation." The differences between them, like the differences between the modes of experience, are not differences of emphasis or of subject-matter; "they are differences of principle" ("CPJ," 214). To accept one theory is to deny the others. The world of jurisprudence is constituted by an unresolved variety of mutually exclusive explanations of the nature of law. This is a situation that philosophy might be expected to remedy, but, on current conceptions of philosophical jurisprudence, it only contributes to the confusion, adding one more dissonant voice to the cacophony.

Oakeshott goes on to consider a number of misconceptions of the philosophy of law, each of which "assumes that a philosophical interpretation of law is merely one interpretation among others, to be pursued if we feel inclined, to be tolerated or dismissed as ineffectual." The most pervasive misconception involves the view that the philosophy of law is the application of some previously thought-out philosophical doctrine to law and legally organized society. The philosophy of law is here conceived of as resting on a philosophy but not as being itself philosophical ("CPJ," 215–16). Another common misconception of the philosophy of law holds that it is normative, involving the consideration of legal rules and arrangements in terms of their goodness and badness and the determination of the end law ought to pursue. The purpose of such a normative philosophy of law is, "not to define the nature of 'right,' but to determine the rightness or wrongness of the legal arrangements of a society." It is clear from what Oakeshott has already said about the nature of ethical thought in *Experience and Its Modes* why he rejects this view of the nature of philosophical jurisprudence. Definition of our moral and legal concepts is one thing, the practical evaluation of these concepts and the construction of a world of value another. "To investigate the nature of a moral criterion is an ethical and a philosophical enquiry; but to determine the goodness and badness of a law involves a moral judgment which the philosopher as such is in no better position to give than any other member of society" ("CPJ," 217–18).

In opposition to these misconceptions of the philosophy of law, Oakeshott recapitulates the idea of philosophy found in *Experience and Its Modes*. Philosophical knowledge, he writes, "is not a special kind of knowledge derived from some special source of information"; it is simply "thought and knowledge without reservation or presupposition." Beginning with "the concepts of ordinary, everyday knowledge," philosophy seeks to extend our knowledge of these concepts by discovering what is implied in them. In Socratic fashion, Oakeshott insists on the continuity between philosophical definition and prephilosophical experience. The philosopher does not begin with universal doubt. Prephilosophical experience is not simply nescience; it implicitly contains a reference to the whole or the totality of experience, and the task of the philosopher is to make this implicit reference explicit. In philosophy, we never pass "from mere ignorance to complete knowledge"; we always pass from what is only half known, what is known confusedly and indistinctly, to what is known more fully and systematically. The process in philosophy "is always one of coming to know more fully and clearly what is in some sense already known" ("CPJ," 345–47).

The essentially Socratic view of philosophy that Oakeshott defends here bears some striking similarities to the outlook of early analytic philosophers such as Moore, Prichard, Carritt, and Ross, who held that philosophy is "not discovery or information or knowledge, not proof or justification, but clarification or analysis of what is already otherwise known." These writers, along with Russell and Wittgenstein, imposed on twentieth-century British philosophy "the axiom that philosophy is a 'second-order' activity of analysis of 'first-order' knowledge."[5] In Wittgenstein's memorable formulation: "[Philosophy] leaves everything as it is."[6]

There is much in this conception of philosophy that Oakeshott could agree with, in this regard differing sharply from Collingwood. Collingwood lamented the influence that the analytic ethical philosophy of Moore and Prichard had had on the moral education of the young. Whereas T. H. Green and other British idealists had given their pupils "ideals to live for and principles to live by," Prichard and his followers "advocated a new kind of moral philosophy, purely theoretical, in which the workings of the moral consciousness should be scientifically studied as if they were the movements of the planets, and no attempt made to interfere with them." It was "the moral corruption propagated by the 'realist' dogma that moral philosophy does no more than study in a purely theoretical spirit a subject-matter which it leaves wholly unaffected by that investigation" that led Collingwood to seek a "*rapprochement* between theory and practice."[7] Such a rapprochement was, of course, explicitly not part of Oakeshott's agenda for moral and political philosophy.

While there are a number of similarities between Oakeshott's view of philosophy and that of analytic thinkers, there are some no less significant differences. That philosophy begins with and analyzes the knowledge contained in our ordinary concepts, so far Oakeshott is in agreement with the analytic view. But for the analytic philosopher, this initial knowledge remains in some sense absolute; it is a datum that philosophy may analyze but never criticize or go beyond. It is just such a view that Oakeshott denies when he asserts that the conclusions of philosophy must be "new"; they must differ from the common-sense notion with which philosophical inquiry begins. "There *must* be disagreement between a concept as it is for, say, common sense, and as it is for philosophy." In the course of philosophical inquiry, the prephilosophical or commonsensical concept with which we begin undergoes radical transformation. For this reason, the conclusions of philosophy cannot be checked by appeal to ordinary experience or common sense. " 'Verification' in philosophical enquiry," Oakeshott writes, pointedly invoking the logical-positivist term of art, "lies always ahead in what the concept is to become, and never behind in what it was when we first began work upon it" ("CPJ," 348–49). Philosophy leaves everything as it is insofar as it makes no direct contribution to the coherence of an abstract world of ideas, but this does not mean that philosophy simply accepts things as they first present themselves, confining itself to mere "analysis."

Two philosophers, according to Oakeshott, exemplify the conception of political philosophy he elaborates in "The Concept of a Philosophical Jurisprudence": Hobbes and Hegel. Oakeshott states this explicitly in a posthumously published manuscript entitled "The Concept of a Philosophy of Politics" (*RPML*, 126, 137). This manuscript makes many of the same points that are found in "The Concept of a Philosophical Jurisprudence," and often in identical language, suggesting that it was written somewhat earlier and mined extensively by Oakeshott for the published article.[8] The manuscript is important because it makes clear that the idea of philosophy that Oakeshott applies to jurisprudence in "The Concept of a Philosophical Jurisprudence" is equally applicable to political philosophy. And it also underlines the intriguing dual influence that Hobbes and Hegel exerted on Oakeshott's conception of political philosophy at this point in his career. I will be examining this dual influence more closely later on in the chapter.

What precisely is the connection between Oakeshott's remarks on the nature of philosophical inquiry and the criticisms he makes of current conceptions of philosophical jurisprudence? The chief defect he discovered in current notions of philosophical jurisprudence was that they conceived of it as merely one among a number of mutually exclusive and equally valid explanations of the nature of law. This defect is remedied in Oakeshott's conception of a philosophical jurisprudence. Such a jurisprudence stands at the end of the process of concrete and critical reflection on the nature of law, having superseded all other limited or partial views; it is at once the most complete explanation of the nature of law and the criterion by which all other explanations must be judged. This process of critical reflection might begin with the essentially abstract definition of law found in, say, analytical jurisprudence; and from there it might pass to wider, more concrete contexts from which to view law, for example, politics, history, economic organization, and social structure. Sooner or later, though, we arrive at a context that does not itself require further explanation, a context that is immune from criticism and cannot be superseded. This, for Oakeshott, is the standpoint of the philosophy of law ("CPJ," 352–53).

The process Oakeshott outlines here is well illustrated in one of his earliest articles, "The Authority of the State" (1929). Addressing himself there to the question of the nature of the state, he observes that we are initially confronted by a multiplicity of different conceptions of the state, and argues—much in the manner of "The Concept of a Philosophical Jurisprudence"—that we must not simply acquiesce in this multiplicity: "the view I wish to suggest is that a complete conception of the state is one which supersedes all others and beside which they appear neither as possible alternatives, nor as contradictions nor as contributions, but as abstractions to be supplanted." He goes on to consider some of the more common conceptions of the state—the state understood as a piece of territory, as a collection of legal or economic persons, as a secular whole, and finally as the political machinery of government—rejecting each as an abstraction from concrete social reality. Where, then, is a concrete conception of the state to be found, a conception that is "self-subsistent" and "carries with it the explanation of itself and requires to be linked on to no more comprehensive whole to be understood"? Only in "the social whole which is correlative to individuals who are complete and living persons; or, in other words, the totality in an actual community which satisfies the whole mind of the individuals who comprise it" (*RPML*, 81–83). Oakeshott here ends up with something like a full-blown Hegelian definition of the state. Indeed, what is interesting about this early article—apart from illustrating the conception of political philosophy that Oakeshott would fully elaborate a decade later in "The Concept of a Philosophical Jurisprudence"—is that it reveals his Hegelianism to be as much a philosophy of explanation as anything else.

Recovering the Tradition of Political Philosophy

"The Concept of a Philosophical Jurisprudence" is for the most part concerned with the metapolitical issue of the nature of legal and political philosophy. It provides little practical guidance on the question of where, as a matter of actual procedure, we might begin today to construct a genuinely philosophical theory of law and civil society. Toward the end of the essay, however, he offers a few suggestive remarks on this score, stating that "the greatest hindrances which stand in the way of a fresh and profitable start with the philosophical enquiry into the nature of law are the prevailing ignorance about what has been accomplished in this enquiry, and the prejudice, that springs from ignorance, that little or nothing has been accomplished." Therefore, he argues that the "first item on our agenda" should be "a thorough reconsideration of the history of the philosophy of law, and in particular of the great texts which belong to that history. . . . The philosophical enquiry into the nature of law is not something we can begin today *de novo*, and spin out of our heads . . . without reference to what has gone before" ("CPJ," 357).

But in order to learn from the history of legal and political philosophy, Oakeshott insists that we must change our attitude toward it. For too long the history of philosophical jurisprudence has concerned itself with the conclusions or opinions found in a philosophical doctrine instead of with the reasons given for those conclusions. A concrete philosophical doctrine "provides a *ratio decidendi* for every *obiter dictum*," and it is with these *rationes decidendi* that the historian of philosophy ought properly to be concerned. Interestingly, Oakeshott calls for a more philosophical approach to the history of legal and political philosophy here, in contradistinction to the traditional historical approach that emphasizes conclusions and "the supposed effects or influence of those conclusions." Indeed, in order to distinguish what he has in mind from conventional history, he speaks of the "tradition" of philosophical jurisprudence, by which he means "the history of philosophical jurisprudence philosophically conceived, seen as a living, extemporary whole in which past and present are comparatively insignificant." This tradition is single and continuous, though our narrow focus on conclusions has blinded us to its unity and continuity. It is a tradition, not "of conclusions or even of questions," but of philosophical inquiry ("CPJ," 358–59).

These ideas on the history of legal and political philosophy are developed more fully in two articles—one on Bentham (1932), and one on

Hobbes (1935)—that Oakeshott wrote some years before "The Concept of a Philosophical Jurisprudence." The Bentham article is mainly an attack on the "new Bentham" of recent scholarship, which has attempted to rehabilitate Bentham by elevating him to the status of a great critical thinker, a philosopher who anticipated a number of recent developments in philosophical and political thought. Oakeshott, who lectured on utilitarianism throughout the 1930s, does not share this view. For him, Bentham is a creature of the eighteenth century, not a precursor to the twentieth, and he is the exact opposite of a critical thinker and a philosopher: he is a *philosophe*. According to Oakeshott, the *philosophe* is characterized by a faith in indiscriminate knowledge and "general credulity." He is also a rationalist. Here Oakeshott provides his first portrait of the disposition that will occupy a large part of his attention in the 1940s and 1950s:

> the *philosophe* is a rationalist, in the restricted sense that he believes that what is made is better than what merely grows, that neatness is better than profusion and vitality. The genius of the *philosophe* is a genius for rationalization, for *making* life and the business of life rational rather than for *seeing* the reason for it, for inculcating precise order, no matter at what expense, rather than for apprehending the existence of a subtle order in what appears to be chaotic. (*RP*, 139)

Oakeshott does not focus on Bentham's rationalism in this essay, however, but on the historical method that has led to such a false estimate of his importance and originality. This method is concerned more with discovering "anticipations" in a thinker's thought than with whether a particular matter is developed subtly or profoundly. It concerns itself exclusively with the conclusions of a philosophical doctrine and with the aftereffects of those conclusions. No wonder Bentham appears as a giant in the history of English thought: he "was an ingenious man, and if we look hard enough we shall certainly find in his works some 'remarkable anticipations' of fairly modern views. But what of it? Does that make him a giant? A thinker like Bentham does not trouble to discriminate or confine himself; he skims the cream" (*RP*, 146).

The preoccupation with effects and influence not only leads us to misjudge the rank of a thinker, it also prevents us from understanding what he actually thought, what his ideas actually were. When we concern ourselves with effects or consequences, we look only to a thinker's conclusions and ignore the *rationes decidendi* that lie behind them. In Bentham's case, his *rationes decidendi* reveal him to be an essentially eighteenth-century thinker. The grounds or reasons of his arguments for cremation, contraception, coeducation, etc., "were all typical of eighteenth-century thought, and nearly all fallacious. For Bentham, so far from having thought out his first principles, had never given them a moment's consideration" (*RP*, 147).

In "The New Bentham," Oakeshott argues that attention to Bentham's *rationes decidendi* allows us to see how conventional a thinker he really was. In his 1935 article on Hobbes, he argues that attention to Hobbes's *rationes decidendi* has the opposite effect, revealing how original and radical a philosopher he actually was. Here too, though, the narrow focus on Hobbes's political opinions and conclusions has obscured what he really has to offer us: namely, "a comprehensive view of the nature of political life." Every man, Oakeshott writes,

> has his political opinions, and sometimes they are opinions which will interest and inspire ages other than his own. But a political philosopher has something more, and more significant, than political opinions: he has an analysis of political activity, a comprehensive view of the nature of political life, and it is this, and not his political opinions, which it is profitable for a later and different age to study. ("TH," 265)

Disregard for the reasons upon which Hobbes's views are based has also led to the misinterpretation of those views. In particular, the failure to appreciate the profoundly systematic character of Hobbes's thought—the tendency to see it as a mere collection of opinions—has prevented scholars from fathoming Hobbes's meaning. Oakeshott gives a number of examples of such misinterpretation, and in each case it is the *moral* reading of an essentially *philosophical* doctrine that leads to error. This appears most clearly in the common contention that Hobbes's political philosophy is grounded on a view of human nature as selfish or egoistic. Oakeshott responds, however, that "the essential selfishness of man is not, in Hobbes, a premise, but (if the doctrine is to be found anywhere) is a conclusion, the result of a long and complicated argument. His premise is a doctrine of solipsism, a belief in the essential isolation of men from one another, and expounded as a theory of knowledge." Hobbes's individualism is ultimately based, not on a moral opinion about human nature, but on a philosophical theory of knowledge, on a "thoroughgoing nominalism and an almost extreme solipsism" ("TH," 273–75).

The antithesis between moral *philosophy* and moral *opinion* that is evident in this example forms the basis of Oakeshott's admiring but not uncritical review of Leo Strauss's *The Political Philosophy of Hobbes: Its Basis and Its Genesis*. This review, entitled "Dr Leo Strauss on Hobbes" (1937), is of particular importance because, in it, Oakeshott confronts a historian of political philosophy with whom he would seem to have a great deal in common. Oakeshott and Strauss both see the history of political philosophy as somehow essential to philosophical inquiry into politics today; both share a keen appreciation of the radical quality of philosophical thought, which they attempt to recover in the political philosophy of the past; and both set themselves against various leveling interpretations that either minimize important differences between past philosophers, overemphasize superficial similarities, ignore subtleties, or search for ahistorical "anticipations." Nevertheless, despite these affinities, Oakeshott ultimately disagrees with Strauss's overall interpretation of Hobbes.

One of the things that no doubt attracted Oakeshott to Strauss's book—which he actually reviewed on three different occasions[9]—was its attempt to replace the traditional positivist image of Hobbes as a naturalistic philosopher engaged in a scientific analysis of politics with an image of Hobbes as a genuine moral philosopher. Though Oakeshott shares this general aspiration with Strauss, he rejects Strauss's specific argument that the original and real basis of Hobbes's political philosophy was a prescientific "moral attitude" upon which Hobbes in his mature writings merely superimposed a scientific form and which he never really abandoned. For Oakeshott, the argument of *Leviathan* constitutes a genuine advance in Hobbes's philosophical thinking, not because it is more "scientific"—to Oakeshott "Hobbes was never a scientist in any true sense . . . his 'science' is conceived throughout as an epistemology"—but because it represents Hobbes's attempt "to find a firmer basis than merely moral opinion" for his political philosophy (*HCA*, 150–53).

Oakeshott also qualifies Strauss's rather grand claim that Hobbes is the originator of a new tradition in political philosophy and the founder of modern political philosophy.[10] He makes two points in this regard. First, though he accepts Strauss's thesis that Hobbes's political philosophy represents a break with the dominant natural-law tradition, he does not see this move as completely unprecedented; Strauss neglects Hobbes's significant affinities with an earlier, Epicurean tradition (*HCA*, 153–54). Second, taking off from Strauss's claim that Hobbes's substitution of will for law became the starting-point for all later political thought, Oakeshott adds that Hobbes still lacked something vital to modern political thought: namely, a satisfactory theory of volition. This lack only came to be remedied in "the union of a reconstituted natural law theory with Hobbes's Epicurean theory—a union indicated in such phrases as Rousseau's 'General Will,' Hegel's 'Rational Will,' and Bosanquet's 'Real Will.'" The programmatic intention of this passage becomes explicit in the next few lines:

> The most profound movement in modern political philosophy is, as I see it, a revivification of the Stoic natural law theory achieved by the grafting upon it an Epicurean theory; it springs from the union of the two great traditions of political philosophy inherited by Western Europe from the ancient world. Its greatness is that it is a genuine theory and not a merely eclectic composition; and that it has not yet succeeded in finding an entirely satisfactory expression is certainly not a sign of its moribund condition. (*HCA*, 157)

Here Oakeshott indicates clearly the direction he thinks philosophical inquiry into politics should take in the twentieth century. The task of contemporary political philosophy is to carry through the theoretical attempt begun by Rousseau and Hegel to synthesize the Epicurean theory of Hobbes with the natural law theory of the Stoics. What exactly this involves is not yet clear. In order to flesh it out, we must examine Oakeshott's relationship to the odd couple of Hobbes and Hegel more closely.

Hobbes, Hegel, and Liberalism

As in his epistemology and metaphysics, so in his political philosophy, Oakeshott's relationship to Hegel cannot be understood apart from the mediating influence of the British idealists. But whereas it was Bradley who exercised the greatest influence on Oakeshott's logic and metaphysics, it was T. H. Green (1836–1882) and Bernard Bosanquet (1848–1923) who shaped his encounter with Hegel in the sphere of political philosophy. Bradley did, of course, write an influential and wonderfully provocative Hegelian essay on "My Station and Its Duties" (the title says it all), but it was Green and Bosanquet who were mainly responsible for taking Hegel's ideas about freedom and the state and adapting them to British political experience.

Green led the way in this regard, enunciating a "positive" doctrine of freedom meant to counter the individualism found in the political philosophies of John Stuart Mill and Herbert Spencer. By freedom, he argued, we "do not mean merely freedom from restraint or compulsion. We do not mean merely freedom to do as we like irrespectively of what it is that we like. . . . We mean a positive power or capacity of doing or enjoying something worth doing or enjoying . . . the greater power on the part of citizens as a body to make the most and best of themselves."[11] Freedom means self-mastery, being determined by our "higher self" over and against our "lower self." The realization of such freedom—that is, of a certain type of moral character determined by our "higher self"— is the ethical end of individuals and of society. Green assumes that there is a harmony of interests between individual and society, that they share a genuinely "common good" defined by his teleological conception of self-development or self-realization. The state plays a crucial role in the achievement of this common good by creating the conditions for the development of our higher capacities. On this basis, Green favored leg-islation protecting labor, regulating health conditions, requiring educa-tion, and restricting the sale of liquor.

New Liberals like L. T. Hobhouse (1864–1929) seized on the reformist aspect of Green's teaching to advocate even wider state action to remedy social ills, but Green himself resisted such enlargement of the state's role. Firmly rooted in Evangelical Victorian values, he worried about the effects of paternalistic measures on the self-reliance and moral charac-ter of individuals. Thus, in his *Lectures on the Principles of Political Oblig-ation* (posthumously published in 1886), he whittled down the political scope of his doctrine of positive freedom by arguing that state action or law should be confined to those external acts that are better done from a bad motive (i.e. fear of punishment) than not done at all.[12] In the end, human beings cannot be *forced* to be free. The state can only indirectly or negatively promote self-realization by removing obstacles to our freedom. Of course, what constitutes an "obstacle" to self-realization—liquor? poverty? capitalism?—remains a fatal ambiguity in Green's theory.

It was left to Green's pupil Bernard Bosanquet to fully develop the Hegelian ideas that Green had introduced into British political phi-losophy. Though Bosanquet's *Philosophical Theory of the State* (first pub-lished in 1899) followed Green in most essentials, it was significantly more Hegelian in its positive assessment of the modern state. Quoting Green's famous reservation against Hegel—"To an Athenian slave, who might be used to gratify a master's lust, it would have been mockery to speak of the State as a realization of freedom; and perhaps it would not be much less to speak of it as such to an untaught and underfed denizen of a London yard with gin shops on the right hand and on the left"—

Bosanquet commented: "The time has gone by for the scrupulous caution which Green displayed in estimating the value of the State to its members."[13]

Like Green, Bosanquet began by rejecting the individualism of thinkers like Bentham, Mill, and Spencer, who saw law or government as "essentially antagonistic to the self or true individuality of man."[14] For these writers, the individual is what it prima facie appears to be, something separate and cut off from everything that surrounds it; and the political problem becomes one of fencing this private individual off from outside social forces and protecting it from the intrusion of government. In Rousseau's notion of the general will Bosanquet found a much more radical and satisfying treatment of the "paradox of self-government." Here the "negative relation of the self to other selves begins to dissolve away before the conception of the common self," and "the negative relation of the self to law and government begins to disappear in the idea of a law which expresses our real will, as opposed to our trivial and rebellious moods."[15]

Bosanquet's greatest contribution to the idealist theory of the state came in his detailed treatment of the "general"—or what he preferred to call the "real"—will. Like Rousseau, Hegel, and Green, Bosanquet distinguished between the conscious, arbitrary, momentary will of the individual and the true, real, or rational will that it implies. He then asked what this distinction can possibly mean: What does it mean to speak of a "real will" that is distinct from my "actual will"? He answered this question by first pointing out the familiar fact that we frequently desire things that would not satisfy us if we got them. What we casually desire from one moment to the next frequently does not correspond to what we would want if we took the future into account or considered our actions in terms of their overall contribution to the systematic whole that is our self. Our "actual" will, which seeks to satisfy momentary wishes and desires, rarely corresponds to our "real" will, which seeks to weave our complex needs and wants into a harmonious whole. Our "actual" will is riven by contradictions that our "real" will seeks to remove:

> A comparison of our acts of will through a month or a year is enough to show that no one object of action, as we conceive it when acting, exhausts all that our will demands. . . . In order to obtain a full statement of what we will, what we want at any moment must at least be corrected and amended by what we want at all other moments; and this cannot be done without also correcting and amending it so as to

harmonise it with what others want . . . Such a process of harmoniz-
ing and readjusting a mass of data to bring them into a rational shape
is what is meant by criticism. And criticism, when applied to our
actual will, shows that it is not our real will; or, in the plainest language, that what we really want is something more and other than at
any given moment we are aware that we will, although the wants
which we are aware of lead up to it at every point.[16]

Like Hegel, Bosanquet identified the "real" or "rational" will with
the state. It is in the laws and institutions of the state that the process
of criticism described in the passage above takes place. Rousseau's
Legislator is only a crude and mythical version of this complex process
by which the "actual" will is slowly disciplined and transformed. In the
state "we find at once discipline and expansion, the transfiguration of
partial impulses, and something to do and to care for, such as the human
self demands." It is there that the individual finds "an outlet and a stable
purpose capable of doing justice to his capacities—a satisfying object of
life."[17] Like Green's, Bosanquet's doctrine of self-realization rests on a
teleological conception of human nature. And implicit in his identification of the "real will" with the state is the contentious claim that the
state can prescribe more satisfactorily than the individual herself the life
that will enable her to realize herself.

Bosanquet's grandiose conception of the state was vigorously attacked
in Hobhouse's *Metaphysical Theory of the State* (1918). Writing in the
shadow of the war, Hobhouse criticized Bosanquet for glorifying the
state and thus inhibiting efforts to change or improve it. This criticism,
however, overlooked many of the nuances of Bosanquet's argument. For
one thing, Bosanquet was careful not to identify the state with "merely
the political fabric": the state "includes the entire hierarchy of institutions by which life is determined, from the family to the trade, and from
the trade to the Church and the University."[18] Indeed, he saw the process
of criticism and improvement described above as taking place largely in
the social sphere. For this reason he was vehemently opposed to any sort
of state socialism and supported the nonstatist approach to provision
for the poor represented by the Charity Organisation Society. Second,
Bosanquet, like Green, argued that, insofar as the state operates through
force, it cannot directly promote the spiritual or moral end of individuals. State action or law must be confined to external actions; its role is
limited to hindering hindrances to self-realization.[19]

Let us return now to Oakeshott. We have seen that he was thoroughly
imbued with the idealist theory of the state in his earliest writings on

political philosophy from the 1920s. He rejected the individualism of Bentham and Mill and embraced instead the idealist doctrine of the interdependence—or, less mildly, the identity—of self and society. His attitude does not seem to change much in the 1930s. In his review of Strauss, as we have seen, he claims that Hobbes's lack of a coherent theory of volition had to some extent been remedied by Rousseau's notion of the general will, Hegel's notion of the rational will, and Bosanquet's notion of the real will. Such idealist reflection represents "the most profound movement in political philosophy." Oakeshott reinforces this view in a 1936 review of a book on Bosanquet, writing that the "so-called Idealist theory of the State is the only theory which has paid thoroughgoing attention to all the problems which must be considered by a theory of the State." He claims that Bosanquet's *Philosophical Theory of the State* remains "the most comprehensive account" of this idealist theory of the state, and picks out for special commendation Bosanquet's "philosophy of the self," which is far superior to "so-called 'individualistic' theories, which are inclined to treat the self as something too important to be examined."[20]

Though clearly sympathetic to the idealist theory of the state, Oakeshott is not uncritical of it. In the same review that he praises it as "the only theory which has paid thoroughgoing attention to all the problems which must be considered by a theory of the State," he also writes that it is "a theory that has yet to receive a satisfactory statement." The study of Bosanquet's *Philosophical Theory of the State* is only a "useful preliminary" to such a restatement.[21] Oakeshott is no less cryptically critical of Bosanquet in a review of J. D. Mabbott's *The State and the Citizen* written more than a decade later. There he remarks that, since the publication of *The Philosophical Theory of the State*, "no general work on political philosophy by an English writer has impressed those interested in the subject as being of first-class importance." This he finds remarkable "because Bosanquet's work did not leave the subject in so firm a state of equilibrium that it was difficult to know in what direction advance was to be made: the book was recognized to have grave defects, though its most important shortcomings were not those which its contemporary critics fastened on."[22]

One wishes Oakeshott had been a little more explicit about the "grave defects" and more profitable direction alluded to in this passage. Bringing to bear the direction in which Oakeshott's own political philosophy was to develop, I would suggest two possible objections he would have to the idealist theory of the state as expounded by Green and Bosanquet. First, I think Oakeshott would have profound reservations about their Kantian doctrine of the limits of state action. This doctrine rests on the double thesis that the moral value of an action lies exclusively in its motive and that state action, operating through force and fear of punishment, inevitably compromises the purity of our motives. Such a doctrine seems to reinstitute at the level of moral motivation the very individualism that the idealist theory seeks to overcome. It is not clear that the law, concretely understood, always operates through force or fear of punishment, or that it inevitably compromises the purity of our motives (whatever that might mean). Mabbott, in the book alluded to above, is very good on this, and Oakeshott seems to endorse his argument.[23] Unfortunately, in his own attempt to determine the limits of state action, Mabbott falls prey to a similar type of individualism by drawing lines around the "private individual" and invoking a distinction between social and nonsocial goods. Oakeshott speaks in full Hegelian voice when he counters:

> The "private individual" as I understand him is an institution, a social, indeed for the most part a legal, creation, whose desires, emotions, ideas, intelligence, are social in their constitution. Nothing, I take it, is more certain than that this individual would collapse, like a body placed in a vacuum, if he were removed from the "external" social world which is the condition of his existence.[24]

The second difficulty I think Oakeshott would have had with Green and Bosanquet's idealist theory of the state involves their teleological conception of human nature and of human self-realization. In Green especially, there is a clear sense of the sort of character we ought to realize and of the "higher self" the state ought to promote. His whole ethical and political philosophy is suffused by the Kantian dualism between duty and inclination; and his identification of self-sacrifice for the sake of the common good with self-realization seems not only excessively ascetic but also to obscure the very real conflicts that can arise between the claims of the individual and the claims of society. Bosanquet is less ascetic than Green and more Hegelian, but he too assumes that there is a "real will," a true human nature, that we ought to realize and that the state ought to promote. He also assumes that the state is in many respects wiser than we are in articulating our "real will" and guiding us to genuine self-realization.

Though Oakeshott does not explicitly reject Bosanquet's and Green's teleological conception of human nature and the purposive character it imposes upon the state in his writings from the 1930s, his divergence from them is implicit in his admiration for Hobbes; implicit, indeed, in his whole Paterian-Epicurean sensibility, so different from Green's cramped and moralistic vision of human perfection. Though in his review of Strauss Oakeshott saw the idealists as redressing the lack of a coherent theory of volition in Hobbes's political philosophy, there is a sense in which Oakeshott himself uses Hobbes's skeptical Epicurean outlook to correct the teleological and rationalistic tendencies of the idealist theory of the state. For Oakeshott, Hobbes (along with Montaigne) embodies the radical, Epicurean individualism that forms the deepest current in modern liberalism. In his 1935 article on Hobbes, for example, he calls Hobbes "the most profound philosophical individualist in the history of political theory." And he claims that, far from being the enemy of liberalism, as he is often portrayed (by Green and Bosanquet, for example),[25] Hobbes "had more of the ground of liberalism in him than even Locke" ("TH," 272).

Oakeshott's elevation of Hobbes over Locke in the liberal pantheon constitutes one of his most novel revaluations. In an article written in 1932, the tercentenary of Locke's birth, he sharply criticizes Lockean liberalism for its "boundless but capricious moderation." Locke, he writes,

> was the apostle of the liberalism which is more conservative than conservatism itself, the liberalism characterised not by insensitiveness, but by a sinister and destructive sensitiveness to the influx of the new, the liberalism which is sure of its limits, which has a terror of extremes, which lays its paralysing hand of respectability upon whatever is dangerous or revolutionary. ("JL," 73)

Perry Anderson cites these lines as evidence of Oakeshott's antiliberalism at this time,[26] but in fact they represent his desire to renovate liberalism by grounding it in a much more radical sense of individuality than that found in Locke. The real crisis of liberalism is that, in its Lockean form, it has become boring:

> The moderate individualism of Locke has no attraction for those who have embraced a radical, an Epicurean individualism. Locke's "steady love of liberty" appears worse than slavery to anyone who, like Montaigne, is "besotted with liberty." Democracy, parliamentary government, progress, discussion, and the "plausible ethics of productivity" are notions—all of them inseparable from the Lockian liberalism—which fail now to arouse even opposition; they are not merely absurd and exploded, they are uninteresting. ("JL," 73)

The other aspect of Locke's political philosophy that Oakeshott has no patience for is his doctrine of natural rights. This has more to do with Oakeshott's Hegelianism, but interestingly he sees Hobbes as having more in common with Hegel on this point than with Locke. Both Hobbes and Hegel, in contradistinction to Locke, understand the civil condition to involve a radical transformation of the natural situation of human beings such that there can be no appeal from the one to the other. Oakeshott indirectly criticizes Locke's naïve "individualism"—understood as an ontological account of the self in society rather than as an ethical ideal—in a discussion of Ernest Barker's Lockean attempt to see "society" as something separable from and independent of the "state." Such a distinction between society and state is a

> relic of that "individualism" in political theory which while it is explicitly fled from is often implicitly succumbed to. And the notion of the State taking up and directing a separable part of the life of Society corresponds closely to the seventeenth century notion that when man entered political society he surrendered, not the whole, but a part of his natural rights—and it is a notion from which Hobbes might have rescued us if we had listened to him.[27]

In addition to clarifying Oakeshott's reasons for preferring Hobbes to Locke, this passage discloses Oakeshott's much more radical approach to political philosophy, in contrast to the love of theoretical compromise that was characteristic of Barker.[28]

Oakeshott's novel interpretation of Hobbes receives its most complete expression in his celebrated Introduction to *Leviathan*, published in 1946. There many of the themes sketched in the essays of the 1930s are developed and gathered into a coherent account of Hobbes's thought. Once again, Oakeshott emphasizes Hobbes's voluntarism and individualism, which he connects to Hobbes's skeptical understanding of "reasoning." Hobbesian reasoning, in contrast to the more substantial Reason of the classical tradition, yields only hypothetical and conditional knowledge and can never provide us with knowledge of ends. This skeptical doctrine of the limits of reasoning entails the replacement of reason by will as the foundation of political authority. Authority thus understood is not hostile to individual liberty but in fact more compatible with it than is the classical notion of Reason and rule by "those who know": "it is Reason, not Authority, that is destructive of individuality." Oakeshott puts this point in the most provocative way possible:

> Hobbes is not an absolutist precisely because he is an authoritarian. His scepticism about the power of reasoning . . . together with the

rest of his individualism, separate him from the rationalist dictators of his or any age. Indeed, Hobbes, without being himself a liberal, had in him more of the philosophy of liberalism than many of its professed defenders. (*HCA*, 67)

Here one can see how Hobbes's skeptical doctrine of authority serves as an antidote to the teleological and rationalistic tendencies of Green and Bosanquet.

One of the things that Oakeshott rejects emphatically is the contention (of Strauss and Macpherson, for example) that Hobbes is a "bourgeois" moralist, the author of a new, "bourgeois" morality, a "bourgeois hedonist."[29] While he is perfectly willing to ascribe such a "bourgeois" outlook to Locke, he does not see this label as remotely capturing Hobbes's robust sense of individuality. In the Introduction to *Leviathan*, he writes: "Man, as Hobbes sees him, is not engaged in an undignified scramble for suburban pleasures; there is the greatness of great passion in his constitution" (*HCA*, 78). But it is in his later essay, "The Moral Life in the Writings of Thomas Hobbes" (1960), that Oakeshott decisively refutes the "bourgeois" interpretation of Hobbes's political philosophy, arguing that Hobbesian man is driven not simply by fear and the desire for security but also by pride, honor, and magnanimity. Though it may at first appear that Hobbes defends the morality of the tame man by making fear of death the primary motive for endeavoring peace, Oakeshott shows that there is evidence in Hobbes's writings of an alternative derivation of the endeavor for peace out of the passion of pride. The presence of this aristocratic element in Hobbes's moral outlook rebuts the simple designation of it as "bourgeois." Moreover, the suggestion of "a single approved condition of human circumstances for all conditions of men" contained in the notion of "bourgeois morality" has nothing to do with Hobbes's "morality of individuality," which involves no such common substantive purpose (*HCA*, 93–94, 127–33).

The Claims of Politics

Oakeshott studiously avoided politics for the better part of the 1930s, that most political of decades. By the fall of 1938, however, after Munich and the sacrifice of Czechoslovakia, the all-engulfing European crisis could not be blinked. Abstract discussions of political philosophy began to seem remote, as Louis MacNeice ironically captured in his *Autumn Journal*:

Good-bye now, Plato and Hegel.
　The shop is closing down;
They don't want any philosopher-kings in England,
　There ain't no universals in this man's town.[30]

In these circumstances, at the suggestion of Ernest Barker, Oakeshott turned his attention to compiling an anthology of documents relating to the most important social and political doctrines of contemporary Europe: representative democracy, Catholicism, communism, fascism, and National Socialism. His purpose would seem to have been to help educated men and women gain clarity about the congeries of social and political doctrines swirling around Europe at the time and affecting both governments and significant numbers of people. There is an embarrassment on Oakeshott's part, however, about the obvious practical purpose that such a book would seem to serve. He claims, rather donnishly, that it is a book "for those who are interested in ideas; and those who are not, need not trouble to turn its pages" (*SPD*, xiv). But clearly people were interested in these ideas not simply for their own sakes but for very immediate, practical reasons. Oakeshott detracts from his purpose by pointing out that the "value of a regime, fortunately, does not depend upon the intellectual competence of its apologists"; but he goes on to concede that, "when a regime chooses to rationalize its practice, chooses to issue an official statement of the social and political doctrine upon which it relies . . . the coherence of such a statement becomes a matter of importance; and if it can be convicted of intellectual confusion, that is not a fault to be brushed aside as insignificant" (*SPD*, xv).

As he wrestles with the union of theory and practice implied in his project but denied by his philosophy, Oakeshott says a number of interesting things about the social and political doctrines he is illustrating, especially liberalism. In the first place, he attributes the existence of so many different social and political doctrines to a "deep and natural dissatisfaction" with the dominant doctrine, liberalism, which has become (echoing the essay on Locke) "intellectually boring." Oakeshott is particularly critical of the philosophical underpinnings of liberalism: its "crude and negative individualism" and "what may be called its moral ideal: 'the plausible ethics of productivity.'" Such a philosophy is not one "anyone could accept nowadays without a radical restatement which has yet to be provided." Despite these criticisms, Oakeshott is clearly sympathetic to what he takes to be liberalism's central principles: "that a society must not be so unified as to abolish vital and valuable differences, nor so extravagantly diversified as to make an intelligently coordinated and civilized social life impossible, and that the imposition of a universal plan of life on a society is at once stupid and immoral" (*SPD*, xvi–xix, xx).

As far as the other doctrines are concerned, Oakeshott tries to be evenhanded, but his conviction that they are all—with the exception of Catholicism—pretty rickety constructions inevitably leaks out. Of Catholicism and its conception of natural law he is genuinely admiring, though, unlike T. S. Eliot, he never seems to have been attracted to the idea of imposing a Christian or Thomist character on society. He speaks of Marxism's "imaginative power"—it will be remembered that Oakeshott was one of the first to lecture on Marx at Cambridge—and even suggests that, "among the new doctrines, [it is] the one from which we have most to learn." Nevertheless, despite its radical criticism of liberalism, communism "appears to preserve unchanged the most questionable element of Liberal Democracy," namely, its materialism. This is true of fascism as well, despite the fact that its criticism of liberal democracy "is far too acute to be merely ignored." Oakeshott finally drops his veneer of neutrality in a footnote, commenting that the "fundamental cleavage" between communism, fascism, and National Socialism, on the one hand, and liberalism and Catholicism, on the other, is that the former "hand over to the arbitrary will of a society's self-appointed leaders the planning of its entire life," whereas the latter "not only refuse to hand over the destiny of a society to any set of officials but also consider the whole notion of planning the destiny of a society to be both stupid and immoral" (*SPD*, xix–xxii).

Oakeshott made one other foray into the political debate of the late 1930s, contributing an essay to a symposium on "The Claims of Politics" published in the September 1939 issue of *Scrutiny*. The question posed to the participants in the symposium was whether those who occupy themselves with art, literature, and higher culture in general— like the contributors to *Scrutiny*—also have an obligation to bring their cultural activity to bear on politics, and in what way. Most of the participants (who included R. H. Tawney and Christopher Dawson) took the view that artists and thinkers do not have an obligation to bring their activity directly to bear on politics, but that they do have some contribution to make to politics in the widest possible sense as encompassing the moral and spiritual values of a civilization.

This is roughly the view Oakeshott takes as well, though he expresses it with a contempt for politics that is missing in the other contributors. He rejects, in the first place, the idea that direct political activity is the only way to contribute to the communal interests of society. Like any good Hegelian, he denies that "non-political" activity is somehow less communal or social than active participation in political activity: "the truth is that nothing we do is unconnected with the life of our society, no activity is private in the sense of being without its place or context in the corporate social life." Indeed, he argues, among the various forms of social or communal activity, politics is one of the least adequate expressions of the communal interests of society: "Politics is a highly specialized and abstracted form of communal activity; it is conducted on the surface of the life of society and except on rare occasions makes remarkably small impression below that surface." Again the influence of Hegel can be discerned in the claim that a "political system is primarily for the protection and occasional modification of a recognized legal and social order. It is not self-explanatory; its end and meaning lie beyond itself in the social whole to which it belongs . . . A political system pre-supposes a civilization." It is at this point that Oakeshott delivers his most withering indictment of political life:

> A limitation of view, which appears so clear and practical, but which amounts to little more than a mental fog, is inseparable from political activity. A mind fixed and callous to all subtle distinctions, emotional and intellectual habits become bogus from repetition and lack of examination, unreal loyalties, delusive aims, false significances are what political action involves. . . . Political action involves mental vulgarity, not merely because it entails the concurrence and support of those who are mentally vulgar, but because of the false simplifica-tion of human life that appears in even the best of its purposes. (*RPML*, 92–93)[31]

The most remarkable thing about this essay is the practical role that Oakeshott goes on to ascribe to art, literature, and philosophy. In contrast to the rather superficial social activity of the politician, the business of the artist, poet, and philosopher is "to create and recreate the values of their society." By this Oakeshott does not seem to have in mind radical, Nietzschean value-creation but, rather, Hegelian self-awareness and immanent critique of the values of society. In the artist, poet, and philosopher, "a society becomes conscious and critical of itself, of its whole self." Their genius is "to mitigate a little their society's igno-rance of itself" and thereby save it from a "corruption of consciousness" (*RPML*, 95–96). This last phrase is borrowed from Collingwood's *Prin-ciples of Art*, which Oakeshott had reviewed enthusiastically in 1938. Without the artist, Collingwood had written, "no community altogether knows its own heart . . . Art is the community's medicine for the worst disease of the mind, the corruption of consciousness."[32] More than just the phrase, though, Oakeshott seems to have adopted Collingwood's general view of the complementarity of theory and practice against his own rigid separation of the two.

It is not just theory and practice that are brought closer together in "The Claims of Politics" but also philosophy and art, both of which are seen as engaged in the same task of recreating the values of society and bringing it to greater self-awareness. This, too, may owe something to Collingwood's *Principles of Art*, which Oakeshott described as "the work of an artist and a philosopher."[33] In *Experience and Its Modes*, Oakeshott briefly (and somewhat cryptically) commented that in art, music, and poetry "we are wholly taken up with practical life" (*EM*, 297), but he did not ascribe to them the function of self-knowledge and protection from the corruption of consciousness that he does in "The Claims of Politics." In this essay, not only does philosophy appear to be more practical than it did in *Experience and Its Modes*, but art appears to be more theoretical.

The most suggestive example of this overlap between philosophy and art in Oakeshott's work is his wonderful little essay, originally delivered as a radio talk in 1947, "*Leviathan*: A Myth." Here Oakeshott argues that Hobbes's *Leviathan* is not only a great work of political philosophy but "one of the masterpieces of the literature and language of our civilization." A civilization is not to be understood as "something solid and external" but as a "collective dream" whose substance is "myth, an imaginative interpretation of human existence, the perception (not the solution) of the mystery of human life." Whereas the project of science "is to solve the mystery, to wake us from our dream, to destroy the myth," the office of literature is to dream the myth of our civilization more profoundly and thus "recreate" it. Though Hobbes's *Leviathan* has often been taken as attempting the former, Oakeshott argues that it really accomplishes the latter. After tracing the Jewish-Christian roots of our civilizational myth, he concludes that there can be no mistaking the character of Hobbes's rendering of the human condition in *Leviathan*: "It is myth, not science. It is perception of mystery, not a pretended solution" (*HCA*, 159–63).

There is one final implication of this argument to be noticed, an implication that Oakeshott does not explicitly draw but that has enormous consequences for his conception of philosophy. By linking philosophy to art and understanding its task to be the recreation of the values of a society or a civilization, Oakeshott has effectively historicized philosophy. By this I do not mean that he has reduced philosophical knowledge to historical knowledge in Collingwoodian fashion, but that he does not see the historical setting of a philosophy—or at least of a political philosophy—as completely extrinsic or irrelevant to it. This marks an important change from the point of view of *Experience and Its Modes*, where Oakeshott claimed that time and place are irrelevant to philosophy, indeed, as irrelevant as they are in science (*EM*, 349). Such a view of the ahistorical character of philosophy can be found as late as the manuscript "The Concept of a Philosophy of Politics" (circa 1937–38), where Oakeshott says of Hobbes's *Leviathan* that it is a book that does not merely offer an "explanation of the origin and character of political life" adapted to its historical circumstances but contains "something which, because it can relevantly be separated from time and place and for other reasons, I should call a philosophy of politics" (*RPML*, 119).

Though Oakeshott nowhere comments directly on this change to a more historical conception of political philosophy, it is intimated in his definition of political philosophy in the Introduction to *Leviathan* as "the relation of political life, and the values and purposes pertaining to it, to the entire conception of the world that belongs to a civilization" (*HCA*, 4). He goes on to characterize this philosophical endeavor as the establishment of the connections between politics and eternity, but it is clear that eternity here has been given a temporal or historical dimension. Though this statement belongs to 1946, it follows directly from the argument of "The Claims of Politics." The historical view of political philosophy that it articulates characterizes Oakeshott's outlook from this point on.

4 Rationalism

Back from the war in 1945, Oakeshott resumed his teaching duties at Cambridge. In 1946, his edition of Hobbes's *Leviathan* appeared, accompanied by his celebrated Introduction. And in 1947, in the newly founded *Cambridge Journal*, he began to publish the antirationalism essays that were to transform him from a well-regarded Cambridge don into a major public intellectual. These essays were remarkable from a number of points of view, but what was most striking about them in terms of Oakeshott's own development was how political and polemical they were. Gone was the purely philosophical voice of *Experience and Its Modes*; in its place appeared the gently—sometimes not so gently—mocking voice of the philosophical polemicist. Among other things, the essays ridiculed the socialist policies of the Attlee government that laid the basis for the postwar welfare state in Britain. As a result, Oakeshott quickly became a lightning rod for a newly energized conservatism in Britain.

Oakeshott was not, of course, the only one criticizing rationalistic and utopian politics in postwar Europe. In Britain, Friedrich Hayek, Michael Polanyi, Karl Popper, Isaiah Berlin, Jacob Talmon, and Herbert Butterfield were all putting forward their own critiques of rationalism, utopianism, and socialist collectivism. In Germany, the neoliberal thinkers associated with the journal *Ordo*—Wilhelm Röpke, Walter Eucken, and Alexander Rüstow—belonged broadly to this anti-utopian trend of thought, as did the German refugees Leo Strauss, Eric Voegelin, and Hannah Arendt. And in France, Raymond Aron and Bertrand de Jouvenel were attacking communism as the "opium of the intellectuals." Contrary to the image of this period as being one in which political theory was dead, the 1940s and '50s saw an efflorescence of political thought springing up in reaction to fascism, communism, and the catastrophic events of World War II. It is a severely foreshortened understanding of contemporary intellectual history that sees political philosophy as being "revived" only with the publication of John Rawls's *Theory of Justice*.

One would not want to press too hard on the similarities between these thinkers, however. Their critiques of rationalism, utopianism, and collectivism rested on widely varying philosophical arguments and assumptions, and they often pointed to different political conclusions. Popper's defense of "piecemeal social engineering" over against "utopian social engineering," for example, breathed an entirely different spirit from Oakeshott's more radical critique of rationalism. The hallmarks of Oakeshott's critique were its profound skepticism and its philosophical sophistication. Though its political implications were undoubtedly conservative, they were not incompatible with a certain understanding of liberal democracy. Nor did Oakeshott's diagnosis of European politics in terms of rationalism remain static during this period. Indeed, we will see that the grounds for his rejection of rationalism subtly shifted in the 1950s from epistemological considerations to more recognizably moral and political ones. After fully analyzing and assessing Oakeshott's critique of rationalism, I conclude the chapter by once again considering his conception of political philosophy, this time in the context of the debate over the status of political philosophy that raged in England—and elsewhere—in the 1950s.

Critique of Rationalism

Before approaching Oakeshott's postwar critique of rationalism, it is worth pointing out that much of its theoretical basis lay in his prewar philosophical outlook. As early as his 1932 essay on Bentham, Oakeshott was speaking of the rationalist as one who "believes that what is made is better than what merely grows" and who possesses a genius "for rationalization, for *making* life and the business of life rational rather than for *seeing* the reason for it, for inculcating precise order, no matter at what expense, rather than for apprehending the existence of a subtle order in what appears to be chaotic" (*RP*, 139). In the concrete logic elaborated in *Experience and Its Modes*, Oakeshott fully justified his understanding of the immanence of reason and his preference for "a subtle order in what appears to be chaotic" over any simple order that is imposed or manufactured from outside. The unity of experience, he argued there, is not of the simple sort that belongs to a class but, rather, the complex unity that belongs to a world or system. It is a unity "in which every element is indispensable, in which no one is more important than any other and none is immune from change and rearrangement. The unity of a world of ideas lies in its coherence, not in its conformity to or agreement with any one fixed idea" (*EM*, 32–33). In a world or system, universal and particular are inseparable. The universal is, in short, a "concrete universal." As will become clear shortly, this logic of the concrete universal forms the philosophical backbone of Oakeshott's critique of rationalism.

The first salvo in this critique was the essay "Rationalism in Politics," which appeared in the second and third issues of the *Cambridge Journal* in 1947. The first few pages of the essay, devoted to the general character and disposition of the rationalist, identified clearly, if somewhat polemically, Oakeshott's target. It was not merely the collectivism and social planning embodied in the policies of Clement Attlee's postwar Labour government, though it certainly included these; rather, it was the whole Enlightenment mentality that seeks to judge everything at the bar of human reason and has no use for authority, tradition, or prejudice: The rationalist "stands (he always *stands*) for independence of mind on all occasions, for thought free from obligation to any authority save the authority of 'reason'. . . . [H]e is the *enemy* of authority, of prejudice, of the merely traditional, customary, or habitual" (*RP*, 5–6). What more than anything else characterizes the rationalist mentality for Oakeshott is its reductive attitude toward experience, its desire to reduce "the tangle and variety of experience to a set of principles," its "irritable nervousness in the face of everything topical and transitory" (*RP*, 6, 7). The rationalist, he writes,

> has no sense of the cumulation of experience, only of the readiness of experience when it has been converted into a formula: the past is significant to him only as an encumbrance. He has none of that *negative capability* (which Keats attributed to Shakespeare), the power of accepting the mysteries and uncertainties of experience without any irritable search for order and distinctness, only the capability of subjugating experience; he has no aptitude for that close and detailed appreciation of what actually presents itself which Lichtenberg called *negative enthusiasm*, but only the power of recognizing the large outline which a general theory imposes upon events. (*RP*, 6)

Oakeshott was mainly concerned with the impact of this reductive, rationalist mentality on politics. Rationalist politics are, above all, ideological politics—the simplicity and (illusory) self-containedness of a set of abstract principles being preferred to the complexity and relative open-endedness of a tradition of behavior. They are also the politics of repair and reform. For the rationalist, "political activity consists in bringing the social, political, legal and institutional inheritance of his society before the tribunal of his intellect"; and "the consciously planned and deliberately executed [are] considered . . . better than what has grown up and established itself unselfconsciously over a period of time" (*RP*, 8, 26). Rationalist politics are also "the politics of the felt need," in which a single problem or purpose is isolated and the entire resources of a society mobilized to solve or pursue it (*RP*, 9). Such a view of politics takes society in wartime as the model for society in peacetime—a view that was common in the 1940s and one which Oakeshott vehemently rejects in a number of places (see, for example, "CBP," 477; *VLL*, 116–17). Finally, rationalist politics are "the politics of perfection" in combination with "the politics of uniformity": the rationalist believes not only that there is a single best (i.e. rational) solution for every political problem but that this solution should be universally applied (*RP*, 9–10).

There is a good deal of Burke in Oakeshott's polemical denunciation of rationalist—what Burke referred to as "metaphysical"—politics. The grounds of Oakeshott's critique of rationalism, however, unlike Burke's, focus on epistemological considerations. The hidden spring of rationalism, he tells us, "is a doctrine about human knowledge." In order to explicate this doctrine, he distinguishes two sorts of knowledge present in all concrete activity: technical knowledge and practical or traditional knowledge. Technical knowledge consists entirely of formulated rules, principles, or maxims; it is the sort of knowledge that can be found in or learned from books, whether they be legal codes, cookbooks, or books containing the rules of method for an intellectual discipline. Practical or traditional knowledge, on the other hand, "exists only in use, is not reflective and (unlike technique) cannot be formulated in rules." No concrete activity, whether it be cookery, art, science, or politics can be carried on simply with a knowledge of the technique; there is always something else—Oakeshott calls it variously style, connoisseurship, artistry, judgment—which tells us not only how and when to apply the rules but also when to leave the rules behind (*RP*, 11–16). This notion of practical or traditional knowledge recalls Aristotle's notion of *phronēsis* and has obvious parallels with Gilbert Ryle's "knowing how" and Michael Polanyi's "tacit knowledge."[1]

The essence of rationalism is that it denies the epistemic value of practical or traditional knowledge, recognizing only technical knowledge. Rationalism consists in the belief in the sovereignty of technique, which is not the same thing as the sovereignty of reason per se. It is important to make this distinction in order to avoid mistaking Oakeshott's critique of rationalism for an attack on reason simply rather than on a certain misunderstanding of reason.[2] The attraction of technique for the rationalist lies in its apparent certainty and self-completeness. Technical knowledge seems to rest on nothing outside of itself, building directly on pure ignorance, the empty (or emptied) mind. But this apparent certainty and self-completeness of technical knowledge is an illusion.

Knowledge of a technique does not spring from pure ignorance; it pre-supposes and is a reformulation of knowledge that is already there. "Nothing, not even the most nearly self-contained technique (the rules of a game) can in fact be imparted to an empty mind: and what is imparted is nourished by what is already there." It is only by ignoring or forgetting the total context of our knowledge that a technique can be made to appear self-contained and certain (*RP*, 16–17).

Like many other critics of rationalism, Oakeshott traces its origins back to the seventeenth century. He sees Bacon and Descartes as the dominating figures in the quest for a "consciously formulated technique of research," a mistake-proof method of inquiry. Nevertheless, their writings also disclose a certain awareness of the limitations of technical knowledge. It was only what was made of their teachings by lesser men that gave rise to modern rationalism. Bacon and Descartes are among "les grands hommes" mentioned in the epigraph of "Rationalism and Politics" who, "en apprenant aux faibles à réfléchir, les ont mis sur la route de l'erreur" (*RP*, 17–22).

In politics, the rationalist's belief in the sovereignty of technique translates into the belief in the superiority of an ideology over a tradi-tion or habit of behavior. Rationalist politics are "the politics of the book" (*RP*, 26–27). The superiority of an ideology, like that of a tech-nique, is thought to lie in its being self-contained, "rational" through and through. This, again, is an illusion. An ideology, far from being self-contained or independently premeditated, itself presupposes a tradition of behavior and is merely an abridgment of it.

It is at this point that Oakeshott criticizes the ideological character of Hayek's *Road to Serfdom*: "A plan to resist all planning may be better than its opposite, but it belongs to the same style of politics. And only in a society already deeply infected with Rationalism will the conversion of the traditional resources of resistance to the tyranny of Rationalism into a self-conscious ideology be considered a strengthening of those resources" (*RP*, 26). Hayek would seem to be a strange figure to attack here, as his critique of rationalism shares so much with Oakeshott's. Like Oakeshott, he criticizes rationalism for its belief in the superiority of what is self-consciously designed over what has "spontaneously" or unselfconsciously grown up. He, too, traces this "constructivist" error back to Descartes. And like Oakeshott, he decries the then fashionable view, exemplified by Karl Mannheim's *Man and Society in an Age of Reconstruction* (1940), that the lessons of war, in which everything is subordinated to a single purpose, should be applied in peacetime.[3] Nev-ertheless, despite these similarities, Oakeshott and Hayek differ profoundly over the role of ideology in politics. In *The Road to Serfdom*, Hayek speaks of the need to rearticulate the ideals and principles of liberal democracy if "we are to succeed in the war of ideologies."[4] Nor is this to be understood as merely a response to the exigencies of war. Years later, in his statement "Why I Am Not a Conservative," Hayek argues that by its "fear of new ideas" and "distrust of theory" conservatism "deprives itself of the weapons needed in the struggle of ideas."[5] It is this ideological dimension of Hayek's thought, as Irving Kristol has remarked, that has made it more congenial to American conservatism than Oakeshott's more skeptical outlook.[6]

What accounts for the remarkable dominance of rationalism in modern European politics? Oakeshott traces the appeal of rationalistic ideologies to the incursion of the politically inexperienced into politics. He gives three examples: the new ruler, the new ruling class, and the new political society. In the case of the new ruler, it was Machiavelli who supplied the need for a technique of politics, a "crib" to make up for the ruler's lack of political education and traditional knowledge. Machiavelli thus takes his place alongside Bacon and Descartes as one of "les grands hommes." And like them, he too showed an awareness of the limitations of technical knowledge that his followers lacked: "to the new prince he offered not only his book, but also, what would make up for the inevitable deficiencies of his book—himself: he never lost the sense that politics, after all, are diplomacy, not the application of a technique." As examples of cribs for new and politically inexperienced classes, Oakeshott cites Locke's *Second Treatise* and the work of Marx and Engels—the latter two providing "for the instruction of a less politically educated class than any other that has ever come to have the illusion of exercising political power." Finally, Oakeshott shows how the circumstances of a new political society such as the United States at its founding favored the emergence of a rationalistic politics based on self-conscious reflection and abstract principles (*RP*, 28–33).

For someone who argues so forcefully against abridged and ideological history, Oakeshott's historical account of the emergence and appeal of rationalism in politics is curiously truncated and uncomplicated. This is not the only time we will observe such simplification in Oakeshott's excursions into history. Can the demand for the rational transparency of political arrangements be ascribed solely to the need for a crib by the politically inexperienced? Here Oakeshott could learn something from his mentor Hegel, who saw the demand that everything be justified at the bar of human reason as a distinctively modern principle, stemming from the Reformation. As Hegel put it in the *Philosophy of Right*: "It is a great obstinacy, the kind of obstinacy which does honour to human beings, that they are unwilling to acknowledge in their attitudes anything which has not been justified by thought—and this obstinacy is the characteristic property of the modern age, as well as being the distinctive principle of Protestantism."[7]

As to the practical effects of the dominance of ideologies in politics, Oakeshott is rather brief in "Rationalism in Politics," suggesting only that it has been disastrous. The gist of his analysis seems to be that we have lost control over our affairs; that modern politics have come to be characterized by an ever increasing irrationality and arbitrariness. This has happened because what the rationalist takes for the whole of knowledge is really only a part, and not the most important part at that. The more we have become enslaved to technique and ideology, the more impoverished our concrete knowledge of how to act and conduct our affairs has become. To paraphrase a passage from another essay: the political energy of our civilization has for many centuries been applied to building a Tower of Babel; and in a world dizzy with political ideologies we know less about how to behave in the public realm than ever before (*RP*, 481). Our moral and political predicament is one of great confusion; and this confusion stems not so much from a pervasive relativism—as Leo Strauss suggested[8]—as from an erroneous belief about the self-sufficiency of technical or ideological knowledge.

Oakeshott fleshed out his analysis of the dangers of ideology in an essay that appeared a year after "Rationalism in Politics" entitled "The Tower of Babel." There the contrast between practical knowledge and technique is depicted in terms of the contrast between customary morality, or the morality of a habit of behavior, and reflective morality, or the morality of the self-conscious pursuit of moral ideals. The chief danger of the latter consists in its tendency to inhibit, undermine, or otherwise paralyze action. Also, whereas customary morality is highly elastic and adaptable—Oakeshott compares it to a vernacular language in this regard—reflective morality is characterized by rigidity and imperviousness to change. In such a morality, a single moral ideal is liable to become an obsession to the exclusion of other ideals. Purity and intellectual coherence are prized above the impure coherence of a complex whole or system. As a result, the society which adopts a reflective morality "in action shies and plunges like a distracted animal"; it suffers from a "chaos of conflicting ideals" and the "disruption of common life" (*RP*, 466–77).

Once again, there are echoes of Burke and his defense of prejudice in this critique of reflective morality. But the echoes of Oakeshott's concrete logic are even more distinct. The life of a society is pictured as a complex whole or system from which reflective morality abstracts now this, now that, isolated moral ideal. In a desperate attempt to impose an artificial unity on society, the moral rationalist ends up disturbing, and even destroying, the complex ecology upon which society rests. Oakeshott raises the possibility that this disruptive, obsessive tendency of reflective morality might be held in check "by more profound reflection, by an intellectual grasp of the whole system which gives place and proportion to each moral ideal." But he goes on to add that "such a grasp is rarely achieved" (RP, 476). The naïve and inevitably less tidy coherence of customary morality proves to be more reliable than the abstract and self-conscious coherence of a morality of ideals.

Of course, Oakeshott regards neither of these forms of morality, taken alone, as a likely, or even desirable, form of moral life. They are ideal extremes, concrete morality consisting in some sort of combination of them both. This is a point that Peter Winch seems to overlook in his otherwise acute criticism of Oakeshott's stark opposition of habitual and reflective conduct.[9] Oakeshott defends a mixed form of morality in which reflection plays a vital, if subordinate, role. In the mixed form of morality in which habit is dominant, he argues, "action will retain its primacy," but reflection will provide morality with "the power to criticize, to reform and to explain itself, and the power to propagate itself beyond the range of the custom of society." Such a mixed form of morality will enjoy "the appropriate intellectual confidence in its moral standards and purposes. And it will enjoy all this without the danger of moral criticism usurping the place of a habit of moral behaviour, or of moral speculation bringing disintegration to moral life" (RP, 477).

A different fate awaits the mixed form of morality in which the self-conscious pursuit of moral ideals dominates—the form that Oakeshott believes now characterizes the moral life of the West. Here moral criticism will have a disintegrating effect on moral habit.

> When action is called for, speculation or criticism will supervene. Behaviour itself will tend to become problematical, seeking its self-confidence in the coherence of an ideology. The pursuit of perfection will get in the way of a stable and flexible moral tradition, the naïve confidence of which will be prized less than the unity which springs from self-conscious analysis and synthesis. (RP, 478)

In this mixed form of morality, moral ideals usurp the place of habits of behavior, and it is a role Oakeshott does not believe they can sustain because moral ideals are themselves the products of a habit or tradition of behavior. Moral ideals do not exist in advance of moral activity; they "are not, in the first place the products of reflective thought . . . they are the products of human behaviour . . . to which reflective thought gives subsequent, partial and abstract expression in words." Torn from the concrete context of a tradition of behavior, moral ideals become increasingly incapable of determining conduct. What efficacy and determinacy they retain derives entirely from the traces of traditional behavior that continue to operate in them. For this reason, a morality in which moral ideals are dominant "is not something that can stand on its own feet" (*RP*, 479–80).

Oakeshott's most elaborate argument for the view that ideals and purposes are never the spring of human activity but merely abridgments of our practical knowledge of how to go about an activity appears in the 1950 essay "Rational Conduct." There he uses the example of Victorian bloomers to criticize the rationalistic understanding of rational conduct as "behaviour in which an independently premeditated end is pursued and which is determined by that end." Bloomers were thought to be the "rational" form of dress for girl bicyclists in Victorian times because their design seemed to spring solely from independent reflection, undistracted by irrelevant considerations such as fashion, custom, or prejudice, on the specific problem of efficiently propelling a bicycle. Oakeshott argues, however, that this was not the case. If the activity of the designers of bloomers was governed simply by independent reflection on the problem of efficiently propelling a bicycle, why did their minds pause at bloomers instead of running on to shorts? The questions these designers were really trying to answer, though they may not have realized it, was the question "What garment combines within itself the qualities of being well adapted to the activity of propelling a bicycle and of being suitable, all things considered, for an English girl to be seen in when riding a bicycle in 1880?" And it is this question, complex (having more than one simple consideration) and tied to time and place, that they succeeded in answering (*RP*, 101–3, 115–16).

Of course, it is not in principle impossible that this more complex and circumstantial end could have been premeditated, but Oakeshott argues that such an end still cannot be considered the spring of activity. Our projects, and not simply the means by which we pursue them, derive from our knowledge of how to conduct an activity. A problem is not something pregiven; it is itself the product of a skillful "knowing how" (to use Ryle's apposite expression). A man who is not already a scientist cannot formulate a scientific problem. Whether a purpose is premeditated or not, it is never the spring of our activity, only a consequence (*RP*, 117–20).

In "Rational Conduct," Oakeshott also begins to disclose more fully the positive view of human activity and rationality that lay behind his critique of rationalism. Having shown that particular actions, problems, and projects all presuppose activity itself, he defines rationality as "faithfulness to the knowledge we have of how to conduct the specific activity we are engaged in." Such faithfulness, however, does not imply that there is nothing to be achieved in activity, no improvement to be made. The knowledge with which we begin is never "fixed and finished"; it is fluid, both coherent and incoherent, and rational conduct is conduct that contributes to and enhances its coherence (*RP*, 121–22). Once again, the echoes of Oakeshott's concrete logic in *Experience and Its Modes* can be heard here. Just as the criterion of experience in that work was said to lie "in its coherence, not in its conformity to or agreement with any fixed idea," so here the criterion of activity, its rationality, is said to consist in the coherence of a complex and fluid whole, not in conformity to some overall purpose.

How does this relate specifically to practical activity? Practical activity, too, begins, ends, and is characterized throughout by coherence. This coherence is not introduced from the outside; nor does it emanate from some external source—a rule, a principle, or a premeditated purpose. Rather, it is coeval with the activity of desiring itself. Nor is desire an empirical or "natural" state antecedent to activity; it "is being active in a certain manner." Desire already exhibits a knowledge of how to manage practical activity. Sometimes this knowledge takes the form of moral approval and disapproval. But, again, approval and disapproval are not to be thought of as somehow coming after desire; they are inseparable from it. Practical activity, then, "is always activity with a pattern; not a superimposed pattern, but a pattern inherent in the activity itself." Oakeshott refers to this pattern as a "current" or a "prevailing sympathy," and he defines a rational action as one that can maintain a place in this current or flow of sympathy. He acknowledges that this current or flow is subject to clog or compromise, but he insists that such a diseased condition cannot be cured by a transfusion of ideals, principles, or purposes, for these (as we have seen) are incapable of generating behavior. Recovery ultimately "depends upon the native strength of the patient; it depends upon the unimpaired relics of his knowledge of how to behave" (*RP*, 124–29).

The positive account of human activity and rationality sketched in "Rational Conduct" is amplified and applied to politics in Oakeshott's famous inaugural lecture, "Political Education," delivered in 1951. Here we finally get a sustained discussion of the idea of tradition that is the counterweight to rationalism. Oakeshott begins the lecture by reiterating his critique of ideology. The claim that a political ideology provides the impetus for political activity cannot be sustained. A political ideology is not the spring of political activity but only the product of subsequent reflection on it. This is the case, for example, with the Declaration of the Rights of Man and with Locke's *Second Treatise*. These did not exist in advance of political practice, they were abridgments of it; they were not prefaces to political activity but postscripts. Nor does freedom, the most idealized of our political ideals, escape Oakeshott's skeptical analysis: "Freedom, like a recipe for game pie, is not a bright idea . . . [it] is nothing more than arrangements, procedures of a certain kind: the freedom of an Englishman is not something exemplified in the procedure of *habeas corpus*, it *is*, at that point, the availability of that procedure" (*RP*, 48–54).

Oakeshott's primary concern is with the theoretical understanding of political activity that is implied in ideological politics. This understanding is defective because it misdescribes what actually goes on in political activity. Ideological politics are not simply undesirable; they are strictly speaking impossible. From this follows the practical defect of ideological politics; for "to try to do something which is inherently impossible is always a corrupting enterprise" (*RP*, 48). The specific corruption promoted by the ideological understanding of politics is the delusion that ideological knowledge alone is sufficient for conducting the activity of attending to the arrangements of a society; the delusion that "a knowledge of the chosen ideology can take the place of understanding a tradition of political behaviour." This corruption is exemplified in what Oakeshott calls "one of the most insidious current misunderstandings of political activity," the misunderstanding in which the "arrangements of a society are made to appear, not as manners of behaviour, but as pieces of machinery to be transported about the world indiscriminately" (*RP*, 55, 63).

Having shown that every ideology rests on or presupposes an already existing tradition of behavior, Oakeshott argues that it is in terms of such traditions of behavior that political activity must be understood. Because a tradition is not something fixed or finished, an inflexible manner of doing things, political activity must be the exploration of what is intimated in a tradition. Oakeshott gives the example of women getting the vote. Here was a case in which what was already intimated in the already achieved legal status of women had yet to be recognized; here was an incoherence calling out for remedy. Natural right or abstract justice had nothing to do with it. The only relevant reason for enfranchising women "was that in all or most other important respects they had already been enfranchised" (*RP*, 56–57).

Politics is (in the now famous phrase) "the pursuit of intimations." Oakeshott uses the word "intimations" because he wants to emphasize that what we have to do within political activity is something less precise and more elusive than logical implications or necessary consequences (*RP*, 57–58). This is central to his notion of tradition and ultimately relates back to his concrete logic. A tradition of behavior is a complex whole that does not point in a single direction, nor is it entirely self-consistent. It has identity, but this identity is of a complex and not a simple nature. A tradition of behavior is, in short, a concrete universal, and Oakeshott evokes its complex many-in-oneness in the following way:

> [A tradition of behavior] is neither fixed nor finished; it has no changeless centre to which understanding can anchor itself; there is no sovereign purpose to be perceived or invariable direction to be detected; there is no model to be copied, idea to be realized, or rule to be followed. Some parts of it may change more slowly than others, but none is immune from change. Everything is temporary.

But that everything is temporary in a tradition does not mean that it provides no criterion for distinguishing between good and bad projects. To be sure, this criterion cannot lie in correspondence to a fixed purpose or principle. But by denying such objectivism, Oakeshott does not lapse into a featureless relativism. The criterion that governs a tradition is coherence. In a passage worthy of Burke, he writes:

> though a tradition of behaviour is flimsy and elusive, it is not without identity, and what makes it a possible object of knowledge is the fact that all its parts do not change at the same time and that the changes it undergoes are potential within it. Its principle is a principle of *continuity*: authority is diffused between past, present and future; between the old, the new and what is to come. . . . Everything is temporary, but nothing is arbitrary. Everything figures by comparison, not with what stands next to it, but with the whole. (*RP*, 61; see also 67–68)

It is because a tradition of behavior is a whole in this complex and concrete way—because it does not disclose a single, unambiguous norm or principle—that politics is also said to be (in another famous phrase) "a conversation, not an argument." The image of conversation is used here to evoke the quality of relationship subsisting between the multiplicity of considerations that compose a single tradition. In navigating a tradition we do not employ deduction, subsumption, or demonstration; these belong to argumentative discourse. Rather, a tradition of behavior presents us with a number of different, frequently competing, always circumstantial considerations or intimations that have to be attended to, weighed, and balanced. "Conversation," like "intimation," evokes the open-endedness and flexibility of this engagement. It does not imply that there are no "arguments" in politics (though Oakeshott does seem to suggest that these arguments will not be over principles or ideologies).[10] He certainly does not conceive of politics "in terms of the pleasant, somewhat idle but also valuable, civilized talk of university dons over their afternoon sherry."[11]

Oakeshott insists that by claiming that politics is the pursuit of intimations he is not recommending a certain style of politics; he is only explaining what actually happens in political activity. Politics can never be anything but the pursuit of intimations. Even so-called revolutionary situations or foundings do not escape this condition. Historical analysis reveals every such "founding"—whether it be the American Founding, the French Revolution, or the Russian Revolution—to be a modification of past circumstances and not a creation *ex nihilo* (*RP*, 58–59). The ideological style, no less than any other style of politics, is bound to tradition and confined to exploring its intimations. This is but the other side of Oakeshott's earlier contention that ideological politics are, theoretically speaking, impossible.

The epistemological aspect of Oakeshott's critique of ideological politics has puzzled many commentators. If, in the end, all politics are necessarily traditionalist, if ideological politics are simply impossible, there would seem to be no reason for preferring one style of politics to another; rationalist politics, though theoretically naïve, would seem to pose no great danger and therefore not to need to be criticized. Oakeshott is partly to blame for this confusion because he consistently downplays the practical importance of his critique. Nevertheless, he does not deny that belief in an erroneous theory can have pernicious practical consequences. Although the theory can produce no concrete piece of behavior to match its prescriptions, it can confuse, throw off, or otherwise corrupt activity. Significantly, he concludes his lecture by mentioning two practical benefits that follow from his analysis of political education:

The more profound our understanding of political activity, the less we shall be at the mercy of plausible but mistaken analogy, the less we shall be tempted by a false or irrelevant model. And the more thoroughly we understand our own political tradition, the more readily will its resources be available to us, the less likely we shall be to embrace the illusions which wait for the ignorant and the unwary: the illusion that in politics we can get on without a tradition of behaviour, the illusion that the abridgement of a tradition is itself a sufficient guide, and the illusion that in politics there is anywhere a safe harbour, a destination to be reached or even a detectable strand of progress. (*RP*, 66)

The issue on which criticism immediately fastened in Oakeshott's lecture was the idea of tradition defended in it. In his vitriolic attack on Oakeshott in the *New Statesman*, Labour intellectual R. H. S. Crossman formulated two of the most common criticisms of this idea. First, he argued, Oakeshott's idea of tradition does not provide a standard by which one tradition can be said to be better than another. It is incapable of judging, for example, between the tradition of British parliamentary democracy and that of Soviet Communism or German National Socialism. Second, why should we assume there is only one tradition in any given state or territory? And if there is more than one tradition, how do we determine which of the rival intimations of the different traditions to pursue?[12]

To the second criticism Oakeshott responds that the tradition he was specifically concerned with in his lecture was the legal structure of a society that is united by its recognition of such a structure (*RP*, 69). Beyond that, he is clear that no tradition intimates only a single thing; every tradition contains within itself a multiplicity of different, and sometimes colliding, intimations. The question then arises: how do we know which intimation among this multiplicity to pursue? And Oakeshott has no ready practical answer to it. "Do you want to be told," he asks, "that in politics there is, what certainly exists nowhere else, a mistake-proof manner of what should be done?" (*RP*, 69) This does not mean that anything goes, or that there is no criterion for distinguishing between good and bad political projects. The criterion to be satisfied, as we have learned, is coherence. But what specifically this predicates is something that cannot be settled in advance of activity. Practical reasoning is always a matter of attending to the multiplicity of considerations that compose a tradition and of striking some sort of balance.

Crossman's first criticism is somewhat more difficult to answer. In some ways it is true that Oakeshott does not provide a standard by which entire traditions may be compared and evaluated. But whether this implies that there is no basis upon which to criticize or evaluate the traditions of German National Socialism or Soviet Communism is less clear. In the first place, it is questionable whether it is even appropriate to speak of "traditions" here, since both of these regimes ruled more through brute force than through political deliberation. But even putting this objection to one side, it is doubtful that either German National Socialism or Soviet Communism can be identified with the whole of the political traditions in which they emerged. Indeed, they seem to represent what Oakeshott calls ideologies—rather severe abridgments of traditions in which one or two elements have been picked out and pursued to the exclusion of all the rest.

Crossman's criticism of Oakeshott's idea of tradition on the basis that it provides no standard by which to distinguish a good tradition from a bad one is merely a specific version of the more general objection to conservatism that, as Hayek has put it, "by its very nature it cannot offer an alternative to the direction in which we are moving."[13] The neo-conservative historian Gertrude Himmelfarb has put forward an interesting variation on this standard objection. She argues that the logic of Oakeshott's traditionalism suggests that we should merely acquiesce in the rootless, anarchic, and anti-authoritarian tendencies of contemporary life (i.e. the 1960s). Oakeshott's idea of tradition leaves the conservative without a critical leg to stand on when the counterculture becomes the dominant culture.[14]

Oakeshott would no doubt reply that Himmelfarb here confuses what has become momentarily dominant in our culture with the whole of our tradition. Our traditional inheritance consists of much more than what lies on the surface of the present. In this regard, Oakeshott would surely agree with Hans-Georg Gadamer's warning—in response to the criticism that traditional knowledge and *phronēsis* are no longer enough in a world characterized by a total chaos of norms and principles—that we must be careful not to "equate Nietzsche's anticipations and the ideological confusion of the present with life as it is actually lived with its own forms of solidarity. . . . [T]he displacement of human reality never goes so far that no forms of solidarity exist any longer."[15]

None of this suggests that there is nothing problematic about Oakeshott's traditionalist model of political activity as it is formulated in his writings up through "Political Education." The central difficulty, however, lies not in the fact that he defends tradition but in how he conceives of tradition and the pursuit of its intimations. Oakeshott is so concerned to refute the false intellectualism of ideological politics that he sometimes seems to exclude ideological debate and argument over principles altogether from politics. It is a strange thing to say of a philosophical idealist, but when it comes to politics Oakeshott sometimes seems to be almost a materialist, or at least an ultrapragmatist. His examples from cookery, cricket, and even legal argumentation only serve to reinforce this pragmatism and obscure the crucial ideological dimension of modern politics. The example of women getting the vote is illuminating in this regard. Is it really true that the only reason for enfranchising women was that in all other respects they had already been enfranchised? Did the principles of justice or political equality really have nothing to do with it? What would Oakeshott say of slavery? Didn't its incompatibility with the principles of the Declaration of Independence constitute a relevant reason for abolishing it?

There is a way in which Oakeshott's valorization of habit, custom, and the unselfconsciousness of tradition is profoundly anachronistic. This may be the way politics were conducted in aristocratic societies, but it is irrelevant to modern democratic societies. This is essentially the point Hegel makes in the passage quoted above: the fundamental principle of the modern age, deriving from the Reformation, is that everything must be justified at the bar of human reason, must be justified by thought. Modern politics are unavoidably ideological, though not necessarily in the negative sense disparaged by Oakeshott. As one early and perceptive critic of Oakeshott put it, "a politician in the highly vocal, argumentative, Western political world . . . is *inevitably* a rationaliser, and his rationalisations obviously invite critical scrutiny. It is really *non-*ideological politics which have become impossible in the West, because a process of critical awareness cannot reverse itself."[16]

Interestingly, Oakeshott's later discussions of tradition and political discourse pay far more serious attention to this ideological dimension of politics. In a reply to one of his critics in 1965, for example, he makes it plain that a tradition consists of general ideas, principles, and norms. His fundamental objection to rationalism now is that it fails to grasp the radical diversity of these ideological beliefs by trying to reduce them to a self-consistent creed or universal norm from which to deduce injunctions. The normative beliefs that compose a tradition, he writes,

are not self-consistent; they often pull in different directions, they compete with one another and cannot all be satisfied at the same time, and therefore they cannot properly be thought of as a norm or a self-consistent set of norms or "principles" capable of delivering to us an unequivocal message about what we should do. . . . Aristotle called them the "admitted goods" and recognized them to be incommensurable.[17]

Given the radically diverse nature of a tradition—Oakeshott calls it a "multi-voiced creature"—political deliberation becomes a matter of striking a balance between competing goods. There is nothing here that precludes ideological debate or arguments over principle. The only thing that is precluded is the belief that such debate is a matter of mathematical demonstration issuing in categorical injunctions.

The unavoidably ideological character of modern politics receives even more emphatic acknowledgment in an essay that seems to come from roughly the same time as the reply above: "Political Discourse."[18] In this essay, Oakeshott explicitly concerns himself with argumentative political discourse and contends that such discourse is always conducted in terms of vocabularies of general ideas that are not inappropriately spoken of as "ideologies." Such discourse also has a "logical design," of which Oakeshott distinguishes two varieties: persuasion and demonstration. Aristotle provides the classic treatment of the first in his *Rhetoric*, showing that persuasive speech is concerned with contingencies rather than necessities, probabilities rather than certainties, and conjectures rather than proofs. The uncertainty that inevitably attaches to persuasive speech, however, has led other thinkers to search for a more demonstrative and apodictic form of political discourse. Oakeshott discusses Plato and Marx in this regard, as well as the social scientists who speak of "the end of ideology," and he leaves us in no doubt that he finds this to be a misguided enterprise: political discourse that "deals in conjectures and possibilities and the weighing of circumstantial pros and cons . . . is the only sort of reasoning appropriate to practical affairs. In this matter Aristotle and Isocrates are better guides than Plato and Marx" (*RP*, 95).

The Tradition of Modern European Politics

Given the importance of tradition in his understanding of politics, it was inevitable that, in order to understand the current political situation more profoundly, Oakeshott would turn his attention to the tradition of modern European politics. Beginning with the posthumously published *The Politics of Faith and the Politics of Scepticism* (most likely written around 1953) and continuing through the essays "On Being Conservative" (1956) and "The Masses in Representative Democracy" (1957) and the lectures on *Morality and Politics in Modern Europe* (1958), he reflected on the historical roots of modern European politics and on the beliefs that nourished or undermined a liberal understanding of politics. In the course of this historical reflection, as we shall see, his diagnosis of modern politics subtly shifts from an emphasis on rationalism as the enemy of free institutions to an emphasis on the anti-individualistic morality of the common good.

Before taking up these writings, it is worth looking at Oakeshott's earliest attempts to connect his critique of rationalism to a defense of liberal institutions. Unlike many other critics of rationalism, Oakeshott does not identify liberalism with rationalism. In a review of Hans Morganthau's *Scientific Man versus Power Politics*, for example, he criticizes Morganthau for making precisely this identification:

> The truth is . . . that parliamentary government and rationalist politics do not belong to the same tradition and do not, in fact, go together. . . . [T]he institutions of parliamentary government sprang from the least rationalistic period of our politics, from the Middle Ages, and . . . were connected, not with the promotion of a rationalistic order of society, but (in conjunction with the common law) with the limitation of the exercise of political power and the opposition to tyranny in whatever form it appeared. The root of so-called "democratic" theory is not rationalist optimism about the perfectibility of human society, but scepticism about the possibility of such perfection and the determination not to allow human life to be perverted by the tyranny of a person or fixed by the tyranny of an idea. (*RPML*, 109)

Oakeshott envisages liberalism here as a countertradition to rationalism. But the question arises, why should we adopt this particular tradition over any of the other alternatives that constitute our inheritance—for example, rationalism itself? Given that our tradition is essentially ambivalent—a point urged by many of Oakeshott's critics, and one which he himself seems to recognize—why choose the liberal strand in it over any of the other strands? The concept of tradition alone does not seem to provide any guidance on this question. And in the absence of any guidance, Oakeshott's liberal politics seem to rest on nothing more than personal preference.

Here, again, there is some confusion about Oakeshott's notion of tradition, though the confusion arises largely from his own failure to make explicit what is involved in this complex notion. A certain ambiguity attaches to Oakeshott's notion of tradition. On the one hand, it refers (in an ordinary way) to the actual beliefs, practices, and institutions in a given society. On the other hand, it refers (in a more technical usage) to a certain set of formal properties characteristic of human experience, knowledge, or activity in general. It is this latter sense that is being invoked when one speaks of tradition—as I have above—as a concrete universal. Here tradition refers not to the past or the merely existent but to the nature of a complex whole and the manner in which it is maintained and integrated. It is because liberalism is a tradition in this more criterial sense that Oakeshott can adopt it over rationalism, which turns out not to be a genuine tradition at all.

The articulation between Oakeshott's notion of tradition and his liberal politics can best be seen in two essays from the late 1940s: "Contemporary British Politics" (1948) and "The Political Economy of Freedom" (1949). In "Contemporary British Politics," Oakeshott is primarily concerned to criticize the idea of central planning espoused by socialists. Central planning, he argues, involves the concentration of power in the hands of the government, and such concentration inevitably leads to despotism. The single most important condition of human freedom is the diffusion of power in a society.

Oakeshott develops his criticism of central planning by distinguishing between two different modes of integration or organization of society. The mode of integration that belongs to a centrally planned society is of a simple and external sort. All power is concentrated in the hands of the government, and the government imposes order on society from the outside, as it were. In contrast to this mode of integration is another of a more complex sort, based on the rule of law. This integration is in terms of rights and duties, which are not, however, to be conceived of as "natural" or absolute. The integration provided by the rule of law is, of course, never perfect or final; enjoyment of the rights and duties that comprise it can lead to dangerous concentrations of power calling for remedy or readjustment. But the key point is that these dangerous concentrations of power must be diffused by means of incremental adjustments in the rights and duties of individuals, never by means of an overhead plan ("CBP," 476–89).

Oakeshott calls the politics he is defending "a kind of perennial politics." The holism and incrementalism that belong to them clearly recall the concrete logic of *Experience and Its Modes* as well as Oakeshott's notion of tradition. Indeed, it is here that we get a clearer idea of just how the idea of tradition functions in Oakeshott's argument.

Tradition is being used here in the criterial sense mentioned above, designating the manner in which a complex whole is maintained and integrated. It is in this sense that Oakeshott's skeptical, perennial, even liberal politics can be said to be traditional. He concludes the essay by recalling us to this understanding of a liberal democracy as a tradition, a way of living. We must not, he urges, think of liberal democracy as an abstract idea or as a fixed body of abstract rights but, rather, as a "living method of social integration, the most civilized and the most effective method ever invented by mankind" ("CBP," 489–90).

This concrete approach to the liberal tradition carries over into "The Political Economy of Freedom." Inquiry into the political economy of freedom obviously presupposes some notion of freedom, but Oakeshott quickly points out at the start of the essay that the freedom he has in mind is not an abstract idea but the concrete way of living we currently enjoy. As in "Contemporary British Politics," he sees the diffusion of power as the most general condition of our freedom. And this diffusion of power appears first in the "diffusion of authority between past, present, and future." In place of Burke's "great primeval contract," Oakeshott invokes his own idea of conversation: "The politics of our society are a conversation in which past, present and future each has a voice; and though one or other of them may on occasion properly prevail, none permanently dominates, and on this account we are free." Again as in "Contemporary British Politics," Oakeshott identifies the rule of law as the method of government, the mode of social integration, best suited to preserving freedom thus understood. And he speaks of the rule of law, along the lines of a tradition, as "control[ling] effectively . . . without breaking the grand affirmative flow of things" (*RP*, 386–90).

The most striking overlap between Oakeshott's conception of a liberal society and his idea of tradition comes, however, in his discussion of the purpose of a free society. Such a society, he tells us, will not find its purpose in any sort of preconceived idea or external goal but, rather,

> in a principle of *continuity* (which is a diffusion of power between past, present and future) and in a principle of *consensus* (which is a diffusion of power between different legitimate interests of the present). We call ourselves free because our pursuit of current desires does not deprive us of a sympathy for what went before. . . . We consider ourselves free because, taking a view neither short nor long, we are unwilling to sacrifice either the present to a remote and incalculable future, or the immediate and foreseeable future to a

transitory present. And we find freedom once more in a preference for slow, small changes which leave behind them a voluntary consensus of opinion . . . and in our perception that it is more important for a society to move together than for it to move either fast or far. . . . We find what we need in a principle of change and a principle of identity. (*RP*, 396–97)

Oakeshott goes on to argue in this essay that the institution of private property is the economic arrangement most compatible with freedom thus understood because it is the least likely to promote dangerous concentrations of power. Two important caveats to Oakeshott's defense of the free market—which in many respects echoes Hayek's—must be noted, however. First, like Hayek, he does not identify economic freedom with laissez-faire. The diffusion of power demands that the government intervene actively to break up monopolies and insure effective competition. Such intervention, however, must be carried out in a manner that is compatible with the structure of our liberty (*RP*, 392–96). Second, and more importantly, market institutions must not be defended merely on the basis of their economic efficiency. Here Oakeshott's understanding of the political economy of freedom diverges from Hayek's. We have already seen Oakeshott complain about liberalism's questionable moral ideal, "the plausible ethics of productivity." Here he insists that "the political economy of freedom rests upon the clear acknowledgement that what is being considered is not 'economics' (not the maximization of wealth, not productivity or the standard of life), but *politics*, that is, the custody of a manner of living" (*RP*, 406).

In "The Political Economy of Freedom" and "Contemporary British Politics," we find Oakeshott trying to conceive of liberal society largely in terms of his critique of rationalism and the idea of tradition underlying it. While not ignoring the issue of freedom, he tends to subordinate it to, or at least place it in the context of, concerns with the stability, coherence, and continuity of a complex society. When we turn to some of Oakeshott's later essays from the 1950s, however, a subtle shift takes place in his outlook, particularly with respect to the grounds on which he defends liberal democracy. Instead of tradition, we now hear a good deal more about individuality; and the liberal political order, characterized by the diffusion of power, the rule of law, and the absence of any overarching purpose, is defended largely in terms of its appropriateness to this historic disposition. Moreover, what Oakeshott opposes to this morality and politics of individuality is not so much ideology any longer as the morality and politics of the common good: the imposition on subjects of a common substantive condition of human circumstance.

As this new articulation of Oakeshott's political teaching suggests different grounds for his defense of liberal political arrangements, so it suggests different grounds for his rejection of rationalism in politics. Whereas in the essays up through "Political Education" Oakeshott rejects rationalism on the basis that it does not accord with human reason properly understood or the logic of human activity, in "On Being Conservative" and the essays that follow it he rejects rationalism on the basis that it does not accord with individuality or human freedom. There has been a displacement in Oakeshott's critique of rationalism away from epistemological considerations to more recognizably moral and political ones. Indeed, one might question whether the word "rationalism," which inevitably directs us to considerations of the theory of knowledge, any longer adequately specifies Oakeshott's target.

The locus of this shift in Oakeshott's thinking about rationalism is his celebrated essay "On Being Conservative" (written in 1956, rejected for publication in *Encounter* by Irving Kristol, and finally published in 1962 as part of *Rationalism in Politics*). The central thrust of this essay is to define a conservatism that does not rest on natural law or any sort of general beliefs about human nature or the universe. The principal targets of the essay are Burke and his modern followers—Russell Kirk, for example[19]—whom Oakeshott believes have tied political conservatism too closely to controversial and even anachronistic speculative and religious beliefs. (Oakeshott's lukewarm attitude toward Burke in this essay contrasts sharply with the Burkean qualities of his earlier essays.) In contradistinction to these "cosmic Tories," Oakeshott makes a thoroughly modern and skeptical defense of the conservative disposition in politics.

He begins with a description of the conservative disposition in general, the chief characteristic of which is "a propensity to use and enjoy what is available rather than to wish for or to look for something else; to delight in what is present rather than what was or what may be." To be conservative is to prefer the present to the past or the future, the familiar to the unknown, the actual to the possible. Further, the conservative has a cautious attitude toward change and innovation. For him there is much to lose, and this makes him unadventurous (*RP*, 407–12).

It is not part of Oakeshott's purpose to unequivocally defend this conservative disposition—a point often missed by readers of this essay. He recognizes that this disposition is not strong among us, nor has it been for the last five centuries or so. We are a people addicted to change and innovation, and Oakeshott does not suggest that we should completely transform ourselves (*RP*, 413–14). Instead, he argues that, even given our current disposition to change and innovation, a conservative disposition with respect to politics and the general rules of conduct makes a great deal of sense. It is not necessary to call upon general beliefs about human nature or the universe to make the conservative disposition in politics intelligible. What makes this disposition intelligible has "nothing to do with a natural law or a providential order, nothing to do with morals or religion"; it involves only

> the observation of our current manner of living combined with the belief . . . that governing is a specific and limited activity, namely the provision and custody of general rules of conduct, which are understood, not as plans for imposing substantive activities, but as instruments enabling people to pursue the activities of their own choice with the minimum frustration, and therefore something which is appropriate to be conservative about. (*RP*, 423–24)

Oakeshott contrasts the conservative attitude toward our current individualistic and pluralistic circumstances—circumstances in which human beings engage in a vast variety of enterprises, entertain a multiplicity of opinions, and in general exercise "an acquired love of making choices for themselves"—with that of the rationalist. The rationalist sees nothing but disorder in all this activity and diversity and attempts to resolve it by imposing a single comprehensive end or purpose on society. The conservative, on the other hand, accepts this individualistic and pluralistic state of affairs and confines government to the role of ruling over it as a referee rules over a game. For the rationalist, government is "an instrument of passion" and "the art of politics is to inflame and direct desire." For the conservative, on the other hand, the business of government is "not to inflame passion and give it new objects to feed upon, but to inject into the activities of already too passionate men an ingredient of moderation" (*RP*, 424–28, 431–33).

These, then, are the alternatives—the "politics of passion" versus the "politics of scepticism"—and Oakeshott leaves us in no doubt that he considers the second to be more appropriate to our circumstances. In a people that is conservative in hardly any other respect, political conservatism makes a great deal of sense. "It is not at all inconsistent," he writes in a sentence that could stand as a motto for the entire essay, "to be conservative in respect of government and radical in respect of almost every other activity." For this reason, he thinks conservatives have more to learn from skeptical individualists like Montaigne, Pascal, Hobbes, and Hume than from the cosmic speculations of Burke (*RP*, 435).

The skeptical conservatism defended by Oakeshott in "On Being Conservative" contrasted sharply with the "new conservatism" emerging in the United States in the 1950s. American conservatism tended to stress the role of ideas in the corruption of modern political life—the title of Richard Weaver's influential conservative tract, published in 1948, was *Ideas Have Consequences*. The modern attack on objective values and their source in transcendent reality had led to a relativism that was defenseless against modern dictatorship and totalitarianism. What was needed was a revival of objective standards in the form of natural law to serve as a bulwark against these political dangers. This was the thrust of John Hallowell's argument in *The Moral Foundations of Democracy* (1954) and of Walter Lippmann's argument in *The Public Philosophy* (1955). Oakeshott wrote a review of the latter book criticizing Lippmann for seeking both the cause and the cure of our current political predicament in intellectual doctrines: abstract ideas are never the source of our conduct, he argued, and what keeps our leaders in check is not a complicated doctrine of natural law but "some simple moral qualities: courage, or perhaps pride, or indifference, or even mere laziness" (*RPML*, 115). It was in this environment that Leo Strauss's diagnosis of modernity in terms of relativism and radical historicism and his call for a return to classical political philosophy came to exert a powerful influence on American conservatives, from Willmoore Kendall to Irving Kristol.[20]

The opposition of the "politics of passion" and the "politics of scepticism" in "On Being Conservative" is not an isolated feature of that essay alone but forms the basis of Oakeshott's historical analyses of modern European politics throughout the 1950s. A version of this opposition first appears in *The Politics of Faith and the Politics of Scepticism*, a manuscript that Oakeshott chose not to publish during his lifetime but that seems to have been written somewhere around 1953. The concern that animates this book is to understand the character of modern European politics as it has disclosed itself since roughly the sixteenth century. And, as in his later writings, most notably the third essay of *On Human Conduct*, Oakeshott argues that this character is not something simple or monolithic but, rather, complex and equivocal. The modern European political consciousness is a divided consciousness, and the politics of faith and the politics of skepticism constitute its poles.

The politics of faith and the politics of skepticism stand for two radically opposed understandings of the activities and office of government in the modern world. According to the first, governing is understood as the pursuit of perfection, where "perfection" denotes "a single, comprehensive condition of human circumstances," whether it be moral virtue, religious salvation, or material prosperity. Implied in such a perfectionist conception of politics is the idea that governing is also an unlimited or "omnicompetent" activity, unconcerned with formalities and positively disposed toward power (*PFPS*, 23–29). Power is in many ways at the heart of this conception of politics. The politics of faith views government as an immense reservoir of power to accomplish its grandiose purposes. Indeed, such a conception of politics only became possible, according to Oakeshott, with the vast increase in the power of governments in early modern Europe. In this latter regard, he interestingly argues—somewhat at odds with the view he takes in later writings— that "the politics of faith is not the parent of a great increase in the quantity of power at the disposal of government, but a child of the circumstantial enlargement of that power" (*PFPS*, 45–46).

Oakeshott sees Francis Bacon as the first and most adventurous theorist of the perfectionist politics of faith. Bacon not only had a vision of human perfection, which he envisaged as the complete mastery of the world and the exploitation of its resources for the benefit of mankind; he also conceived of government as the agent of this perfection, for which purpose he thought it should be endowed with unlimited power. In this regard, Oakeshott distinguishes Bacon's ambitious perfectionist politics from Machiavelli's more modest understanding of the activity of governing as "the exercise of power for maintaining order and securing the continuance of the political community." In Machiavelli, "there is no hint of a minute and brooding authority engaged in the tireless direction of all the activities of the subject" (*PFPS*, 52–57). In addition to the Baconian technological project, Oakeshott identifies two other influential versions of the politics of faith: the religious and the economic.

The politics of skepticism is in all respects the opposite of the politics of faith. It, too, is the creature of the "circumstantial enlargement" of the power of European governments in the fifteenth and sixteenth centuries. But instead of dreaming of all that might be done with this newly acquired power, the politics of skepticism set itself the task of specifying more narrowly the purpose toward which such power might be used. According to this skeptical conception of politics, governing is a limited and specific activity. It is not concerned with perfection or truth but only with reducing the occasions for conflict among individuals who, pursuing a vast variety of enterprises, are apt to come into conflict with one another. Governing here is understood to be a judicial, not a managerial, activity; and the image of the ruler is that of a referee, not that of a "leader" (*PFPS*, 30–34). Oakeshott associates a number of thinkers with this skeptical understanding of politics, but the names that appear most frequently in connection with it are those of Montaigne, Pascal, Hobbes, Hume, and Burke. The repeated invocation of the last-named thinker in this book confirms that it was probably written before 1954, when Oakeshott's attitude toward Burke began to become more ambivalent.

An important implication of Oakeshott's analysis of modern European politics in terms of the duality of the politics of faith and the politics of skepticism is that it answers those critics who claim that the logic of Oakeshott's traditionalism dictates that we must simply acquiesce to the rationalism that has come to dominate modern politics. Oakeshott's analysis suggests that the modern political tradition is not so one-dimensional and that it intimates two very different understandings of the office and activities of government. If our situation is not as happy as the optimistic believers in historical progress suggest, neither is it as dire as some radical critics of modernity fear. Against those for whom the cloud of the politics of faith seems "to have hung over us for so long that it fills the whole sky and darkens the whole earth"—one thinks here of Heidegger and those political philosophers, like Strauss and Arendt, who were influenced by his monolithic account of modernity—Oakeshott asserts that "the politics of faith are not, and never have been, the only, or the only significant, style and understanding of politics which the history of the modern world discloses" (*PFPS*, 66). In a review from the same time as *The Politics of Faith and the Politics of Skepticism*, Oakeshott criticizes Eric Voegelin for making precisely this mistake when he reduces the history of modern politics to the history of Gnostic or perfectionist politics: "Perhaps the most serious defect of the whole account is the underestimate of the strength and vitality throughout modern European history of what may be called neo-Augustinian politics as both the partner and opponent of Gnostic politics."[21]

The politics of faith and the politics of skepticism, then, are the poles of the modern European political consciousness; and they have stamped our understanding of the activity of governing in the modern world as well as the political vocabulary we use to describe it—words such as "right," "security," and so forth—with ambiguity. But Oakeshott does not write to eliminate this ambiguity. The conclusion he particularly wishes to avoid is "the fruitless conclusion that a virtuous politics would seek simplicity and 'shun ambiguous alloy'" (*PFPS*, 18). This constitutes one of the most interesting aspects of this posthumously published book, serving as a corrective to what sometimes appears as a sterile purism and hostility to ambiguity in Oakeshott's later writings. Neither the politics of faith nor the politics of skepticism, according to Oakeshott, constitutes a self-sufficient or concrete understanding of politics in the modern world. Each, taken by itself and in an uninhibited form, displays a self-destructive character (*PFPS*, 91–92).

That Oakeshott makes this argument in connection with the perfectionist politics of faith does not, of course, surprise us. But that he makes it in connection with the politics of skepticism does seem noteworthy, especially in light of the highly procedural and formalistic character of his later writings. The skeptical style of politics, he argues here, while eminently suitable to static conditions of society, is "sluggish" and unprepared when it comes to genuine emergencies; and in its moderateness, it is incapable of evoking love or gratitude from its subjects. Most important of all, the skeptical style of politics seems strangely irrelevant in the current activist climate of politics. In this climate, "the sceptical style must appear as an unintelligible piece of sophistication" or, worse, an expression of frivolity (*PFPS*, 105–10).

Given the self-destructiveness of both the politics of faith and the politics of skepticism taken by themselves, Oakeshott concludes that our task today should be, not to opt for one or the other of these extremes, but to preserve and exploit the complexity and ambiguity of our political tradition. To this end, he resuscitates Halifax's *Character of a Trimmer* (published in 1688) as the character most appropriate to our situation. The "trimmer" is one who does not put all the weight of a ship on one side or point the sail in a single direction but who constantly makes adjustments in response to particular circumstances in order to keep the boat on an even keel. In terms of the dichotomy that defines our political tradition, the trimmer will be concerned to prevent our politics from running to either of the extremes of faith or skepticism and to cultivate a middle region between them. This does not mean, however, that the trimmer will always be simply in the middle. In our current circumstances, for example, which Oakeshott sees as dominated by the politics of faith, the trimmer will throw his weight to the other side of the boat and seek to renew the skeptical pole of our politics (*PFPS*, 121–28).

The analysis of modern European politics begun in *The Politics of Faith and the Politics of Passion* is continued in Oakeshott's 1957 essay "The Masses in Representative Democracy" and his 1958 Harvard lectures on *Morality and Politics in Modern Europe*. The principal change in these later writings is that Oakeshott no longer characterizes the poles of the modern European consciousness in terms of the dichotomy of

faith and skepticism but—in keeping with the shift in his thinking
noted above—in terms of the dichotomy of individuality and anti-
individuality. This change is accompanied by a more ideological edge to
Oakeshott's historical account. The politics of perfection are no longer
seen as springing from hubristic overreach but from moral failure.

   This ideological aspect of Oakeshott's analysis is especially evident in
"The Masses in Representative Democracy." Significantly, Oakeshott
begins his historical inquiry into the "masses," not with the emergence
of the "mass-man," but with the emergence of the "individual" at the
dawn of the modern era. This reflects the general point of view of the
entire essay: the preeminent event in modern European history is not,
as Ortega y Gasset contended, the "accession of the masses to complete
social power" but, rather, the emergence of the modern "individual";
the mass-man is a wholly derivative character. Oakeshott traces this
seminal event to the end of the medieval period when the tight-knit
character of corporate and communal life was beginning to break up.
Italy figures prominently in the story, and he quotes Burckhardt, to
whom his account obviously owes a great deal: "At the close of the
thirteenth century Italy began to swarm with individuality; the ban laid
upon human personality was dissolved; a thousand figures meet us, each
in his own special shape and dress." This historic disposition to cultivate and enjoy individuality gradually spread to Northern Europe—
Montaigne is cited as one of its earliest and greatest exemplars—and it
eventually imposed itself profoundly on European conduct and belief.
No department of life remained unaffected by it (*RP*, 363–67, 370,
382–83).

   There are two areas, according to Oakeshott, in which this experience of individuality was clearly reflected; first, in the field of ethical
theory (Hobbes and Kant are cited as notable theorists of the morality
of individuality); and second, in a certain manner of governing and
being governed, a manner that came to be called "modern representative democracy" and received its most perfect expression in "parliamentary government." Oakeshott's account of this manner of government
characteristically does not emphasize political participation so much as
the necessity of "an instrument of government capable of transforming
the interests of individuality into rights and duties." Individuality is not
natural, it is a great human achievement; and what this achievement
required in the first place was an instrument of government capable of
asserting the interests of individuality against already existing feudal
rights and privileges. Such an instrument was ultimately found in
"sovereign" legislative bodies. From these came a law "favourable to the

interests of individuality," providing the "detail of what became a well-understood condition of human circumstance, commonly denoted by the word 'freedom'" (*RP*, 367–69).

Such was the revolution that overtook European sentiments, morals, and politics from roughly the thirteenth century to the seventeenth. But not everyone responded to the new circumstances in quite the same way. What excited some appeared to others as a burden. And in these latter Oakeshott discerns the outline of a character quite opposed to the emergent "individual": namely, the "individual *manqué*." Before this character could become the mass-man, however, one further ingredient was needed: a feeling of moral inferiority, which was the inevitable consequence of the moralization of individuality. To the individual *manqué*'s already acute feelings of inadequacy in the field of conduct was now added "the misery of guilt." And from this feeling of guilt sprang a more militant character, the "anti-individual," who sought to "escape from [his] predicament by imposing it upon all mankind." It is this passion for uniformity, fueled by *ressentiment*, that is the key to the character Oakeshott is investigating. The anti-individual did, of course, eventually discover that he belonged to the most numerous class in European society, thus becoming the mass-man, but it is his resentful, anti-individualistic disposition, not his numbers, that ultimately define the mass-man (*RP*, 370–73).

Oakeshott goes on to argue that the anti-individual generated a morality and a politics to correspond to his character. Instead of celebrating liberty and self-determination, he stressed equality and solidarity. The nucleus of the new morality was "the concept of a substantive condition of human circumstance represented as the 'common' or 'public' good." And this became the basis of the anti-individual's conception of the office of government: "To govern was . . . to impose and maintain the substantive condition of human circumstance identified as 'the public good.'" Parliamentary government, with its ancient procedures and inherent skepticism about final goals, proved to be peculiarly unsuited for this task; therefore it was replaced by results-oriented "popular government." The image of the ruler ceased to be the referee and became instead the "manager" and the "leader" (*RP*, 374–80).

Oakeshott's account of the morality and politics of the mass-man leaves much to be desired. While it possesses a certain Nietzschean polemical appeal, it is sadly deficient as a historical account of the central tension in modern European politics. By tracing the values of equality and community back to the *ressentiment* of the anti-individual, Oakeshott hardly does justice to these ideas and their place in the modern political consciousness. While one may agree with him that "the event of supreme and seminal importance in modern European history remains the emergence of the human individual in his modern idiom" (*RP*, 381), this does not mean that all other, competing values in our political tradition—values such as equality, fraternity, fairness, security, etc.—can be reduced to the resentful psychology of those unable to bear the burdens of individuality. It is strange to see such a powerful critic of ideological history producing such an egregious example of it.

Of greater significance in "The Masses in Representative Democracy" is Oakeshott's treatment of the other pole in the modern political consciousness, the one corresponding to the historic disposition of individuality. First, there is the clear recognition that this disposition *is* historic and not natural. Second, there is a historical richness and nuance to Oakeshott's account of this disposition that is altogether missing from his account of the disposition of the anti-individual. And finally, Oakeshott's obvious sympathy for the disposition of individuality and his tying of liberal democracy to it contrasts sharply with the attitude of conservative liberals like Hayek (or Himmelfarb) who have deep reservations about the romantic cult of individuality associated with thinkers like Wilhelm von Humboldt and John Stuart Mill.[22] Oakeshott does not agree with Mill on many things, but on the value of individuality and its central place in the understanding of liberal democracy they speak with one, eloquent voice.

The Death of Political Philosophy?

In England in the 1950s, there began to appear a whole genre of essays with titles like "The Decline of Political Theory," "Is Political Philosophy Dead?" and "Does Political Theory Still Exist?"[23] In his introduction to a collection of essays entitled *Philosophy, Politics and Society* (1956)—a collection that kicked off with Oakeshott's inaugural lecture on "Political Education"—Peter Laslett made the definitive pronouncement: "For the moment, anyway, political philosophy is dead."[24] Who had killed it? For most of the authors of these obituaries, the culprit was not difficult to identify: it was the school of linguistic analysis at Oxford, which reduced all philosophical problems to "puzzles" thrown up, not by actual moral issues or political arrangements in the world, but by the language we use to describe them. The leading figures of this school were Gilbert Ryle and J. L. Austin, whose careful attention to ordinary language also derived support from the Wittgenstein of the *Philosophical Investigations* (published in 1954).

The most ambitious attempt to apply the method of linguistic analysis to the issues of political philosophy was T. D. Weldon's *The Vocabulary of Politics* (published in 1953). Weldon gave a good, if unself-conscious, description of the new philosophical method on the first page of his book:

> During the last century there has occurred a great change in the methods and aims of professional philosophers in this country and in the United States. . . . What has happened is that philosophers have become extremely self-conscious about language. They have come to realize that many of the problems which their predecessors have found insuperable arose not from anything mysterious or inexplicable in the world but from the eccentricities of the language in which we try to describe the world.[25]

Weldon went on to show that the attempts by traditional political philosophers from Plato to Hegel to demonstrate that one form of political organization is superior to another all rest on a variety of errors about language; likewise the attempt to ground our political preferences in metaphysical foundations. The fundamental error made by all these philosophers was the error of supposing that there is some unchanging essence that corresponds to words in our political vocabulary like "state," "individual," "rights," "law," "freedom," and so forth. Weldon argued that abandoning this essentialism and the quest for metaphysical foundations for our moral and political preferences does not lead to subjectivism, however; rather it opens the way to more discriminating and fruitful empirical inquiries into our political values and institutions.

In a review of *Philosophy, Politics and Society*—which included an essay by Weldon summarizing the main points of his book—Irving Kristol decried the effects of linguistic analysis on political philosophy. Sarcastically titling his review "A Philosophy for Little England," Kristol argued that the essays in Laslett's collection—with the exception of Oakeshott's inaugural lecture—modeled "a new kind of political philosopher, one with a deep anti-political bias, who violently disclaims not only political intentions but political wisdom as well." Concerned only with eradicating "nonsense" and exposing fallacies, the linguistic political philosopher ignores "all those questions about the Good Society and Justice and Political Morality which, if they are only academic table-talk in England, are very substantial matters elsewhere in the world."[26] Three years after Kristol's review, the Popperian philosopher and anthropologist Ernest Gellner bludgeoned home the same point in his vituperative assault on British linguistic philosophy, *Words and Things*. Taking as his text Wittgenstein's statement that "philosophy leaves everything as it is," Gellner condemned linguistic philosophy for abdicating "any kind of normative role" and failing to provide any sort of guide for political life.[27]

Where does Oakeshott stand in relation to this 1950s debate over the nature of political philosophy? It is clear that he would not have much sympathy for Kristol's and Gellner's call for a more politically engaged philosophy. What about the more modest and academic stance of linguistic philosophy? Though obviously not an analytic philosopher himself, having come out of the very different British Hegelian tradition, there are ways in which Oakeshott's conception of philosophy dovetails with that of the analytic school. As I pointed out in chapter 3, Oakeshott agreed with analytic philosophers that philosophy does not discover new knowledge or provide a justification for our beliefs but, rather, clarifies what to some extent we know already. He certainly would not disagree with Weldon's statement that "it is not the job of philosophy to provide new information about politics, biology, physics or any other matter of fact. Philosophical problems are entirely second order problems."[28] There are times when Oakeshott can even sound a bit like an analytic philosopher; for instance, in this passage from "Political Education": "the patient analysis of the general ideas which have come to be connected with political activity—in so far as it succeeds in removing some of the crookedness from our thinking and leads to a more economical use of concepts, is an activity neither to be overrated nor despised" (*RP*, 66).

Further supporting his affinities with analytic philosophy, Oakeshott wrote a fairly positive review of Weldon's *Vocabulary of Politics* and a wholly admiring review of Ryle's *Concept of Mind*.[29] He begins the former review in a way that Kristol would undoubtedly have found to be frivolous in a characteristically English way: "This is a light-hearted book, and is all the better for being so: philosophy is getting rid of one's phlegm, and this should not be a very solemn exercise." He goes on to praise Weldon for his critique of the notion that it is the task of philosophy to provide theoretical foundations for our political beliefs. And he is clearly sympathetic with Weldon's attempt to show that, once we have disposed of the illusion of absolute standards, we are not driven to skepticism or subjectivism but can formulate empirical questions that are far more helpful as guides to political practice than are abstract political doctrines. The one objection Oakeshott has to Weldon's book is that it treats past philosophers like Plato, Aristotle, Hobbes, and Hegel as being far more naïve and unselfconscious than they really were. In this regard, he finds Weldon's interpretation of Hegel to be particularly grotesque.

The last point is not merely an incidental criticism but suggests the important differences that ultimately divide Oakeshott from analytic philosophers like Weldon, despite some superficial similarities. Though Oakeshott can agree with the analytic critique of the pretensions of philosophy with respect to practice, he ultimately does not subscribe to the overly modest role attributed to philosophy by the analytic school—what Peter Winch (following Locke) called the "underlabourer conception of philosophy."[30] The philosophers he admires—Plato, Aristotle, Hobbes, Spinoza, and Hegel—are decidedly not underlaborers. Though philosophy for Oakeshott begins with and analyzes the knowledge contained in our ordinary concepts—or ordinary language—it does not regard this initial knowledge as an absolute datum against which to check our results but as a partial understanding in need of radical transformation in order to become fully understood. Philosophy may be second-order knowledge, but it does not play second fiddle to the first-order knowledge upon which it operates.

All of this is implied in what Oakeshott calls—in a manuscript written sometime around 1949—the "radically subversive" character of philosophic reflection. Borrowing an image from J. D. Mabbott's *The State and the Citizen* (1948)—which Oakeshott reviewed twice in 1949—he likens philosophic reflection to ascending a tower with windows at every level. As we climb higher and higher, our view of the landscape changes radically; so radically that it would be absurd to speak of "applying" the view from the higher levels to that of the ground level or of "checking" the former against the latter. What defines the philosopher is not reaching the top of the tower—significantly, Oakeshott states that there "is no top to this tower," i.e., there is no absolute knowledge—but the predisposition to keep climbing and resist all temptations to arrest one's ascent. The political philosopher is someone who accepts the invitation to climb the tower or be radically subversive without reserve. It is precisely this radically subversive character of philosophic reflection on politics that distinguishes Plato's *Republic*, Hobbes's *Leviathan*, Spinoza's *Ethics*, and Hegel's *Philosophy of Right*. All are concerned with detecting "the permanent character of political activity," though "permanent" here refers to what political activity "*becomes* when given a place in an intelligible universe." Oakeshott's variation on Wittgenstein's saying that "Philosophy leaves everything as it is" thus goes like this: "Political philosophy . . . is saying something concerned with political activity such that, if true, things will be as they are; not as they were when we first caught sight of them, but as they permanently are" (*RPML*, 140–52).

Oakeshott clearly uses "permanent" in a peculiar sense here, and we must be careful not to construe it in contrast with "historical." He does not understand political philosophy as the endeavor to envision an eternal or essential state corresponding to an immutable human nature; rather, it is the attempt to elucidate a view of politics that corresponds to our historic circumstances. In the case of modern political philosophy this means—as Oakeshott makes increasingly clear in his writings from "On Being Conservative" on—elucidating a view of the office of government that is appropriate to "subjects who desire to make choices for themselves, who find happiness in doing so and who are frustrated in having choices imposed on them" (*MPME*, 84). In his 1959 Harvard lectures, Oakeshott cites Locke, Kant, Smith, Burke, Bentham, and (equivocally) Mill as notable theorists of the morality and politics of individuality, but he criticizes them for trying to ground this morality and politics in metaphysical theories of human nature and natural law instead of simply recognizing it as the correlate to a historic disposition: "the best of the writers in this idiom are, I think, those who have pitched their expectations low, that is, those who have not lost sight of the fact that what they were doing is no more than exploring a theory of government appropriate to certain historical circumstances" (*MPME*, 83–85). The reference to "pitching expectations low" here is somewhat misleading. It gives the impression that Oakeshott is invoking the underlaborer conception of philosophy cherished by the linguistic school of analysis; in fact he means only to distance himself from a certain sort of grand metaphysical theorizing. The difficulty and complexity of his position, as I have tried to convey in this section, is that he tries to steer a course between these two conceptions of political philosophy, one of which promises too much and the other too little.

Because it is more tempting to assimilate Oakeshott's conception of political philosophy to the one that promises too little, I want to close this chapter by once again suggesting why we should not. In the first place, more than of philosophical analysis, Oakeshott is a great admirer of philosophical imagination, a quality he associates above all with Hobbes and Hegel. In a review from 1951, Oakeshott praises Santayana's *Dominations and Powers* for this quality, calling it "an achievement of philosophical imagination such as we have become unaccustomed to in these days of minute analysis."[31] Second, Oakeshott's practice as a political philosopher is far from modest. Though he may not talk about eternity, his attempt to make sense of morality and politics in Europe "for the last five centuries or so" is nothing if not ambitious. One of the complaints that run through the essays on the death of political philosophy in the 1950s is that there has not appeared a grand synthetic work of political philosophy in the twentieth century, nothing since Bosanquet's *Philosophical Theory of the State*. As we shall see, Oakeshott undertakes to provide such a synthetic statement in *On Human Conduct*.

5 The Conversation of Mankind

During the period of his rationalism writings, from the late 1940s to the early 1960s, Oakeshott did not confine his attention to politics but meditated seriously on what (he thought) lay beyond the sphere of politics: namely, education, art, and historical inquiry. Indeed, the negative point that unifies his treatment of these cultural activities is precisely that they are not political and therefore must not be politicized. It is in this context that he develops his image of culture as a conversation between the various modes of discourse that compose our civilization. He laments, however, that in recent times the conversation has become "boring" because it has come to be dominated by the voices of practical activity and science: "to know and to contrive are our preeminent occupations" (*RP*, 493). Against this artificial contraction of "the conversation of mankind"—a phrase he takes from Hobbes's *Leviathan*[1]—Oakeshott defends the autonomy of the voices of history and art, and he defines the university as a place where the voice of practice is silent and the voice of science is not allowed to drown out all others.

Education and Conversation

Oakeshott's essays on education form one of the most attractive aspects of his philosophy. They evoke an ideal in which a human being, emancipated from the narrowing necessity of practical life, takes possession of the whole of her spiritual inheritance—what Oakeshott, following Dilthey, calls the *geistige Welt*—and thereby becomes more of a human being. It is an ideal that Oakeshott, like his contemporary F. R. Leavis, saw as increasingly threatened by modern technological and materialistic civilization, reinforced by governmental policies like the Robbins Report of 1963. Hence, the tone of his essays alternates between lyrical evocation of liberal education at its best and ferocious sarcasm directed at the transformation of schools into adjuncts of technological and commercial civilization.

It is the polemical tone that predominates in Oakeshott's earliest essay on education, "The Universities," published in the *Cambridge Journal* in 1949. The target of Oakeshott's attack is a book entitled *The Crisis in the University* by Walter Moberly. The diagnosis of the universities offered in this book is fairly typical of the time, resembling in many respects Leavis's diagnosis in "The Idea of the University."[2] Like Leavis,

Moberly argues that in our "large-scale, mechanical civilization" the universities are failing to provide the kind of moral and spiritual guidance that is necessary if we are not to succumb to the aimless drift that characterizes the technological ideal. This failure is largely owing to the fact that the current university curriculum has degenerated into a welter of specialisms and no longer provides an integrated view of the world or coherent *Weltanschauung*. Moberly's diagnosis is not eccentric, and Oakeshott succeeds in making it look ridiculous—as Moberly's later reply in the *Cambridge Journal* makes clear[3]—only by a fair amount of distortion and exaggeration. Nevertheless, the polemic has value insofar as it brilliantly exposes certain cliché ways of thinking.

The first thing that Oakeshott focuses on in Moberly's book is the relationship between the university and the world that it presupposes. For Moberly, as for Leavis, the world is in desperate straits, under the sway of materialism and technology, and the universities are called upon to provide an ethical orientation or spiritual ideal to save it from itself. For Oakeshott, this reading of our situation is "at once too alarmist and too optimistic." As he sees it, our situation "is far more desperate than Sir Walter thinks," and therefore there is no reason to be alarmed about what we cannot change: "a more profound diagnosis of our situation (such, for example, as appears in F. G. Juenger's book, *Die Perfecktion der Technik*) would offer no place for the optimism that supposes a 'revolution' can be conducted which would 'save' us." In a remarkable passage, Oakeshott discloses the pessimistic outlook that lies at the bottom of his quietistic ideal of the university as "a place apart":

> When what a man can get from the use and control of the natural world and his fellow men is the sole criterion of what he thinks he needs, there is no hope that the major part of mankind will find anything but good in this exploitation until it has been carried far enough to reveal its bitterness to the full. This . . . is not an argument for doing nothing, but it is a ground for not allowing ourselves to be comforted by the prospect, or even the possibility, of a revolution. The voyager in these waters is ill advised to weigh himself down with such heavy baggage; what he needs are things that will float with him when he is shipwrecked. (*VLL*, 109–10)

For Oakeshott, the conflict between the university and today's world under the sway of materialistic technology is "absolute" (*VLL*, 111–12), and he is critical of any attempt to bridge it. He criticizes Moberly, for example, for having anything good to say about the doctrine of "scientific humanism," a doctrine C. P. Snow would defend ten years later in his famous lecture on "The Two Cultures." For Oakeshott, the doctrine of scientific humanism "turns out to be a naïve assertion of the plausible ethics of indiscriminate productivity, a simple-hearted worship of power, an innocent bowing down before the mighty course of events. It turns out to have no criterion for helping us to know when we are not hungry" (*VLL*, 112–13). With science as a means to power and the exploitation of the earth's resources the university ought to have nothing to do.

Oakeshott's most trenchant criticisms of Moberly come in connection with the issue of the integration of the curriculum. To prevent the degeneration of the curriculum into a miscellaneous assortment of specialisms, Moberly suggests that the university must provide "a synoptic, integrated view of the moral and intellectual world," a "unified conception of life," a *Weltanschauung*, a synthetic doctrine that does for our age what St Thomas's *Summa* did for his (*VLL*, 121–22). Oakeshott finds nothing in all this but nonsense. In the first place, no such integration of the world of knowledge is currently available to us. Second, no such integration is necessary for the university to exercise its function. There is a way in which the various specialisms can come together in a meaningful way in the university without being integrated from above by some sort of *Weltanschauung*.

It is at this point that Oakeshott introduces (for the first time) the notion of "conversation" (*VLL*, 126, 134). He elaborates on the idea in a talk he gave for the BBC one year after the publication of "The Universities." Though "the world of learning may have the appearance of a fragmentary enterprise," he comments in "The Idea of a University," it need not call upon "a sticky mess called 'culture'" to fill in the interstices between the various branches of knowledge:

> The world of learning needs no extraneous cement to hold it together; its parts move in a single magnetic field, and the need for go-betweens arises only when the current is gratuitously cut off. The pursuit of learning is not a race in which the competitors jockey for the best place, it is not even an argument or a symposium; it is a conversation. And the peculiar virtue of a university (as a place of many studies) is to exhibit it in this character, each study appearing as a voice whose tone is neither tyrannous nor plangent, but humble and conversable. A conversation does not need a chairman, it has no predetermined course, we do not ask what it is "for," and we do not judge its excellence by its conclusion; it has no conclusion, but is

always put by for another day. Its integration is not superimposed but springs from the quality of the voices which speak, and its value lies in the relics it leaves behind in the minds of those who participate. (*VLL*, 98)

There is one point in "The Universities" where Oakeshott leaves polemic behind and evokes, in one of the most beautiful passages ever written about liberal education, what he calls the "great and character-istic gift of the university . . . the gift of an interval":

Here was an opportunity to put aside the hot allegiances of youth without the necessity of acquiring new loyalties to take their place. Here was an interval in which a man might refuse to commit himself. Here was a break in the tyrannical course of irreparable human events; a period in which to look round upon the world without the sense of an enemy at one's back or the insistent pressure to make up one's mind; a moment in which one was relieved of the necessity of "coming to terms with oneself" or of entering the fiercely trivial par-tisan struggles of the world outside; a moment in which to taste the mystery without the necessity of at once seeking a solution. . . . One might, if one were so inclined, reduce this to a doctrine about the character of a university; one might call it the doctrine of the interim. But the doctrine would be no more than a brief expression of what it felt like to be an undergraduate on that first October morning. Almost overnight, a world of ungracious fact had melted into infinite possibility; we, who belonged to no "leisured class," had been freed for a moment from the curse of Adam, the burdensome distinction between work and play. What opened before us was not a road but a boundless sea; and it was enough to stretch one's sails to the wind. (*VLL*, 127–28)

From this lyrical height Oakeshott once again descends to polemic, tracing what he considers to be the real crisis in the universities to an influx of students unprepared to take advantage of the opportunity to "stretch one's sails to the wind" offered by a university. One of the least attractive features of Oakeshott's philosophy of education is its refusal to consider the claims of equity or what he scornfully refers to as "social justice." He dismisses Moberly's suggestion that, in the past, universi-ties like Oxford and Cambridge have been bound up with "privilege" and a "leisured class"—hence the reference in the passage quoted above to "we, who belonged to no 'leisured class.'" And his characterization of the new class of students entering universities in the postwar years is a grossly distorted caricature: "The leaders of the rising class are consumed with a contempt for everything which does not spring from their own desires, they are convinced in advance that they have nothing to learn and everything to teach, and consequently their aim is loot—to appropriate to themselves the organization, the shell of the institution, and convert it to their own purposes" (*VLL*, 120, 130).

More than a decade passed before Oakeshott returned to the subject of university education in the 1961 essay "The Study of 'Politics' in a University." In this essay, along with the essay "Learning and Teaching" (originally delivered as a lecture in 1965), Oakeshott provides a more positive account of his conception of education. Both essays begin with a characterization of education in general as an initiation into an inheritance composed of emotions, beliefs, images, ideas, languages, skills, and practices—"what Dilthey called a *geistige Welt*." This inheritance is a historic achievement and therefore contingent, miscellaneous, and not perfectly coherent. Education is learning to see oneself in the mirror of this historic and contingent inheritance. This is not an affront to human autonomy or self-realization; indeed, seeing oneself in the mirror of a historic inheritance is the only way human beings can genuinely realize or make the most of themselves (*RP*, 187–88; *VLL*, 45–50).

From this characterization of education in general, Oakeshott goes on to consider the specific education appropriate to a university. He does so by contrasting university education to school education and vocational education. In the latter two types of education, the knowledge to be acquired has the character of something already achieved, fixed and finished, inert, and authoritative. It consists of the sort of information that can be found in encyclopedias, textbooks, training manuals, and now the internet. In university education, on the other hand, the knowledge to be acquired appears as something to be explored and investigated, not merely accepted. Oakeshott employs the distinction between a "language" (or manner of thinking) and a "literature" (what has been said from time to time in a "language") to bring out the contrast he has in mind. Both in school and in vocational education, it is mainly a literature that is being studied; students are required to master a body of information, not to understand the manner of thinking that generated it. In university education, on the other hand, it is the language or manner of thinking of the historian or the scientist, not simply the results of their activity, that occupies the attention of the student.

In "Learning and Teaching," Oakeshott uses a slightly different distinction—between "information" and "judgment"—to bring out the distinctive character of university education, or at least of the education that imparts what he considers to be the most important aspect of our inheritance. Information refers to the "explicit ingredient of knowledge," consisting of the authoritative and relatively inert facts and rules found in dictionaries, encyclopedias, manuals, and textbooks. Judgment refers to the "tacit or implicit component of knowledge" that, like connoisseurship, cannot be specified in propositions. It is the "knowing how" that necessarily accompanies the "knowing what" of information in any concrete skill or ability. Though he acknowledges that there is an element of judgment and connoisseurship in every concrete activity, Oakeshott claims that this element is "immeasurably greater" in the activities that form the basis of a university education: art, literature, science, history, and philosophy. It is in these activities especially that we become acutely aware of considerations of style as well as of the intellectual virtues of patience, accuracy, economy, and elegance (*VLL*, 50–62).

When Oakeshott turns his attention to the study of politics in a university, the reader is not unprepared for the conclusions that follow from his analysis. The study of politics in a university should concern itself with "languages" and not "literatures," and it should be an education that focuses more on "judgment" than on "information." The explanatory languages that Oakeshott finds most relevant to the study of politics in the university are those of history and philosophy, the quest for a science of politics having failed to yield anything remotely resembling a scientific mode of thinking. Unfortunately, this is not the direction that the study of politics has taken in universities. From the moment politics was introduced into the university curriculum, it was taught in a manner appropriate to a vocational education. Information was imparted that "could have no conceivable interest to anyone except those whose heads were full of the enterprise of participating in political activity or to persons with the insatiable curiosity of a concierge." To this were added works of political philosophy that were read in a manner that Oakeshott describes as "a mixture between the manner in which one might read an out-of-date textbook on naval architecture and the manner in which one might study a current election manifesto." Though this has long been recognized as inadequate, Oakeshott claims that the study of politics in universities has never shaken its original vocational and practical orientation (*RP*, 207–18).

Oakeshott's last writings on education, "Education: The Engagement and Its Frustration" (1972) and "A Place of Learning" (1974), reiterate many of the themes from his earlier writings. Once again, education is understood as an initiation into a historic inheritance or *geistige Welt*, though now Oakeshott uses the language of *On Human Conduct* to describe this transaction. Education, he tells us, is the "distinguishing mark of a human being." The freedom that is inherent in being human consists in the fact that "human beings are what they understand themselves to be," and this implies that they are what they learn to become. A human being "has a history but no 'nature'" (*VLL*, 17–23, 63–65). Because this is so, human self-understanding is inseparable from appropriating and learning to participate in a historic inheritance or "culture." In the context of liberal education, this culture consists of a variety of languages by which we understand the world and ourselves: the languages, for example, of natural science, history, philosophy, and poetic imagination. The relationship between these languages is not argumentative or hierarchical but conversational. We may think of the components of a culture, Oakeshott writes,

> as voices, each the expression of a distinct and conditional understanding of the world and a distinct idiom of human self-understanding, and of the culture itself as these voices joined, as such voices could only be joined, in a conversation—an endless unrehearsed intellectual adventure in which, in imagination, we enter a variety of modes of understanding the world and ourselves and are not disconcerted by the differences or dismayed by the inconclusiveness of it all. And perhaps we may recognize liberal learning as, above all else, an education in imagination, an initiation into the art of this conversation in which we learn to recognize the voices; to distinguish their different modes of utterance, to acquire the intellectual and moral habits appropriate to this conversational relationship and thus to make our *début dans la vie humaine*. (*VLL*, 28–29, 37–39)

This is a beautiful passage, and these late essays on education, especially "A Place of Learning," are full of them. But as in the earlier essays, there is also a note of bitterness in these essays that occasionally explodes into derisive scorn. Oakeshott ridicules the Deweyan child-centered approach to education, which seeks to replace "school" as a place where children learn under "conditions of direction and restraint designed to provoke habits of attention, concentration, exactness, courage, patience, and discrimination" with "an arena of childish self-indulgence" where learning is reduced to "experimental activity," personal "discovery," and "group discussions" (*VLL*, 71–73). But by far his greatest contempt is reserved for the project of substituting "socialization" for education. Here education is understood, not as an initiation into a historic cultural inheritance, but as integration into current society, an apprenticeship to commercial and industrial life. Oakeshott sees the 1963 Robbins Report on higher education, which greatly expanded the universities in Britain and created the polytechnics, as a particularly egregious example of this project of substituting socialization for education. And he sounds a rare apocalyptic note when assessing the corruption of the educational engagement that this project has brought about: "The design to substitute 'socialization' for education has gone far enough to be recognized as the most momentous occurrence of this century, the greatest of the adversities to have overtaken our culture, the beginning of a dark age devoted to barbaric affluence" (*VLL*, 31–32, 78–93).

In his excoriation of the project of transforming education into an adjunct of modern technological society, Oakeshott resembles no one more than his famously vituperative contemporary, F. R. Leavis. One can imagine that Oakeshott must have delighted in Leavis's wonderful skewering of C. P. Snow's 1959 Rede Lecture on "The Two Cultures," with its philistine and thoroughly unselfconscious endorsement of the ideal of technological progress and economic productivity.[4] Oakeshott actually refers in one place to "the silly doctrine of the 'two cultures'"; and, like Leavis, he is quite suspicious of the role played by science in the university curriculum, not because it doesn't represent a legitimate mode of intellectual inquiry, but because it tends to be pursued in a purely utilitarian and vocational fashion and often represents itself as "the model of all valid human understanding" (*VLL*, 32–33, 88–89). Interestingly, the Robbins Report referred approvingly to Snow's diagnosis of the two cultures.[5]

Oakeshott does not follow Leavis, however, in seeing the university as the solution to our problems, providing direction in the face of cultural "drift" and "disintegration" and serving as a coordinating and unifying "centre of consciousness."[6] As we have seen, Oakeshott does not think the world can necessarily be saved from the pervasive sway of technology and the materialistic exploitation of the earth's resources; he certainly does not saddle the university with the role of savior. Instead, he sees the university at its best as "a place apart" where one can find respite from the "*danse macabre* of wants and satisfactions" that currently dominates the world (*VLL*, 93).

Here Oakeshott's difference with current conservative theories of education also becomes clear. (It is unnecessary to point out that his conception of liberal education has nothing in common with the highly politicized conception of knowledge and education of the multicultural left.) The alarmist reflections of Leo Strauss's disciple Allan Bloom in *The Closing of the American Mind: How Higher Education has Failed*

Democracy and Impoverished the Souls of Today's Students (the title says it all) would no doubt strike Oakeshott as another, and slightly more hysterical version of the crisis mentality he criticized in Moberly. The name Bloom gives to our crisis is "relativism," and he looks to the universities to provide "a unified conception of life" to save democracy and the souls of students. From this point of view, Oakeshott's notion of conversation appears unduly frivolous, a kind of fiddling while Rome burns. Nor would Oakeshott's educational philosophy seem to have much in common with the projects of moral and cultural literacy associated with William Bennett and E. D. Hirsch. Here the *geistige Welt* appears as an itemized list of inert cultural facts or moral lessons with every vestige of what Oakeshott calls "judgement" completely squeezed out.

As attractive as Oakeshott's philosophy of education is, it is not without its difficulties. The most glaring of these is its failure to balance its obvious concern with intellectual excellence with any sort of consideration of equity or of other purposes education might serve in a democratic society. This failure is evidenced in Oakeshott's unflattering portrait of the "rising class" as concerned only with "looting" the universities, as well as in his opposition to the expansion of educational opportunities aimed at in the Robbins Report. It is with some justice that Noel Annan comments that in Oakeshott's educational writings "there is a relentless refusal to acknowledge the facts of life."[7]

Though in many places Oakeshott displays an insensitivity to the complexity of the social problem in modern education, there is one place where he captures with deadly and depressing accuracy the circumstances in our contemporary world that make it exceedingly difficult for the young to respond to the invitation of liberal education. The passage, which comes at the end of "A Place of Learning," is worth quoting at length and marks a fitting conclusion to our discussion of Oakeshott's philosophy of education:

> The world in which many children now grow up is crowded, not necessarily with occupants and not at all with memorable experiences, but with happenings; it is a ceaseless flow of seductive trivialities which invoke neither reflection nor choice but instant participation. A child quickly becomes aware that he cannot too soon plunge into this flow or immerse himself in it too quickly; to pause is to be swept with the chilling fear of never having lived at all. There is little chance that his perceptions, his emotions, his admirations and his ready indignations might become learned responses or be even innocent

fancies of his own; they come to him prefabricated, generalized and uniform. He lurches from one modish conformity to the next . . . seeking to lose himself in a solidarity composed of exact replicas of himself. From an early age children believe themselves to be well-informed about the world, but they know it only at second-hand in the pictures and voices that surround them. It holds no puzzles or mysteries for them; it invites neither careful attention nor under-standing. . . . This world has but one language, soon learned: the language of appetite. . . . It is a language composed of meaningless clichés. It allows only the expression of "points of view" and the cease-less repetition of slogans which are embraced as prophetic utterances. Their ears are filled with the babel of invitations to instant and unspecified reactions and their utterance reproduces only what they have heard said. Such discourse as there is resembles the barking of a dog at the echo of its own yelp. (*VLL,* 41)

The Voice of Poetry

Although the image of conversation makes its first appearance in Oakeshott's writings on education, it receives its most memorable expression in the essay "The Voice of Poetry in the Conversation of Mankind" (originally published in 1959). Here Oakeshott brings out clearly the implications of this image for his theory of knowledge in general.

In *Experience and Its Modes,* the various forms of experience—history, science, and practice—were understood to be abstractions from the con-crete whole of experience. Though Oakeshott resisted the Hegelian temptation to determine the exact degree of abstraction in each of the modes and thus arrange them in a logical hierarchy, he nevertheless measured the modes against the concrete whole of experience pursued by philosophy and found them to be self-contradictory and incoherent. From the concrete standpoint of philosophy, the modes merely dis-tracted from the pursuit of an absolutely coherent world of experience and therefore needed to be avoided or rejected.

In "The Voice of Poetry," the monism of *Experience and Its Modes* is abandoned and replaced by the pluralism implied in the image of con-versation. "In a conversation," Oakeshott writes, "the participants are not engaged in an inquiry or a debate; there is no 'truth' to be discov-ered, no proposition to be proved, no conclusion sought. . . . [T]he con-versation itself does not compose an argument" (*RP,* 489). In the language of *Experience and Its Modes,* there is no absolutely coherent world of experience to be achieved, against which the various modes can be judged deficient. Indeed, the modes can no longer be understood (as Spinoza understood them) as modifications of or abstractions from the concrete whole of experience: "in this conversation there is . . . no voice without an idiom of its own: the voices are not divergencies from some ideal, non-idiomatic manner of speaking, they diverge only from one another" (*RP*, 497).

All of this implies a very different conception of philosophy from the one defended in *Experience and Its Modes*. Philosophy can no longer be understood as "experience without presupposition, reservation, arrest or modification" (*EM*, 2). Indeed, Oakeshott now writes: "I do not myself know where to place an experience released altogether from modality or a world of 'objects' which is not a world of images and is governed by no considerabilities" (*RP*, 512). Nor can philosophy be charged with examining the various modes of experience to determine whether they fulfill the criterion of coherence and rejecting them if they don't. In the pluralistic conversation envisaged in "The Voice of Poetry," "there is no symposiarch or arbiter; not even a doorkeeper to examine credentials. Every entrant is taken at its face-value and everything is permitted which can get itself accepted into the flow of speculation. And voices which speak in conversation do not compose a hierarchy" (*RP*, 490). Though deprived of its critical authority vis-à-vis the modes of experience, philosophy nevertheless retains a special, "parasitic" status in the conversation: it reflects on the "quality and style of each voice" and on the "relationship of one voice to another," but "it makes no specific contribution" to the conversation (*RP*, 491).

From this preliminary discussion of the "meeting-place" of human activities in terms of the image of conversation, Oakeshott moves on to the central concern of his essay, namely, poetry, under which name he comprehends all the various arts: painting, sculpture, music, dance, literature, and so forth. What makes the consideration of poetry particularly urgent in our current circumstances, he argues, is that the conversation of mankind has become "boring" owing to the domination of the voices of science and practice, the latter in the form of politics. In the Preface to *Rationalism in Politics*, he suggests another reason for his consideration of poetry: it is "a belated retraction of a foolish sentence in *Experience and Its Modes*." I will take this latter remark as a point of departure for my discussion.

The foolish sentence Oakeshott refers to is this: "For in [art, music and poetry], in the end, we are wholly taken up with practical life" (*EM*, 297). He does not amplify on this sentence but merely drops a footnote in which he quotes a passage from Rilke's early collection of stories *Die Letzten* (The Last Ones):

> Art is childhood. Art means not to know that the world already exists, and to make a world: not destroying what is found already existing, but simply not finding anything to hand. Nothing but possibilities and wishes. And then, suddenly, fulfillment, summer, the sun. Involuntarily, without making any words about it. Never completing, never having the Seventh Day. Never seeing that all is good. Dissatisfaction is itself youth.[8]

It is no doubt the references to incompletion and dissatisfaction in this passage that lead Oakeshott to quote it in support of his view that art belongs to practical experience. According to the argument of *Experience and Its Modes*, practical experience can never definitively reconcile the discrepancy between "what is" and "what ought to be"; "permanent dissatisfaction . . . is inherent in practical experience" (*EM*, 303–4).

So much can be gathered from Oakeshott's not so much foolish as cryptic sentence on art in *Experience and Its Modes*. There are clues in some of his other early writings, however, that suggest why he initially identified art with practical experience. In these writings, we often find Oakeshott speaking of practical life at its best or most intense in poetic terms. This is what he takes from Pater, who saw art as *the* activity that confers "the highest quality" on our moments and "simply for those moments' sake."[9] In the essay "Religion and the World," for example, it is sometimes difficult to tell whether Oakeshott is speaking of poetry or religion when he identifies the latter with "living sensibility," "present insight," "a more daring and sensitive way of living," a life that carries "in each of its moments its whole meaning and value." It is significant that almost all the evidence for this religious sensibility comes from poetry—Wordsworth, Goethe, Pater, and, in the final lines of the essay, Shelley's elegy for Keats. It is a highly poeticized conception of religion that Oakeshott presents in this essay—and, as we shall see, in *On Human Conduct*. And it is perhaps because he sees such a close connection between poetry and religion that he was initially led to assign the former, like the latter, to practical experience.[10] In *Experience and Its Modes*, he comments that the "most thoroughly and positively practical life is that of the artist or the mystic" (*EM*, 297).

It is important to point out that, by identifying poetry with practical life, Oakeshott does not mean to suggest that poetry should somehow be practical, imparting moral lessons or inciting political action. Rilke would not be the poet to quote if this were the case. It is not that

Oakeshott wants to assimilate poetry to the utilitarian calculus of practical life, but precisely the opposite: he sees poetry as elevating practical life above the utilitarian domain of means and ends and "external achievement." Here again Pater provides the clue. Pater could at one and the same time hold the doctrine of art for art's sake and still ascribe to art the highest practical—even moral—function. As he put it in his essay on Wordsworth: "To treat life in the spirit of art, is to make life a thing in which means and ends are identified: to encourage such treatment, the true moral significance of art and poetry."[11] The art of life is to treat one's life as a work of art.

By the late 1930s, perhaps under the influence of Collingwood—whose *Principles of Art* he enthusiastically reviewed in 1938—Oakeshott seems to have moved away from this Paterian understanding of the relation between art and life. In "The Claims of Politics" (1939), he argues that, while poetry can make no direct contribution to politics or the life of society—as the politically engaged poetry of the 1930s tried to do—it nevertheless makes an indirect contribution by recreating the values of society: "the genius of the poet and the artist and to a lesser extent of the philosopher is to create and recreate the values of their society. In them a society becomes conscious and critical of itself, of its whole self." By equipping society with self-knowledge and thus recreating its values, the artist and the poet protect society from the most damaging of corruptions that can visit it, the "corruption of its consciousness" (*RPML*, 95). Commentators have argued whether Oakeshott's position on art in "The Claims of Politics" marks a retreat from or a continuation of his identification of art with practical life in *Experience and Its Modes*, but this misses the real nature of the shift from the earlier to the later position. It is not that art has become any more or less practical in "The Claims of Politics" but that it has acquired a more social function. In contrast with his earlier, Paterian individualism, Oakeshott now views art in Hegelian fashion as the self-consciousness of the social whole.

As noted in chapter 3, Oakeshott takes the concept of the "corruption of consciousness" from Collingwood's *Principles of Art*. Because this work defends the expressive theory of art that Oakeshott will later explicitly reject in "The Voice of Poetry," it is worth examining its basic argument. According to Collingwood, art is not mere representation (which would reduce it to a "craft" or technical skill); nor is it in the service of practice (art as "magic"); nor does it exist merely to be enjoyed or give delight (art as "amusement"). Art is the expression of emotion. This formula must be understood properly, however. Collingwood does not mean to suggest that a work of art is a mere means to the expression of preconceived emotions: "the artist has no idea what the experience is which demands expression until he has expressed it. What he wants to say . . . becomes clear to him only as the poem takes shape in his mind, or the clay in his fingers."[12] Nor are the emotions the artist expresses merely his own; they are also those of his audience and ultimately of his community. By expressing the emotions of his community, which exist prior to expression in only a confused and obscure state, the artist makes his community conscious of itself and protects it against the "corruption of consciousness" that consists in disowning or failing to grasp one's own emotions. This is what a poet like Eliot does in *The Waste Land*. The artist

> tells his audience, at risk of their displeasure, the secrets of their own hearts. His business as an artist is to speak out, to make a clean breast. . . . As spokesman of his community, the secrets he must utter are theirs. The reason why they need him is that no community altogether knows its own heart; and by failing in this knowledge a community deceives itself on the one subject concerning which ignorance means death. . . . Art is the community's medicine for the worst disease of mind, the corruption of consciousness.[13]

With this background, we may now return to the argument of "The Voice of Poetry." As already mentioned, one of the motivating reasons for Oakeshott's philosophical consideration of poetry is that the conversation of our civilization has come to be dominated by the voices of science and practice. Therefore, in order to locate the specific place that poetry occupies on the map of human activity, he first says something about the places occupied by practical and scientific activity. What he has to say about these two activities largely echoes what he said about them in *Experience and Its Modes*, though instead of speaking of modes of thinking he now speaks of modes of imagining, and instead of worlds of ideas he speaks of worlds of images. In practical activity we move around in a world composed of images of desire and aversion as well as of approval and disapproval. Practical activity is the world *sub specie voluntatis* and *sub specie moris*. The images that compose the world of science, on the other hand, are independent of our hope and desires; they are characterized by universality, communicability, and impersonality. The world of science consists exclusively of images that are measurements; it is the world *sub specie quantitatis* (*RP*, 495–508).

In contrast to both science and practice, Oakeshott defines poetry as the activity of "contemplating" or "delighting." Pater, who also defined art as contemplation, gives a concise description of what Oakeshott has in mind when he uses these terms: "a type of beholding for the mere joy of beholding."[14] Beyond that, Oakeshott maintains that poetic images, unlike those found in science or practice, are "mere images," images that do not invoke the distinction between fact and not-fact or truth and falsity. (It is worth observing that the monistic scheme of *Experience and Its Modes* had no room for such a world of "mere" images or ideas, a world unreferred to reality.) Nor do poetic images provoke either moral approval or disapproval; they only provoke intransitive delight. The poet does not seek to convey some deep moral or spiritual truth about the human condition: he "arranges his images like a girl bunching flowers, considering only how they will appear together" (*RP*, 509–17).

Oakeshott's view of poetry as the contemplation of images for the sheer joy of contemplating them sets itself against two common beliefs that hold venerable positions in the history of aesthetics: first, the belief that poetry has beneficial practical or moral effects; and second, the belief that poetry is somehow connected with truth. In rejecting the first belief, Oakeshott of course finds himself in good company: from Kant, who claimed that aesthetic pleasure is purely "disinterested" and unconnected with practical usefulness, to Oscar Wilde, who declared that "all art is quite useless." Closer to home, Edward Bullough, a fellow Caius man for whom Oakeshott wrote a lengthy obituary, defended a version of the doctrine of art for art's sake, finding the distinctive principle of aesthetic experience in the "psychical distance" from objects that enables disinterested contemplation.[15] In an example that Oakeshott would have liked, Bullough illustrates his concept of psychical distance by contrasting the practical attitude toward a fog at sea with the aesthetic attitude. Whereas the former sees only danger in the fog and is filled with anxiety, the latter relishes the milky opacity of the fog, the creamy smoothness of the water, and "the strange solitude and remoteness from the world."[16]

Oakeshott undoubtedly makes a valid point when he denies that art is practical or useful or moral in any sort of direct sense, but he sometimes carries this point to absurd (or at least not obvious) conclusions. For example, he denies that we can legitimately subject the conduct and character of Anna Karenina, Lord Jim, Iago, or the Duchess Sanseverina to moral approval or disapproval (*RP*, 520). This may be true in some literal sense—these are, after all, fictional characters—but surely we can consider these characters in terms of their moral qualities, which may provoke approval or disapproval, admiration, contempt, or pity.[17] There are many authors who deny that poetry can have any direct moral or practical effect—for example, Schiller, Wordsworth, Keats, Shelley,

Arnold, Pater, and even Bullough—who nevertheless affirm that poetry can refine our sentiments, enlarge our sympathies, and quicken our sensibilities. Collingwood, too, rejected the notion of art as propaganda or in the service of practice—what he called "magical" art—but he still maintained that art plays a crucial role in protecting society against the "corruption of consciousness." Interestingly, Oakeshott explicitly denies that art can fulfill this latter practical function, thus repudiating the view that he took in "The Claims of Politics" (*RP*, 533).

With respect to the contention that poetry conveys truth, or (as Keats's Grecian urn put it) that beauty is truth, Oakeshott proceeds once again by construing it in an implausibly literal manner. He denies that poets are engaged in describing actual cows, cornfields, midinettes, May mornings, graveyards, or Grecian urns. This is not news. And he wonders how the concept of truth applies to images such as Yeats's "O sea-starved hungry sea," a nonsense verse from the sixteenth century, or Anna Karenina (*RP*, 522). Admittedly, it is difficult to apply the concept of truth to an isolated line of verse or to a poem that strives to make nonsense, but this is not necessarily the case with Oakeshott's third example, that of Anna Karenina. Does not the power of this character lie in her emotional truth, the fact that she reflects real emotions or a real tension between emotions?

Oakeshott recognizes that there are less improbable versions of the view that poetry is connected with truth. Perhaps the most important of these is the view that poetry is an expression of emotional experience. Unfortunately, Oakeshott considers this view in its most improbable form. He denies that a poem like "Dejection: An Ode" is an attempt to excite dejection in the reader, and he denies that such a poem can be understood as the mere expression "of an already clear mental image": "A poet does not do *three* things: first experience or observe or recollect an emotion, then contemplate it, and finally seek a means of expressing the results of his contemplation; he does *one* thing only, he imagines poetically" (*RP*, 525). But this has nothing to do with the theory of art as expression that, say, Collingwood expounds. For Collingwood, the arousing of emotion belongs to art misunderstood as magic or amusement. And, as we have seen, he rejects the notion of art as a mere means to the expression of preconceived emotions. For Collingwood, too, a poet does not do three things but only one: express or put into language the inchoate emotions that belong to our individual and collective existence.

Oakeshott claims that if there is any poem that should fit the expressive theory it is Keats's *Ode to Melancholy*, and yet it doesn't. Once again he reduces the expressive theory to a caricature. He argues that the "poem could have been composed by a man of sanguine temperament who never himself felt the touch of melancholy" (*RP*, 526). But this commits the error of what Collingwood calls "aesthetic individualism," suggesting that the emotions the artist expresses are merely his own and not those of his audience and community. Nor is it clear that someone who had never experienced the intense longing to escape into ideal beauty and the ultimate futility of that longing—the experience at the heart of *Ode to Melancholy*—could write this poem. Oakeshott also argues that the poem is not designed to arouse melancholy in the reader, but this, as we have seen, is not a necessary element in the expressive theory. Finally, he argues that the poem is not about the emotion symbolized in the word "melancholy," which is true but says nothing about whether the poem is not about a complex emotion for which the word "melancholy" stands as an abstract and inadequate symbol. None of this is to say that the expressive theory of art is necessarily the correct theory, only that Oakeshott has not refuted it in its most plausible form.

Recognizing that his highly formalist understanding of poetry threatens to isolate it in the conversation of mankind, Oakeshott suggests that there are intimations of contemplative imagining in practical life that make possible a "common understanding" between them. In love and friendship, for example, we seem to leave behind the imperatives of utility and moral approval and disapproval that characterize practical life: "Friends and lovers are not concerned with what can be made out of each other, but only with the enjoyment of one another. . . . The relationship of friends is dramatic, not utilitarian." In the experience of Kantian "moral goodness," too, we seem to find "a release from the deadliness of doing and a possibility of perfection, which intimates poetry" (*RP*, 536–38). By building a bridge from practical life to poetry in this way, Oakeshott also seems to allow for the possibility that poetry may exercise a subtle effect on practical life: "Having an ear ready for the voice of poetry is to be disposed to choose delight rather than pleasure or virtue or knowledge, a disposition which will reflect itself in practical life in an affection for its intimations of poetry" (*RP*, 540). Here a shadow of the sentiment expressed in the "foolish sentence" from *Experience and Its Modes* survives in Oakeshott's "belated retraction."

Would that Oakeshott had followed up the suggestions contained in his acknowledgment of the converse between poetry and practice. As it is, "The Voice of Poetry" articulates an aesthetic formalism that too severely circumscribes the practical and intellectual significance of art. While the essay serves as a salutary corrective to simplistic theories of art that value it only for its edifying character or its social and political utility, it nevertheless fails to do justice to the complex relationship that subsists between poetry and truth and poetry and practice. In many ways, the earlier "Claims of Politics" represented a more promising approach to the nature of art. There, without making it the mere adjunct of politics, Oakeshott showed how art could not only promote formal "delight" but also contribute to society by mitigating its ignorance of itself. As one of the purest worshippers of poetic beauty once wrote:

> Sure not all
> Those melodies sung into the world's ear
> Are useless; sure a poet is a sage;
> A humanist, physician to all men.[18]

The Voice of History

The other voice in the conversation of mankind that Oakeshott, throughout his career, was concerned to rescue from the monological tendencies of science and practice was the voice of history. In 1958, a year before he published "The Voice of Poetry," he published an essay entitled "The Activity of Being an Historian," in which he revisited the form of knowledge he had treated so illuminatingly and boldly in *Experience and Its Modes*. Though the analysis of history in this essay follows closely the earlier analysis in *Experience and Its Modes*, there is one important difference. In keeping with the nonhierarchical conception of the relationship between philosophy and the other forms of experience articulated in "The Voice of Poetry," history is here investigated as a "coherent manner of thinking about the world" (*RP*, 152) and not judged as an abstract or defective mode of experience from the standpoint of a notional concrete whole. Oakeshott continues to speak of history as a "mode" of experience, but his conception of modality has changed from the absolute idealist conception defended in *Experience and Its Modes*. No longer is modality understood in terms of abstraction from or modification of the concrete whole but, rather (as he puts it most perspicuously in *On History*), as "the conditions of relevance that constitute [an enquiry as] a distinct kind of enquiry and distinguish it both from an inconsequential groping around in the confusion of all that may be going on and from similarly distinct enquiries of other kinds" (*OH*, 2).

In addition to this change, there had also been an explosion of interest in the philosophy of history in Britain in the 25 years that separated "The Activity of Being an Historian" from *Experience and Its Modes*. An important landmark in this explosion of interest was the posthumous publication of Collingwood's *The Idea of History* in 1946. Collingwood's ill-health and untimely death in 1943 prevented him from completing the book on the problem of historical knowledge that he had long intended to write. Nevertheless, the fragments of which *The Idea of History* is composed give a fairly clear idea of the central tenets of Collingwood's theory of history: first, that history is sharply distinguished from natural science in being concerned with the "inside" or "thought-side" of events ("all history is the history of thought"); and second, following from this, that history "is the re-enactment of past thought in the historian's own mind."[19]

Oakeshott wrote a generous review of *The Idea of History*, commenting that, "unfinished and scrappy as it is, it is enough to show that if [Collingwood] had been unhindered by ill-health and early death he could have done for historical knowledge something like what Kant did for natural science." He also praised Collingwood as an imaginative historian of ideas who grasped that the task of the historian of ideas is "to understand a writer more profoundly than the writer understood himself, just as the task of the historian of feudal society (for example) is to understand that society more profoundly than anyone who merely enjoyed it could understand it."[20] This was a strange thing to say of a thinker whose central historiographical doctrine was that history consisted in the *reenactment* of the thought of past individuals in the historian's own mind. Indeed, in later writings, Oakeshott explicitly attacks Collingwood's doctrine of historical reenactment for precisely failing to appreciate that the task of the historian is to understand "men and events more profoundly than they were understood when they lived and happened."[21]

It is interesting to contrast Oakeshott's criticism of Collingwood here with the one made by Leo Strauss in his essay "On Collingwood's Philosophy of History." Strauss focuses on Collingwood's contention that in reenacting the thought of the past the historian must also criticize it from the standpoint of the present. Such a procedure, he argues, prevents the historian from carrying out her true task, namely, understanding an author exactly as he understood himself.[22] Despite his sharp difference with Oakeshott on the nature of the task of the historian, Strauss makes a point against Collingwood that Oakeshott would undoubtedly have agreed with. He relentlessly exposes the Whiggish elements in Collingwood's philosophy of history, pointing to those passages in *The Idea of History* where Collingwood suggests that scientific history views the past from the standpoint of the historian's present, showing how that present has come into existence.[23] In these passages, Collingwood is guilty of reading the past backwards in a way that Oakeshott condemns as emblematic of a practical, rather than a historical, past.

Whatever their specific differences, in the postwar debate in Britain over the nature of history, Oakeshott and Collingwood were generally lumped together as idealist philosophers who rejected positivism and sought to establish the autonomy of historical knowledge vis-à-vis natural science. Their attack on positivism, however, did not go unanswered. Philosophers like Karl Popper tried to formulate a theory of scientific and causal explanation that would apply to both history and natural science.[24] The *locus classicus* of this attempt to understand history in terms of the categories of scientific explanation was Carl Hempel's 1942 article "The Function of General Laws in History." There Hempel argued that historical explanations invoke, either implicitly or rudimentarily, general laws that link events in a causal fashion.[25] This came to be called the "covering law model" of historical explanation, and it was hotly debated among philosophers in the 1940s and 1950s. Philosophers like Morton White, Maurice Mandelbaum, and Patrick Gardiner tried to refine the model, and philosophers like William Dray, Alan Donagan, W. B. Gallie, and Arthur Danto rejected it, often exploring narrative as an alternative form of explanation.[26]

One of the more notable attempts to refute the positivistic conception of history was made by Isaiah Berlin in "Historical Inevitability"—the essay Berlin originally delivered as a lecture at the London School of Economics in 1953 and for which Oakeshott gave his famously ironic introduction. In this essay, Berlin argued against the "notion that one can discover large patterns or regularities in the procession of historical events"; the idea that history is determined, not by individuals, but by "vast impersonal forces," either teleological or causal. The names Berlin associated with this deterministic notion of history ranged from Bossuet, Schelling, and Hegel to Condorcet, Comte, Marx, Spengler, and Toynbee.[27]

In arguing against such metaphysical and positivistic philosophies of history, Berlin was certainly in agreement with Oakeshott, but his reasons for rejecting them were quite different from Oakeshott's. Whereas Oakeshott stressed the distinction between the historical and the practical pasts, Berlin argued that historical determinism was problematic precisely because it was inconsistent with the way we ordinarily speak and think about moral and practical action. Historical explanations are compelling only insofar as they accord with our practical experience and our ordinary concepts of moral responsibility, what Berlin calls our "sense of reality." For this reason, he rejected Herbert Butterfield's (and Oakeshott's) contention that historians should refrain from passing moral judgments on historical actors and actions, agreeing instead with Strauss that value judgments are intrinsic to the writing of history: "Purely descriptive, wholly depersonalized history remains what it has always been, a figment of abstract theory, a violently exaggerated reaction to the cant and vanity of earlier generations."[28]

One of the principal targets of "Historical Inevitability" was the controversial historian of the Russian Revolution E. H. Carr, with whom Berlin had a running debate over historical determinism throughout the 1950s and who happened to be in the audience when Berlin delivered his lecture at the LSE.[29] Carr responded to Berlin's attack in his enormously popular—and incredibly muddled—lectures, delivered in 1961, entitled *What Is History?* The lectures began with the uncontroversial observation—backed up with references to Collingwood and Oakeshott—that an "element of interpretation enters into every fact of history." Carr went on to develop this uncontroversial observation, however, in a highly controversial and relativistic direction, advising readers of history to "study the historian before you begin to study the facts," and "before you study the historian, study his historical and social environment." On the issue that divided him from Berlin, Carr affirmed that history involves the study of causes—though Berlin had never really denied this. What was truly controversial was the criterion of historical significance he adduced for the historian's choice of which causes to emphasize in her account: relevance to the future. History is "inevitably a success story." The historian is ultimately interested in who or what ultimately wins out in history and constructs her account to highlight the events that caused or contributed to this successful outcome.[30] Berlin, in his review of Carr's book, referred to this as the "big battalion" view of history.[31]

Oakeshott did not review *What Is History?*, but in 1951 he had reviewed the first volume of Carr's monumental *History of Soviet Russia*, the preface of which already contained hints of what Oakeshott called "Mr. Carr's very curious notions of how to write history." He focused on two aspects of Carr's historiographical approach. First, Carr's "unfortunate" tendency to write history backwards, which allows only the victors onto the stage and relegates the lost causes and eliminated human beings to the wings. "A bias in favour of what is successful," Oakeshott writes, "is far more corrupting than any merely partisan bias"; and "history as a success story is always abbreviated history."[32] Second, Oakeshott criticizes Carr for adopting the eccentric point of view and "extraordinarily private language" of the actors in the Russian Revolution, thus failing to perform the essential task of translating them out of the idiom of practice into that of history. In opposition not only to Carr but also to Collingwood's doctrine of historical reenactment, Oakeshott writes: "The historian is the maker of his events; they have a meaning for him which was not their meaning for those who participated in them, and he will not speak of them in the same way as they spoke." The art of writing history is "the art of understanding men and events more profoundly than they were understood when they lived and happened."[33]

The 1950s and '60s produced not only a great deal of theorizing about the nature of history in Britain but also a great number of distinguished and methodologically self-conscious historians: Marxists like Moses Finley, Christopher Hill, E. P. Thompson, Raymond Williams, and Eric Hobsbawm; controversialists like Hugh Trevor-Roper and A. J. P. Taylor; and less easily categorized writers like J. H. Plumb, Lawrence Stone, and Geoffrey Elton. But the historian with whom Oakeshott shared the deepest affinity was his old friend from Cambridge, Herbert Butterfield. Butterfield's 1931 essay on *The Whig Interpretation of History* defended the ideal of studying history for its own sake that Oakeshott also defended in *Experience and Its Modes*; and it attacked many of the same historical fallacies that Oakeshott attacked: the interpretation of the past with reference to the present; the tendency to abridge history; the quest for origins; and the passing of moral judgments on historical actors and actions.

Oakeshott reviewed three of Butterfield's books between 1949 and 1957: *The Origins of Modern Science: 1300–1800* (1949), *Man on His Past* (1955), and *George III and the Historians* (1957). He was particularly impressed by the first book, which attempted to relate the history of modern science in an unWhiggish way. Instead of reading this history as a success story in which only the positive achievements are significant—as Carr might have done—Butterfield made a point of bringing to the surface the lost causes, dead ends, and unsuccessful attempts that are every bit as important to a genuinely historical understanding of science. Oakeshott praises Butterfield for avoiding the trap of reading the past backwards, as well as for recognizing that "history is the enemy of the lonely great, the strange and unexpected, in persons as well as in events" and therefore accounts for change in terms of the principle of "continuity."[34] Oakeshott also endorses Butterfield's criticism in *George III and the Historians* of Lewis Namier's enormously influential approach to history, which attempted to explain individual actions and beliefs exclusively in terms of a somewhat deterministic "structure of politics."[35]

I have gone into some detail with respect to postwar British reflection on history in order to show how large historiographical issues bulked at the time that Oakeshott wrote "The Activity of Being an Historian" and in order to highlight the distinctiveness of Oakeshott's approach to them. We may now turn to the argument of "The Activity of Being an Historian," which echoes many of the themes sounded in the reviews discussed above. Interestingly, Oakeshott begins by putting to one side the issue that exercised so many of his contemporaries, namely, the attempt to understand history as "an inquiry designed to make past events intelligible by revealing them as examples of general laws." Instead, he focuses on the more fundamental issue of differentiating the historical attitude toward the past from the practical attitude, for it is the practical attitude toward the past that is "the chief undefeated enemy of 'history.'" The attempt to convert history into a scientific enterprise and discover general laws or causes has more often than not been motivated by practical interests (*RP*, 152–53, 172, 180).

The chief difference between the practical attitude toward the past and the historical attitude is that the former views the past in relation to the present, whereas the latter studies the past for its own sake. The practical person "reads the past backwards," showing how it has contributed to, explains, or justifies the present. The historian, on the other hand, does not view the past in relation to the present, does not seek to explain events in terms of their relation to subsequent events, and regards nothing as noncontributory (*RP*, 162, 168–69).

None of this is very surprising, given what Oakeshott has already said about the distinction between the practical past and the historical past in *Experience and Its Modes* and his various reviews from the 1940s and '50s. What *is* surprising is the number of statements about the past that Oakeshott would exclude from authentic history on the basis of this distinction. For example:

He died too soon.
King John was a bad King.
The death of William the Conqueror was accidental.
The Pope's intervention changed the course of events.
The evolution of Parliament.

In a genuinely historical past, Oakeshott comments, "no man dies too soon or by 'accident'; there are no successes and failures"; there are no good and bad Kings, "good" and "bad" being judgments that belong to practical discourse; to speak of the "evolution of Parliament" is clearly to read the past backwards and invoke practical notions of progress; and the "Pope's intervention did not change the course of events, it *was* the course of events." Lest we think that these exclusions render the activity of the historian all but impossible, Oakeshott quotes a passage from Maitland that exemplifies the nonteleological and thoroughly contingent understanding of history he is defending (*RP*, 162–63, 169–70, 173).

The distinction between the historical past and the practical past, according to Oakeshott, suggests the true rationale why certain types of inquiry are considered to be inappropriate to genuine historical analysis: for example, the inquiry into origins, which involves reading the past backwards; the inquiry into recent or contemporary history, which rarely (as we saw with Carr) emancipates itself from the idiom of practice; and of course the passing of moral judgments on historical actors and actions. It also suggests why Collingwood's (and to some extent Berlin's) understanding of the task of the historian as the reenactment of past thought and action cannot be correct. The task of the historian is "to understand past conduct and happening in a manner in which they were never understood at the time; to translate action and event from their practical idiom into an historical idiom" (*RP*, 175–80).

Oakeshott closes his essay by stressing the difficulties involved in achieving a genuinely historical attitude toward the past, especially in our current circumstances. We like to think of ourselves as living in a particularly historically minded age, but this is not the case: "Our predominant interest is not in 'history' but only in retrospective politics. And the past is now more than ever a field in which we exercise our moral and political opinions, like whippets in a meadow on a Sunday afternoon." It is not altogether surprising that we rarely achieve a thoroughly historical attitude toward the past, for this attitude "is the product of a severe and sophisticated manner of thinking about the world," creating a world that is utterly unlike the world of practical interests and affections in which we feel so at home: "It is a complicated world, without unity of feeling or clear outline: in it events have no over-all pattern or purpose, lead nowhere, point to no favoured condition of the world and support no practical conclusions. It is a world composed wholly of contingencies" (*RP*, 181–82). To inhabit such a world habitually might pose a danger to practical life, as Nietzsche envisioned in his *Advantage and Disadvantage of History for Life*, but for

Oakeshott this is the last thing we need to fear in our politically minded and eminently unhistorical age.

The complete working out of the theory of history sketched in "The Activity of Being an Historian" would not appear for another 25 years. When "Three Essays on History" was published in 1983 in the volume *On History and Other Essays*, the interest in the philosophy of history that had been so intense in the 1950s and '60s had died down somewhat, and as a consequence the book did not make much of a splash. This was unfortunate, for *On History* represents one of the most profound treatments of history in the twentieth century. In it, Oakeshott distilled over 50 years of reflection on the problem of historical knowledge going all the way back to *Experience and Its Modes*. If, as Collingwood remarked, the chapter on history in that book represented "the high-water mark of English thought upon history," then *On History* only raised the level higher, engaging with philosophers of history from Heidegger to Hempel and historians from Burckhardt to Braudel. Better than any work I know, it dramatizes the delicate and difficult task of historical construction by which the historian endows the past with a circumstantial intelligibility.

The first of the three essays on history is concerned with the idea of the past that belongs to history. And since the past is merely a way of reading the present, Oakeshott begins with the present with which we are most familiar upon opening our eyes, the present of practical activity, of conceiving and satisfying our wants. This practical present is never, of course, merely present but projects into the future; the tense of practical activity is always present-future. And it is from this present-future that we form our first ideas of the past, a past that is in one way or another connected with our practical self-understanding and activity. Some philosophers, notably Heidegger, have claimed that there is no other world than this present-future of practical activity, the *Lebenswelt*, and that therefore there is no other past than the practical past. But Oakeshott rejects this claim to the unconditionality of the present-future of practical activity; no activity altogether escapes the modality or conditionality of human understanding (*OH*, 7–27).

History, too, constructs its past out of the present, but it is a present of a very different sort than that found in practical activity. It is a present composed of surviving artifacts and utterances that the historian views as evidence from which to infer a past that has not survived. Whereas for the historian these survivals are not-yet-understood objects— "complex and ambiguous identities, delicately balanced compositions of equivocal likelihoods"—whose authentic characters remain to be established, for the practical person they are "emblematic characters and episodes" to be used to respond to our current situations, a storehouse of "symbolic and stereotypic *personae*, actions, exploits and situations" that can be called upon to make sense of our current practical engagements: "Here are Cain and Abel, Moses, Horatius, Caesar crossing the Rubicon, Athanasius at Nicea, Canute on the seashore, King Arthur, Wilhelm Tell, Luther at Worms, Nelson putting his telescope to his blind eye at Copenhagen, Robin Hood, Captain Oates, Davy Crockett, and here is Colonel Custer making his last stand" (*OH*, 27–44). Much labor, skill, and intelligence are required to render these surviving artifacts and utterances useable as evidence for a historical inquiry—labor, skill, and intelligence that are stinted in positivist accounts of the "facts of perception" with which history is alleged to begin.

Establishing the authentic characters of the survivals and vestiges of the past, however, is only the beginning of the historian's inquiry. The next step is to infer from these authenticated survivals a past of "occurrences" understood to be what actually happened. Historians often bring these occurrences together to form what Oakeshott calls a "historical situation," a snapshot of a past *mentalité*, a past social, economic or political structure, or a past moral, religious, or cultural practice. Notable examples include Burckhardt's *Civilization of Renaissance Italy*, Bloch's *Feudal Society*, Namier's *Structure of English Politics on the Accession of George III*, and Braudel's *The Mediterranean and the Mediterranean World in the Age of Philip II*. Though Oakeshott acknowledges that such situational identities often confer considerable intelligibility on the past, he argues that they ultimately represent "an unstable level of historical understanding." The historian of course recognizes that the anatomized historical situation is not something permanent or unmediated, but no effort is made "to abate the mystery of its appearance upon the scene, to investigate the mediation of its emergence or to trace the vicissitudes of its evanescence." The flow of past events is "here halted and made to gyrate in a notional interval between coming and going" (*OH*, 52–62).

The remedy for this static form of historical understanding lies in constructing the past, not in terms of anatomized situational identities, but in terms of historical events. In Oakeshott's somewhat specialized vocabulary, a historical event is an occurrence or situation "understood in terms of its emergence; that is, understood as an *eventus* or outcome of what went before." But since "what went before" itself consists only of historical events, "the historical character of an event is the difference it made in a passage of circumstantially and significantly related historical events" (*OH*, 62). Nothing is fixed or solid here; all is mediation and difference. Indeed, Oakeshott sounds positively Derridean when he describes the antecedent events in terms of which a subsequent event is understood as "differences, each understood in terms of the difference in an assembled confluence of differences which comprise the conditions of the coming into being of a subsequent and which converge to constitute its historical character" (*OH*, 98). Reading the late Oakeshott, like reading the late Henry James, can be a vertiginous experience.

What is the nature of the "significant relationship" between historical events that Oakeshott alludes to in the passage above? It will be remembered that an answer to this question was something that critics found missing in Oakeshott's early account of history in *Experience and Its Modes*. Here he tries to flesh out what he referred to there as the "intrinsic relationship" between historical events. As in *Experience and Its Modes*, he rejects the contention that this relationship can be understood as a causal relationship. The problem with Popper's and Hempel's covering law model of historical explanation is that it treats the "facts" that emerge from the complicated process of historical construction and inference that Oakeshott has described as if they were empirically given, awaiting only to be brought under a causal law: "it assumes to be already known what it is the purpose of an historical enquiry to ascertain." Beyond this, the covering law model treats historical occurrences not as complex mixtures of particularity and genericity but as abstract kinds or generic instances (*OH*, 72–82).

Instead of causality, Oakeshott understands the significant relationship between historical events in terms of "contingency." A contingent relationship is one of "touch" and does not require "the glue of normality or the cement of general causes" to hold events together. He uses the image of a "dry wall" (of the sort found in the countryside around his Dorset cottage) to bring out the nature of such contingent relationship: "stones (that is, the antecedent events) which compose the wall (that is, the subsequent event) are joined together, not by mortar, but in terms of their shapes" (*OH*, 94). He goes on to characterize this relationship between historical events in terms of the idea of historical change. Rejecting models of change in terms of a changeless essence, a teleological purpose, or an organic process, he invokes the idea of "continuity" to characterize the complex identity-in-difference that constitutes historical change. Once again, he seeks the unity of "an assemblage of historical differences," not in some extrinsic purpose or unchanging essence, but "in some intrinsic quality of the assemblage itself" (*OH*, 97–115).

Oakeshott's answer here to what he calls "the central question in any account of historical understanding" (*OH*, 70) does not differ radically from the answer he gave 50 years earlier in *Experience and Its Modes*. The main difference lies in his greater acceptance of the artificiality, what he earlier called the "designated" character, of the historical individual. There is no suggestion here that "the only explanation of change relevant or possible in history is simply a complete account of change" (*EM*, 143), as if an ideal historical explanation would be an explanation of the totality of history. He writes: "any past which is to acquire an intelligible historical identity must be abstracted from the flux and inconsequence of all that was going on then and there, and this procedure of abstraction is recognized when an historical past is specified as an answer to an historical question" (*OH*, 62). Nor does this necessary abstraction in history convict it of being a defective mode of experience from the standpoint of some notional presuppositionless, unmodified, or unconditional experience. As we have seen, there is no such experience in the conversation of mankind.

6 Civil Association

In 1975, Oakeshott published *On Human Conduct*. This was the systematic work of political philosophy he had long envisaged. As far back as the 1925 manuscript, "A Discussion of Some Matters Preliminary to the Study of Political Philosophy," he had meditated on what would be involved in a complete political philosophy, and this concern was reflected in the various propaedeutics to a political philosophy that he wrote in the ensuing years—from "The Concept of a Philosophical Jurisprudence" in 1938 to the manuscripts on "The Concept of a Philosophy of Politics" (circa 1937–38) and "Political Philosophy" (circa 1948–49). The major work toward which these writings gestured, however, was puzzlingly deferred. The postwar rationalism writings certainly did not constitute a complete political philosophy, being concerned for the most part with the narrower and more negative task of critiquing ideological politics and central social planning. It was only in Oakeshott's reflections on modern European politics in *The Politics of Faith and the Politics of Scepticism* (circa 1953), "The Masses in Representative Democracy" (1957), and the Harvard lectures on *Morality and Politics in Modern Europe* (1958) that the central themes of *On Human Conduct* began to emerge, but even here they were not given anything like the systematic treatment demanded by Oakeshott's exacting conception of philosophy.

When *On Human Conduct* finally did come out, the 74-year-old Oakeshott poignantly remarked in the Preface that the "themes explored here have been with me nearly as long as I can remember; but I have left the task of putting my thoughts together almost too late" (*OHC*, vii). He had worked on the book steadily since the mid-1960s. A letter to Ken Minogue from 1967 (from which I quoted earlier) gives a good idea not only of the difficulties Oakeshott encountered in writing *On Human Conduct* but also of the philosophical ambition that lay behind it:

> I am not going to get this finished as quickly as I hoped. Not only have I lost the faculty of rapid writing, but I am finding a vast discontent with a good many of the ideas which used to knock about in my head fairly agreeably, and what is worse (for these can always be replaced by others) I am finding that what I thought I had clear is, when I come to it, just about as clear as mud. So the alternative I face each morning at 9am is either to do a bit of what is called

skirting round the difficulties (which I can't quite bring myself to do: perhaps in another year or two) or to sit glassy eyed watching for a glimmer of light at the end of a long, long dark passage. It takes time. But I've invented something of a new vocabulary, which I hope will carry me through, but I never know that it isn't going to fall apart in my hands.[1]

Everything about the final product suggests that Oakeshott regarded this as his culminating achievement, from the book's austerely grand title and analytical table of contents to its formal style and Latin vocabulary. With what disappointment, then, he must have read the initial reviews of the book, which were generally quite negative.[2] Much of the criticism focused on the form of the book, its abstract and stipulative character, its lack of direct argumentation and coyness about drawing normative conclusions. Alan Ryan wrote that *On Human Conduct* confirmed the long-held suspicion that Oakeshott "regards argument as rather vulgar," refusing to engage in anything "so low-minded as overt ratiocination." Nevertheless, Ryan conceded that the book was "subtle, elegant, and elusive" and disclosed "the distinctive quality of Oakeshott's thinking about politics, a quality which lies in the style, the leisurely pace, the flow of ironic asides, not the argumentation." He also said the book was written in "a prose that makes Proust look like a telegraph operator."[3] Less kind was Hanna Pitkin, who complained that the book was "rigidly dogmatic, assertive, and idiosyncratic almost to the point of being crotchety."[4] Most unkind of all was G. J. Warnock, who, speaking for the Oxford school of linguistic philosophy, did not even deign to mention what Oakeshott's book was about but simply dismissed it as not being philosophy at all because "it contains almost nothing in the way of *argument*."[5]

Such criticisms were not altogether unjustified. The style of *On Human Conduct* is in fact abstract, and its argument often appears to proceed by stipulative definition instead of explicit argumentation. (In this latter regard, *On Human Conduct* differs sharply from the youthful and more combative *Experience and Its Modes*.) Nevertheless, it is a profound work of political philosophy and altogether worthy of being the crowning achievement of Oakeshott's distinguished career. Its aim is to provide a complete philosophical account of the mode of association that Oakeshott had sketched in earlier essays under the rubric of the politics of skepticism or individuality in contradistinction to the politics of passion or the common good. The book consists of three connected essays: the first investigates the essential presuppositions of civil association, namely, freedom and morality; the second contains the theory of civil association proper; and the third considers the place of civil association in constituting and understanding the equivocal character of the modern European state. Oakeshott's theory of civil association may be profitably considered as a contribution to liberal theory, and so, in the final section of the chapter, I discuss it in relation to the contemporary debate over liberalism as it has developed from Rawls and his progeny through Sandel, Macedo, Raz, Galston, Berlin, and Rorty.

Freedom and Morality

In the first essay of *On Human Conduct*, Oakeshott elaborates a teaching about human freedom that serves as the basis of his liberal theory of civil association. Though it cannot be doubted that individual freedom was always at the heart of Oakeshott's political vision, it is only in *On Human Conduct* that he finally provided a philosophical account of it. It will be remembered that, early on in his career, Oakeshott celebrated Hobbes for making will the basis of the state but criticized him for lacking a coherent theory of volition. He went on to cite Rousseau's doctrine of the "general will," Hegel's doctrine of the "rational will," and Bosanquet's doctrine of the "real will" as notable attempts to overcome this deficiency in Hobbes's political philosophy. The teaching on human freedom that Oakeshott develops in the first essay of *On Human Conduct* can be understood as his own, original contribution to this idealist effort. With it he attempts to overcome the atomism of traditional liberal theory by conceiving of human freedom or agency in such a way that its qualification by morality and law need not entail its being compromised. The teaching also allows him to establish limits to state action without appealing either to natural rights (à la Locke) or to the incompatibility of legal compulsion with moral motivation (à la Kant, Green, and Bosanquet).

Before entering on his theory of freedom, Oakeshott, in typical fashion, considers the nature of theorizing. As he did in *Experience and Its Modes*, he begins by rejecting the empiricist distinction between mediate and immediate experience, between understanding and the datum of understanding. There is no "immediate datum" from which understanding may be said to begin; understanding always "begins in an already understood." And the process of understanding is basically one in which an already understood comes to be more profoundly and explicitly understood. At a certain stage in this process, we come to occupy what Oakeshott calls a "platform of conditional understanding," where previously picked out identities are explored and mapped in terms of their relationships to one another. At this stage, the identities themselves remain unproblematic and unquestionable. A more critical attitude toward them, however, is also possible. Instead of simply relating identities to one another as unproblematic "facts," a theorist may also try to enhance their intelligibility by understanding them in terms of their conditions or postulates. In doing so, she comes to occupy a new, and in some sense superior, platform of conditional understanding. Examples of this kind of theoretical engagement include the natural sciences, the historical sciences, and the philosophical disciplines of ethics, aesthetics, and political philosophy (*OHC*, 2–10).

This is not, however, the end of the process. For these new platforms of conditional understanding may themselves be questioned and investigated in terms of their postulates. To this unconditionally critical process of exploring experience in terms of its postulates Oakeshott gives the name "philosophy." This to some extent echoes the definition of philosophy in *Experience and Its Modes* as "experience without presupposition, reservation, arrest or modification," but Oakeshott makes it clear here that the unconditionality of philosophy does not consist in its being completely free of conditions or in its arriving at unconditional theorems; "what constitutes its unconditionality is the continuous recognition of its conditions." Nor, in keeping with the idea of conversation enunciated in "The Voice of Poetry," is the relationship between philosophy and the modes of experience any longer conceived of as being antagonistic or competitive. Oakeshott no longer characterizes the various arrests of experience as lacking in self-consciousness or denying the unconditional engagement of philosophical understanding: "The theorist who drops anchor here or there and puts out his equipment of theoretic hooks and nets in order to take the fish of the locality, interrupts but does not betray his calling. . . . the theorist who interrogates instead of using his theoretic equipment catches no fish" (*OHC*, 11). This applies to the conditional theorizing of the political philosopher, who is now referred to as a "self-consciously conditional theorist," one who "has a heavenly home, but . . . is in no hurry to reach it. If he is concerned to theorize moral conduct or civil association he must forswear metaphysics" (*OHC*, 25).

There are two further points Oakeshott wishes to make about the conditional engagement to understand an identity in terms of its postulates, both of which are relevant to his own conditional engagement to theorize human conduct. The first concerns the distinction (as it is now commonly formulated) between interpretive "understanding" and scientific "explanation." Oakeshott argues that, in order to become a subject of theoretical inquiry, a going-on must be unambiguously identified as belonging to one of two categories: it must be recognized either as an exhibition of intelligence (e.g. a biologist at work) or as an nonintelligent instance (e.g. a wave breaking on the shore). Each category predicates very different sorts of inquiry and very different conditions to be inquired into. In the first case, the conditions will be "practices," which require to be learned or understood in order to be participated in (e.g. religious beliefs, rituals, traditions, etc.). In the second, the conditions will be "processes," which need not be learned or understood in order to be operative (e.g. the law of gravitation, chemical decomposition, etc.). As with the distinction he drew in *Experience and Its Modes* between history and science, the distinction Oakeshott draws here between goings-on identified as exhibitions of intelligence and goings-on recognized as instances of nonintelligent processes is not to be understood as an ontological distinction between different kinds of object, for example, mind and body, or spirit and nature. Rather, it is "a distinction within the engagement of understanding, a distinction between 'sciences.'" And as he did in *Experience and Its Modes*, he picks out psychology and sociology as two inquiries that suffer from categorial confusion, resembling "darkling plains where ignorant armies clash by night" (*OHC*, 12–15, 20–25).

The second point Oakeshott makes with respect to theoretical understanding concerns its relationship to the conditional understanding it seeks to theorize. Here we encounter, once again, Oakeshott's sharp distinction between theory and practice. He argues that, even though the understanding of the theorist is undoubtedly superior to the conditional understanding that she theorizes, the former cannot take the latter's place. The postulates in terms of which a theorist understands the identities of a conditional platform of understanding are not principles from which correct performances may be deduced. To use theoretical knowledge in this way to direct practical activity is the spurious engagement of the "theoretician." Oakeshott illustrates his point with a wry rereading of Plato's allegory of the cave that rejects Plato's contention that the understanding of the philosopher, alleged to be unconditional, is not only superior to but a substitute for every other conditional or cave understanding, arguing instead that the cave dwellers are right to regard the philosopher who poses as a political expert as an imposter (*OHC*, 25–31).

With these metatheoretical issues disposed of, Oakeshott now turns his attention to the central issue of human freedom. He begins by specifying that the freedom with which he is initially concerned is the freedom that is inherent in human conduct. "Freedom" here denotes a formal condition of all conduct recognized to be human; it does not refer to "the quality of being substantively 'self-directed' which an agent may or may not achieve"—what is more properly called "self-determination" or "autonomy." Such formal freedom consists in the fact that human conduct is an exhibition of intelligence, by which Oakeshott does not mean to suggest that human conduct is notably reflective, self-conscious, or rational, only that it involves understanding (which may, of course, be implicit) and that it must ultimately be learned. His concern is to distinguish human conduct, not from spontaneous, habitual, or irrational conduct, but from a genetic, psychological, or otherwise nonintelligent "process." Human conduct is a matter of beliefs, understandings, and meanings, not of biological impulses, organic tensions, or genetic urges (*OHC*, 32, 36–37, 89).

From this initial postulate of the intelligent character of human conduct, Oakeshott develops a thoroughly hermeneutic and historical conception of agency. The world inhabited by a free agent is "composed entirely of understandings": the situation that he confronts in action is an understood situation, not a brute or natural datum; and the satisfaction that he seeks is an understood, not a merely natural, satisfaction. Echoing a point he made in his educational writings, Oakeshott writes: an agent "is what he understands himself to be," and "his contingent situations are what he understands them to be . . . He has a 'history,' but no 'nature'; he is what in conduct he becomes." Nor, he adds, is this history to be understood as "an evolutionary or teleological process. . . . [T]here is no ultimate or perfect man hidden in the womb of time or prefigured in the characters who now walk the earth" (*OHC*, 36–41).

Oakeshott refers to human conduct insofar as it relates to agents responding to their understood situations by choosing specific actions aimed at understood satisfactions under the general rubric of "self-disclosure." What makes such self-disclosure particularly hazardous is that the satisfaction sought in it consists largely of the contingent responses of other agents. Conduct *inter homines* consists mainly of transactions between agents. But these transactions are not by themselves self-sufficient or self-explanatory. They "postulate more durable relationships between agents which are not themselves transactions but are the conditional context of all such transactions." These "more durable relationships" Oakeshott calls "practices," which he defines as any set of considerations, manners, uses, customs, conventions, maxims, principles, or rules that governs or "adverbially" qualifies human actions and relationships. Examples include relationships, such as those of friends, neighbors, and husband and wife; ways of life, such as the stoic *apatheia* and medieval chivalry; and complex modes of discourse, such as science, history, poetry, and philosophy. What all these practices have in common is that they specify procedural or adverbial conditions to be subscribed to in acting; they do not specify substantive performances or actions (*OHC*, 35–36, 39, 44, 54–56).

It is precisely on account of this adverbial character of practices that they do not compromise what Oakeshott has defined as the freedom inherent in agency. A practice "prescribes conditions for, but does not determine, the substantive choices and performances of agents." The "practical" is only an aspect of any action and must always be accompanied by a substantive action chosen by an agent. This is true even of those rules and procedures that have the appearance of forbidding, and not merely adverbially qualifying, substantive actions or choices—for example, criminal laws. "A criminal law," Oakeshott insists, "does not forbid killing or lighting a fire, it forbids killing 'murderously' or lighting a fire 'arsonically.'" Also, because they are adverbial qualifications and not specific commands, the requirements of a practice cannot simply be "obeyed" or "disobeyed"; "they are subscribed to or not subscribed to" (*OHC*, 55–58, 68, 90–91).

What Oakeshott theorizes under the rubric of "practice" coincides with what he previously theorized under the rubric of "tradition." The problem with "tradition" was that it suggested to many—though this was clearly not intended by Oakeshott—a fixed pattern of substantive conduct blindly or habitually "obeyed."[6] In other words, it obscured precisely the adverbial character that Oakeshott seeks to bring out with his notion of a practice. He further elucidates this adverbial character by analogizing a practice to a language. In *Rationalism in Politics*, the acquisition and use of a tradition of behavior was compared to the acquisition and use of a natural language. In *On Human Conduct*, the analogy of language becomes even more prominent. Like a language, a practice

does not impose upon an agent demands that he shall think certain thoughts, entertain certain sentiments, or make certain utterances. It comes to him as various invitations to understand, to choose, and to respond. It is composed of conventions and rules of syntax, and it is continuously invented by those who speak it, and using it is adding to its resources. It is an instrument to be played upon, not a tune to be played. (*OHC,* 59)

Having distinguished two sorts of human relationship—"transactional" relationship, in which agents seek substantive satisfactions in the responses of other agents, and "practical" relationship, in which these transitory transactions are adverbially qualified by procedures— Oakeshott proceeds to draw a further distinction between two sorts of "practical" relationship, two sorts of practices. On the one hand, there are practices that "are designed to promote the success of the transactions . . . they govern," practices that are "instrumental to the achievement of imagined and wished-for satisfactions." An office routine, the rules for making pastry, and the arrangements composing an economy are all examples of this sort of instrumental or prudential practice. On the other hand, there are practices that are not instrumental to any particular purpose or enterprise. Such practices Oakeshott calls "moral" practices. A morality is "a practice without any extrinsic purpose," whose conditions are subscribed to "in seeking the satisfaction of any want." It is "the *ars artium* of conduct; the practice of all practices; the practice of agency without further specification" (*OHC,* 60–62).

Many critics have found Oakeshott's identification of morality with a nonpurposive or noninstrumental practice arbitrary and questionable. Though he doesn't provide much argument for it, the basic intuition seems to be the Kantian one that there must be a distinction between moral and prudential conduct. If moral conduct is reduced to prudential conduct, as in utilitarianism, the force and meaning of the adjective "moral" is still to seek. There is something profoundly Aristotelian in Oakeshott's philosophical procedure in *On Human Conduct,* as he himself points out.[7] It is a procedure not of reduction but of progressive differentiation and specification, in which the intuitive distinctions of ordinary consciousness are more precisely and explicitly formulated. With respect to morality, this procedure initially leads him to side with Kant over the utilitarians. But his final position is less Kantian than Hegelian.

The Hegelian dimension of his conception of morality emerges clearly when Oakeshott invokes once again the analogy of language. A moral practice is like a language, he writes, "in being an instrument of understanding and a medium of intercourse, in having a vocabulary and a syntax of its own, and in being spoken well or ill." Moreover, like a language, it is a wholly historic achievement, reflecting the historic self-understandings of its speakers. There are many such languages in the world, and "this plurality cannot be resolved by being understood as so many contingent and regrettable divergencies from a fancied perfect and universal language of moral intercourse." That such a resolution should have been attempted, however, Oakeshott does not find surprising, since "human beings are apt to be disconcerted unless they feel themselves to be upheld by something more substantial than the emanations of their own contingent imaginations." But for the "modest mortal with a self to disclose and a soul to make," the availability of a "familiar and resourceful moral language (and one for which he may hope to acquire a *Sprachgefühl*)" will be more than enough (*OHC*, 62–64, 80–81).

What more than anything else the analogy of a moral practice to a language highlights is the wholly colloquial or vernacular character of a morality. A morality is not something above our daily existence that we bring to bear on our actions through an act of reflective effort; rather, it is a medium for conduct without which no action or utterance could take place. A morality does not somehow supervene on the more primary or natural activity of desiring or instinctual gratification; it is a language within which the pursuit of any satisfaction takes place, a knowledge we are never without. Over and over again, Oakeshott stresses the vernacular character of a moral practice; the fact that it is a "living and vulgar language" continuously used by agents to disclose and enact themselves, to understand and interact with others. Moral conduct is not "lurching from perplexity to perplexity," nor is it "solving problems"; it is "agents continuously related to one another in the idiom of a familiar language of moral converse" (*OHC*, 62–64). Oakeshott sums up his entire, Hegelian point of view in a passage criticizing the romantic notion of "moral autonomy" implicit in Kant's writings and explicit in vulgar versions of existentialism:

> What is called "moral autonomy" does not require moral choice to be a gratuitous, criterionless exercise of a so-called "will" (an isolated *meum*) in which a lonely agent simultaneously recognizes or even creates a "value" for which he is wholly responsible and places himself under its command, thus miraculously releasing himself from organic impulse, rational contingency, and authoritative rules of conduct. . . . Human conduct is not first having unconditional wants . . . and then allowing prudential reason and moral sensibility to indicate or to determine the choice of the actions in which their satisfaction is sought; it is wanting intelligently (that is, in recognition of prudential and moral considerations) and doing this successfully or not so successfully. (*OHC*, 79–80)[8]

Up to this point, Oakeshott has discussed human conduct solely in terms of "self-disclosure," that is, agents disclosing themselves in actions aimed at procuring imagined satisfactions composed primarily of the responses of other agents. But there is another aspect of human conduct that concerns, not the imagined and wished-for satisfaction of an action, but the "motive" or "sentiment" in which the action is performed. This aspect Oakeshott refers to as "self-enactment," and he maintains that a moral practice is no less concerned with it than with self-disclosure. A moral practice specifies the conditions not only of moral self-disclosure but also of virtuous self-enactment. There is nothing merely "private" or "subjective" about motives; they, no less than actions, are governed by the compunctions of a common language and practice. Nevertheless, we tend to judge our fellows less strictly or exactingly with respect to self-enactment than with respect to self-disclosure, not because we are indifferent to one another's exploits in self-enactment, but because of our ultimate ignorance of one another's motives and the sense that in ordinary intercourse these motives affect us less than outward actions (*OHC*, 70–77).

In virtuous self-enactment the episodic and diurnal character of self-disclosure is somewhat abated: "There is at least the echo of an imperishable achievement when the valour of the agent and not the soon-to-vanish victory, when his loyalty and fortitude and not the evanescent defeat, are the considerations" (*OHC*, 84). Nevertheless, even here the inconclusiveness and dissatisfaction inherent in practical life is not completely escaped. It is only when self-enactment takes the form of religious faith that "the deadliness of doing" is finally overcome. Oakeshott concludes the first essay of *On Human Conduct* with an achingly beautiful account of the nature of religious self-enactment, in which he returns to the themes of some of his earliest essays, especially "Religion and the World." Just as there he characterized religion as the rejection of the worldly standard of external achievement and the attempt to live a life that carries "in each of its moments its whole meaning and value" (*RPML*, 31–32), so here he characterizes it as the sentiment in which "the fugitive adventures of human conduct . . . are graced with an intimation of immortality . . . and the transitory sweetness of mortal affection, the tumult of grief and the passing beauty of a May morning [are] recognized neither as merely evanescent adventures nor as emblems of better things to come, but as *aventures*, themselves encounters with eternity" (*OHC*, 85). From first to last, Oakeshott's conception of religion remained a highly poetic and Paterian one.

Civil Association

The key to Oakeshott's understanding of civil association is the idea of a moral practice developed in the first essay of *On Human Conduct*. Civil association is, most fundamentally, association or relationship in terms of a moral (i.e. noninstrumental) practice. By defining civil association in this way, Oakeshott is able to overcome the atomism that has dogged liberal theory from Locke to Mill. A moral practice—and hence, civil association—does not compromise the freedom inherent in human agency because it does not determine the substantive choices of agents but only prescribes procedural or adverbial conditions to be taken into account when choosing and acting. Far from being an external limit on agency, a moral practice is indispensable to it. There is no agency that is not an acknowledgment of a moral practice, just as there is no utterance that is not in any language in particular. Freedom and morality mutually imply one another.

Throughout the second essay of *On Human Conduct*, Oakeshott contrasts his understanding of civil association as a moral, noninstrumental practice to the more familiar understanding of it in terms of the joint pursuit of a common purpose or interest. To this latter mode of association he gives the name "enterprise association," and he mentions a number of difficulties involved in identifying civil association with it. First, there is "the difficulty of specifying a common purpose in terms of which to distinguish civil relationship from all other enterprise relationship." There is nothing in common purposes such as general prosperity or devotion to a set of religious beliefs, for example, to distinguish *civil* association from a business enterprise or a religious community. Nor can ends such as "security" or "peace" serve to specify the distinctive common purpose of civil association. Security and peace, Oakeshott argues, are not substantive purposes at all; they are not specific satisfactions sought for themselves but conditions that make possible the pursuit of substantive satisfactions. Finally, and most importantly, enterprise association is unable to accommodate the compulsory character that belongs to civil association, at least in the context of the modern state. Enterprise association is necessarily voluntary relationship. The members of such an association, if they are not to compromise their inherent freedom, must acknowledge its common purpose as their own and be able to extricate themselves from the relationship whenever they choose to do so. To make an enterprise association compulsory would be to deprive an agent of that "freedom" or "autonomy" that is the condition of agency (*OHC*, 114–19).

Insofar as civil association is a moral practice, it can also be understood as a vernacular language of intercourse. The "language of civility," Oakeshott concedes, is not spoken on every occasion—it is not, for example, the language in which lovers converse—but "it is never wholly put by," and "there is no situation *inter homines* to which it cannot relate." Nor is this characterization of civil association in terms of a vernacular language of intercourse to be thought of as a mere or vague analogy. For Oakeshott, it constitutes "the essential character of the civil condition." He claims that "the investigation of this condition has flourished only when it has been tied to a reading of its character in which it is recognized as agents exploring their relationships in terms of a language of understanding and intercourse which is native to and continuously re-enacted by those who use it" (*OHC*, 122–24).

As important as the identification of civil association as a moral practice is, it alone does not suffice to specify the nature of civil association. Oakeshott argues that civil association is to be understood not simply as a moral practice but as a special kind of moral practice: it is moral practice "composed entirely of rules; the language of civil intercourse is a language of rules; *civitas* is rule-articulated association" (*OHC*, 124). In his later reply to his critics, Oakeshott sums up the differences between civil rules (or laws) and other moral considerations:

> [Civil rules differ from other moral considerations] in being subject to enactment, repeal and alteration in an authorized procedure, in that the conditions they prescribe are narrower, less demanding, and more precisely formulated, in there being an authoritative procedure for determining whether or not an agent in acting has adequately subscribed to these rules, and in there being known penalties attached to inadequate subscription and an apparatus of power to enforce them.[9]

With the identification of civil association as relationship in terms of noninstrumental rules (or laws), we have arrived at what might be called the *differentia* of civil association. Oakeshott himself regards this feature as the most significant of civil association. It has also been, he comments, the most difficult feature "to identify and get into place" (*OHC*, 181). One of the chief concerns of *On Human Conduct* is to provide a precise definition of the nature of law, that is, of the rules appropriate to civil association. In this regard, it bears comparison not only with the great philosophies of law of Hobbes, Kant, and Hegel, but also with the more recent positivist theories of Hans Kelsen, and H. L. A. Hart. With Hart especially, whose *Concept of Law* appeared in 1961, Oakeshott shares a number of views on the nature of law, though he ultimately diverges from Hart in refusing to sever the necessary connection between law and morality and in conceiving of legal relationship in terms of moral relationship.

Oakeshott begins his inquiry into civil law, or, as he now refers to it, *lex*, by considering the nature of rules in general, of which the rules of a game provide a fairly clear picture. He enumerates four basic features, many of which point up the difference between rules and commands. Like Hart, and for many of the same reasons, Oakeshott rejects the "command theory" of law, which received its most unambiguous statement in the jurisprudence of John Austin. The first feature is that a rule is an authoritative assertion and not a theorem. Unlike a maxim or a piece of advice, a rule does not argue, and its validity does not depend on its being found reasonable, worthwhile, or desirable. It may of course be argued about and its desirability debated, but a rule in itself does not invoke approval; it calls only for assent. Second, a rule is general or abstract. Unlike a command, for example, it is not addressed to an assignable agent; nor is it used up or exhausted in a single performance. Third, again unlike commands, "rules do not enjoin, prohibit, or warrant substantive actions or utterances"; they prescribe adverbial considerations to be subscribed to or taken into account in choosing performances, considerations that "cannot themselves be 'obeyed' or performed." Fourth, rules are recognized in terms of their authority, not in terms of the consequences of their observance or nonobservance (*OHC*, 124–27; *OH*, 126–30).

While the rules of civil association resemble the rules of a game in many ways, there is one crucial difference: whereas a game is an engagement that itself constitutes a relationship, there is no such common engagement in the civil condition. The members of a civil association, now referred to as *cives*, unlike the players of a game, are related solely in terms of their common recognition of rules. This also distinguishes *cives* from the members of an enterprise association, who may observe rules but are not related in terms of rules; they are related instead in terms of a common choice or purpose. Oakeshott claims that "the most important postulates of *civitas* stem from [the] consideration" that rules are the sole terms in which *cives* are related. The first of these postulates is that the rules of civil association (*lex*) compose a self-contained system identifying its own jurisdiction. This is necessary because *lex*, unlike the rules of a game or an enterprise association, is "not imposed upon an already shaped and articulated engagement" but "relates those who are not, as such, otherwise related" (*OHC*, 116–17, 128–30).

Apart from the systematic character of *lex*, civil association postulates a procedure by which the abstract and general rules that compose *lex* are related to contingent situations (adjudication), a procedure whereby these rules can be deliberated in terms of their desirability (legislation), and an apparatus to enforce these rules and exact penalties where they have been inadequately observed (ruling). Oakeshott has interesting things to say on each of these heads, but we need not go into the details here. About the deliberative engagement that belongs to legislation he will have much more to say when he discusses "politics" (*OHC*, 130–46).

The conditions discussed so far relate to civil association primarily as a system of rules—a system Oakeshott now refers to as *respublica* or the public concern. But civil association, he argues, is not simply relationship in terms of a system of rules; it is relationship in terms of a certain manner of recognizing rules, namely, "the recognition of rules as rules." To recognize a rule as a rule is not to recognize it in terms of approval or disapproval; a rule does not cease to be obligatory simply because we do not approve of it. Nor is it recognition of a rule in terms of the consequences—benefits or rewards—of subscribing or not subscribing to it; hope or fear may be *motives* for subscription, but they are not the *grounds* of the obligation to subscribe. To recognize a rule as a rule is to recognize it in terms of its *authority*, and to recognize subscription to it as an *obligation*: "Civil authority and civil obligation are the twin pillars of the civil condition" (*OHC*, 148–49).

Oakeshott's preoccupation with the problem of authority of course goes all the way back to his earliest writings on Hobbes. Like Hobbes, he now argues that civil authority has nothing to do with the desirability—utility, wisdom, rationality, or justice—of the conditions of *respublica*. Recognizing the authority of *respublica* is simply accepting its conditions as binding regardless of whether one approves of them or not. *Respublica* is not a perfectly rational or systematic construction— there is no "single ultimate rule of recognition" (contra Hart), nor is there "an unconditional and unquestionable norm from which all others derive their authority" (contra Kelsen). And if it is asked "how a manifold of rules, many of unknown origin . . . not infrequently neglected without penalty, often inconvenient, neither demanding nor capable of evoking the approval of all they concern, and never more than an imperfect reflection of what are considered to be 'just' conditions of conduct may be acknowledged to be authoritative," Oakeshott answers matter-of-factly that "authority is the only conceivable attribute it could be indisputably acknowledged to have" (*OHC*, 149–54).

Oakeshott's Hobbesian doctrine of authority obviously entails the rejection of the natural-law teaching that holds that the authority or validity of *lex* derives from its conformity with some sort of "natural," "rational," or "higher" law—the "neoplatonic" view that *lex injusta non est lex*. For Oakeshott, authority and desirability are not the same thing, and authority and justice are distinct considerations: *lex injusta* may indeed still be authentic *lex*. Nevertheless, he acknowledges that there are certain formal conditions inherent in civil law as such—"rules not arbitrary, secret [or] retroactive . . . the independence of judicial proceedings," etc.; what Lon Fuller referred to as "the internal morality of law"[10]—to which a law must conform if it is to be a valid law. In respect of these conditions, but only in respect of these conditions, "it may perhaps be said that *lex injusta non est lex*" (*OHC*, 153; *OH*, 140, 155–56).

Because civil authority and its counterpart, civil obligation, do not argue, persuade, or invoke approval, they have frequently been thought to pose a threat to the moral autonomy of human beings. Oakeshott argues, however, that this is not the case, for reasons ultimately relating back to his distinctive understanding of moral autonomy and the freedom inherent in agency. Civil authority and obligation do not compromise the moral autonomy of human beings, first, because civil law or *lex* does not specify substantive actions but only adverbial considerations to be taken into account when choosing and acting. The prescriptions of *lex* "are not expressions of 'will' and their injunctions are not orders to be obeyed." The second reason civil authority and obligation do not compromise the freedom or autonomy inherent in agency has to do with their being distinguished from approval or desirability. It is precisely because recognizing the authority of *respublica* does not involve approval of its conditions that the freedom inherent in agency— which Oakeshott here reformulates as "the link between belief and conduct"—is preserved: "in acknowledging civil authority *cives* have given no hostages to a future in which, their approvals and choices no longer being what they were, they can remain free only in an act of dissociation" (*OHC*, 157–58).

In the passages of *On Human Conduct* under discussion, we find perhaps the clearest statement of the intimate relationship Oakeshott sees between freedom and authority. This relationship receives its most memorable expression in the comment on Hobbes that I have already quoted several times: "Hobbes is not an absolutist precisely because he is an authoritarian"; "it is Reason, not Authority, that is destructive of individuality" (*HCA*, 67). Oakeshott's reflections on freedom and authority may also be usefully compared with the tradition of idealist political philosophy I considered in chapter 3. The core of the idealist project consisted in the attempt to reconcile the authority of the state with individual freedom by basing that authority, not on the consent of the individual, but on her "real" or "rational" will. While Oakeshott certainly follows Hegel, Green, and Bosanquet in rejecting individual consent as the basis of authority, he nevertheless does not identify authority with the "real" or "rational" will of the individual, at least not when this will is conceived of teleologically. His reconciliation of freedom and authority depends instead (as we have seen) on showing that civil authority does not compromise the formal freedom inherent in agency. In this regard, he diverges most sharply from his British Hegelian predecessors—Hegel himself is more ambiguous—whose doctrine of the "real will" does seem to point to a substantial and teleological doctrine of human nature, and whose doctrine of authority therefore does not clearly distinguish between authority and wisdom.

Though acknowledgement of the authority of the rules of *respublica* does not entail recognition of them as desirable, Oakeshott does not deny that these rules may be considered in terms of their desirability. The only thing that *respublica* precludes is that either of these considerations be confused with or substituted for the other. In civil association, authority and desirability or approval are always distinguished. This is one of the things that differentiates it, not only from enterprise association, but from other noninstrumental, moral practices, where authority and approval are difficult to distinguish. In most moralities, the "recognition of a moral virtue is itself the approval of the conditions it specifies for conduct; these conditions may be forgotten or neglected, but to dislodge them is nothing other than a withdrawal or qualification of approval." In other words, in a morality there does not exist, as there does in civil association, an authorized procedure by which a virtue or a norm of conduct may be deliberately enacted or repealed (*OHC*, 158–61). This, and not the fact that civil law relates to external actions while morality relates to internal motives (as Kant argued), is what differentiates civil association from other, less specific moral practices.[11]

The engagement of deliberating the conditions of *respublica* in terms of their desirability Oakeshott calls "politics." He puts this word in inverted commas to distinguish what he means by it from all the other meanings the word has accrued over time. "Politics" relates exclusively to civil association, and this means that it is confined to deliberating specifically *civil* desirabilities. "Engagement in politics," Oakeshott contends, "entails a disciplined imagination. It is to put by for another occasion the cloudy enchantments of *Schlaffraffenland*, the earth flowing with

milk and honey and the sea transmuted into ginger beer, it is to forswear the large consideration of human happiness and virtue . . . and to
focus attention upon civility" (*OHC*, 164). Less rhetorically, politics in
civil association is not concerned with the promotion of substantive purposes, interests, or doctrines because civil association is not concerned
with these things. Civil politics is only concerned with the custody,
maintenance, and desirability of a system of moral, noninstrumental
considerations (*OHC*, 168–73).

Apart from this formal condition of politics, Oakeshott argues that
political deliberation is a contingent and circumstantial engagement, not
a demonstrative or deductive one. This, of course, was the theme of
Rationalism in Politics, and Oakeshott here reiterates many of the points
he made in that work. Once again he rejects natural law and unconditional principles as criteria for political deliberation, defending instead
a more historical, though not necessarily relativistic, understanding of
the process in political activity. In language reminiscent of *Rationalism
in Politics*, he speaks of the political deliberation of civil conditions as
"an exploration of intimations" for which there exists no "mistake-proof
manner" of proceeding. Nor is there any end to this activity: "every
adjustment of a *respublica* is a disturbance of tensions which hold it
together and is liable to bring thitherto concealed discrepancies to the
surface." There are, in short, no "final solutions" in politics (*OHC*, 173,
178–80).

Of course, the most important consideration in political deliberation
concerns the justice or "rightness" of a law. Apart from his discussion of
the justice inherent in *lex*, however, Oakeshott does not have a great
deal to say on this topic in *On Human Conduct*. It is only in his later
essay on "The Rule of Law" that he devotes serious attention to the
fundamental issue of justice. There he argues—against Hobbes and
others—that the formal principles inherent in civil law do not exhaust
the considerations in terms of which the justice of law may be deliberated: "the *jus* of *lex* cannot be identified simply with its faithfulness to
the formal character of law." The criterion by which the justice of a law
is determined must be sought outside of positive law. Nevertheless,
Oakeshott rejects natural law as an inadequate interpretation of this criterion. Natural law has proved to be too indeterminate to serve as a
useful criterion of justice, and the attempt to surmount this difficulty
by formulating the natural law in terms of some readily available principles—a bill of rights or a fundamental law—has not overcome the
defect. Such principles have been "more often than not . . . the occasion
of profitless dispute" (*OH*, 140–43, 157–60).

Fortunately, civil association—and the rule of law that defines it—does not require a set of demonstrable, unambiguous, universal criteria by which to determine the *jus* of *lex*. Beyond the formal principles inherent in the idea of a legal order, Oakeshott argues, civil association "may float upon the acknowledgement that the considerations in terms of which the *jus* of *lex* may be discerned are neither arbitrary, nor uncontentious, and that they are the product of a moral experience which is never without tensions and internal discrepancies." The criterion by which the *jus* of *lex* is determined is thus historical, the reflection of the historic moral-legal self-understanding of the association. But Oakeshott is quick to delimit the scope of this historic moral-legal imagination: it must be "focused narrowly upon the kind of conditional obligations a law may impose" and should not concern itself with more general moral considerations such as those relating to the motives of our actions. Civil prescriptions "should not conflict with a prevailing educated sensibility capable of distinguishing between the conditions of 'virtue,' the conditions of moral association ('good conduct'), and those which are of such a kind that they should be imposed by law ('justice')" (*OH*, 143, 159–61).

On the relationship more generally between morality and the law—which had been famously debated by Lord Devlin and H. L. A. Hart in connection with the Wolfenden Report on Homosexual Offences and Prostitution—Oakeshott has remarkably little to say, though it is perhaps possible to extrapolate his views from his discussion of justice. Given his claim that the laws of civil association ought to reflect the historic moral-legal understanding of its members, it would seem that he rejects the view of liberal thinkers such as John Rawls, Ronald Dworkin, and Bruce Ackerman that civil law should be totally neutral with respect to the substantive moral beliefs of citizens. The noninstrumental character of civil laws certainly precludes their being designed to promote moral virtue or religious salvation as substantive purposes of civil association. But noninstrumentality is not exactly the same thing as neutrality. It seems perfectly possible for noninstrumental civil laws to reflect what might be called the "standards of civility" that belong to any particular civil association, the substantive beliefs a community might have about what constitutes decent or indecent, acceptable or unacceptable, offensive or inoffensive, behavior.[12]

Oakeshott's views on distributive justice, a subject much discussed between 1970 and 1980 in the writings of Rawls, Dworkin, Ackerman, and Robert Nozick, are more easily ascertained. He argues simply that there is no place for distributive justice in civil association. Distributive justice posits a substantive condition as the end of civil association and thus contradicts its defining noninstrumental character. With respect to Rawls's and Ackerman's theories of distributive justice, Oakeshott writes: "Here *lex*, if it exists at all, is composed of regulations understood in terms of the consequences of their operation and as guides to a substantive state of affairs" (*OH*, 156 n13; see also *OHC*, 153 n1). Rawls and Ackerman thus theorize a kind of enterprise association; they are engaged in exploring that idiom of the modern state to which Oakeshott gives the name "teleocracy." This suggests that their own interpretation of what they are doing may be mistaken. Claiming to have expelled teleology and utilitarianism from their theories, they seem to end up incorporating these commitments implicitly.

I will have more to say about Oakeshott's relationship to contemporary liberal theory at the end of this chapter. A more pressing concern for us now is whether his conception of civil association represents anything real. Is it possible to distinguish civil association from enterprise association as sharply as Oakeshott does? Does it make any sense to speak of civil association and civil law as purely procedural, noninstrumental, and devoid of purpose? Much of the criticism of Oakeshott's theory of civil association has revolved around questions such as these that suggest the theory may be excessively formalistic. Is it?

Let us begin with the question whether the distinction between civil association and enterprise association is as sharp as Oakeshott draws it: Isn't civil association dedicated to *some* purpose in the final analysis, whether it be peace, security, freedom, or (as the Declaration of Independence has it) life, liberty, and the pursuit of happiness? Oakeshott clearly does not think so, but his argument is brief and needs to be fleshed out. With respect to peace and security, he simply asserts that they "are not substantive purposes and they do not specify enterprise association" (*OHC*, 119; see also *OH*, 161). What he seems to mean is that peace and security are not specific substantive satisfactions sought for their own sakes but, rather, formal conditions that make possible the pursuit of specific substantive satisfactions. While peace and security certainly characterize civil association, they do not remotely specify extrinsic purposes to be pursued through specific policies requiring substantive performances of citizens. Of course, there are circumstances in which peace and security do become the substantive purposes of an association—civil war, for example, or foreign invasion—but in these circumstances a civil association is transformed into at least a partial enterprise association.

Oakeshott follows a roughly similar strategy in rejecting freedom and happiness as substantive purposes for civil association. The freedom inherent in agency is, of course, something that civil association does not compromise, even when the association takes on a compulsory form. But this freedom hardly constitutes a substantive purpose that civil association pursues by formulating specific policies or requiring substantive actions on the part of agents: "this 'freedom' does not follow as a consequence of [civil association]; it is inherent in its character" (*OH*, 161). As for happiness, it is not a substantive end or purpose at all but, like Hobbes's "felicity," a formal condition "in which the performances of agents continuously achieve their wished-for outcomes (whatever they may be)." As Oakeshott wittily observes: "I cannot *want* 'happiness'; what I want is to idle in Avignon or hear Caruso sing" (*OHC*, 53–54). If, on the other hand, by "happiness" is meant the substantive condition of "prosperity," then we no longer have to do with civil association at all but with enterprise association.

We may now turn to the other version of the formalism charge, which questions whether civil laws are or can be as procedural or purposeless as Oakeshott suggests. Judith Shklar argues, for example, that civil laws are never purely procedural, never completely without purpose; even the rules of the road, which come closest to meeting this formalistic criterion, have the purpose of preventing collisions.[13] And John Liddington, while conceding that the law of contracts may have the formal character Oakeshott ascribes to *lex*, argues that criminal laws are never merely procedural but always prohibit substantive actions. Alluding to Oakeshott's claim that a criminal law does not forbid killing or lighting a fire but only killing "murderously" or lighting a fire "arsonically," Liddington contends that any substantive law could be redescribed in such adverbial terms: a law limiting free speech, for example, might be reformulated as prohibiting speech engaged in "bourgeoisly."[14]

As compelling as these objections seem to be on the surface, they misconstrue what Oakeshott means by the noninstrumental or nonpurposive character of civil law. Clearly, he cannot mean that civil laws are not designed to achieve certain purposes—for example, preventing fires, murders, or collisions. But civil laws do not operate by imposing these purposes on agents or prescribing specific actions to bring them about. Rather, they operate by imposing adverbial conditions to be taken into account as agents pursue purposes of their own choosing.[15] Shklar's example of the rules of the road, contrary to her intention, provides a helpful illustration. That such rules are designed to prevent collisions does not make them purposive in the way Oakeshott means to exclude. The rules of the road do not impose destinations on drivers; they merely impose conditions to be taken into account by drivers whatever their

destinations may be. This is manifestly not the case with laws that prohibit agents from engaging in "bourgeois" (or, for that matter, "unbour-
geois") conduct. It is, of course, possible to redescribe such instrumental
laws in adverbial terms, as Liddington demonstrates, but this only
proves that any insight can be rendered useless by being taken too
literally.

That civil association constitutes a *possible* mode of human relationship, however, does not exhaust the questions that might be asked of it.
Perhaps an even more important question is whether it constitutes a
practicable or desirable mode of association in the circumstances of the
modern state. As Oakeshott himself puts this question: Is civil association anything "more than a logician's dream, a kind of geometrical
theorem composed of related axioms and propositions?" And if it is,
"what place, if any, does it occupy in the practical engagement in the
history of human hopes, ambitions, expectations or achievements in
respect of association" (*OH*, 149). It is to this historical question that he
turns in the third essay of *On Human Conduct*.

The Equivocal Character of the Modern State

In the second essay of *On Human Conduct*, Oakeshott was concerned
with civil association as an ideal mode of human relationship or "ideal
character." Civil association was said to be "ideal," not because it represents some sort of utopia, but because it is an identity that has been
"abstracted from the contingencies and ambiguities of actual goings-on
in the world" (*OHC*, 109). Throughout the second essay—most obtru-
sively in his substitution of archaic Latin expressions for the ambiguous vocabulary of modern politics—Oakeshott never allows us to forget
that civil association is an *ideal* mode of association, in no way to be
mistaken for a specification of a modern state. Why he adopts this
somewhat formalistic procedure only becomes clear in the third essay
of *On Human Conduct*, where we learn that the modern state is not a
single, unambiguous type of human association but, rather, a tension
between two different types, namely, civil association and enterprise
association.

The historical inquiry Oakeshott pursues in the third essay harks
back to the related inquiries from the 1950s: *The Politics of Faith and
the Politics of Scepticism*, "The Masses in Representative Democracy,"
and the Harvard lectures on *Morality and Politics in Modern Europe*.
Here, as there, he specifies that the theme he is concerned with is the
mode of association that a modern European state constitutes, a theme

closely correlated with the beliefs that have been entertained about the office and engagements of government. This theme must be sharply distinguished from two others in the history of European political thought. The first concerns the beliefs in virtue of which a government is recognized to have authority; beliefs relating to the "constitutions" of government. Though an important theme for political reflection, the constitutional shape of a government has nothing to do with the character of its engagements or the mode of association of the state. The second theme that lies outside of Oakeshott's historical inquiry concerns the power of government, reflection on which can be found in the administrative histories of European states. Though this theme is certainly connected with that of the mode of association of a state and the office of its government, it nevertheless is not identical with it and can therefore be left to one side (*OHC*, 188–97).

Borrowing from the great German legal historian Otto von Gierke and his English pluralist disciple Frederick Maitland, Oakeshott organizes his historical account around two ideas or analogies that were used in late medieval Europe to understand the puzzling and exceedingly ambiguous experience of the emergent state: the ideas of *societas* and *universitas*. Drawn from Roman private law, these words denoted two different modes of association. A *societas* was an association in which the members were joined, not in the pursuit of a common purpose, but only in the common acknowledgment of noninstrumental rules of conduct, and they remained distinct despite being associated. A *universitas*, by contrast, was an association dedicated to a common purpose in which the members gave up some of their distinctness and constituted in important respects a single "person"; examples included churches, guilds, and universities. These terms pointed to two very different understandings of the state. A state understood in terms of *societas* was a state governed by noninstrumental law—what Oakeshott in the second essay called a "civil association" and here refers to as a "nomocracy." A state understood in terms of *universitas*, on the other hand, was an enterprise association in which law was understood to be instrumental to a purpose and government to be the management of that purpose—a "teleocracy" (*OHC*, 199–206).

Oakeshott's central contention is that, while neither of these understandings taken alone can identify the modern state, when taken together they provide a framework within which the complexity and essential ambiguity of the modern state can be understood. "A state," he writes, "may perhaps be understood as an unresolved tension between the two irreconcilable dispositions represented by the words *societas* and *universitas*. . . . [T]he thesis I propose to explore is that it is this tension, and not any of the others celebrated in current political discourse, which is central to the understanding of a modern European state and the office of its government" (*OHC*, 200–1).

He begins his account with the intimation of this tension in the late medieval realm. On the side of *societas* there was the ruler of the medieval realm, the king, who was understood to be, not a *grand seigneur* or a lordly proprietor of a domain, but the keeper of the peace and (eventually) the supreme dispenser of justice. The slow extension of royal justice in the medieval realm resulted finally in its being recognized as an association in terms of law. But there were other features of the medieval realm that suggested *universitas* as the most appropriate analogy in terms of which to understand it. An "unpurged relic of lordship" remained embedded in the office of the king. And the sacerdotal authority that originally belonged to the Pope and included the power to control education (*potestas docendi*) was gradually appropriated by the civil ruler (*OHC*, 206–13, 218–24).

From the medieval realm Oakeshott turns to the modern state, which emerged in the sixteenth century as a "sovereign" association, emancipated from external authorities (such as the Church and the Empire) as well as from competitors at home (such as ungovernable feudal magnates), and capable of emancipating itself from its legal past (wherein lay its imprescriptibility). Such sovereignty did not, however, determine whether a state was to be understood as a *societas* or a *universitas* (*OHC*, 224–29). Among the circumstances that pointed to the former analogy was the rather miscellaneous composition of most European states. Each was composed of a vast variety of persons and peoples differing in language, beliefs, customs, aspirations, and purposes. None even came close to constituting a "community," much less a "nation." A European state, at least on the surface, did not appear to be very promising material from which to make a *universitas* (*OHC*, 233–34).

In addition to this somewhat external circumstance, Oakeshott mentions another that pointed even more decisively in the direction of understanding a state in terms of *societas*: the emergence of a new disposition or sentiment in Europe, namely, the disposition to cultivate and enjoy individuality, or, as he puts it here, the disposition to cultivate and enjoy the freedom inherent in agency. As he did in his earlier writings, Oakeshott argues that toward the end of the Middle Ages, as the bonds of corporate, communal life were beginning to dissolve, the unsought and inescapable freedom inherent in agency came to be regarded not simply as a condition to be acquiesced in but as "the emblem of human dignity . . . a condition for each individual to explore, cultivate, to make the most of, and to enjoy as an opportunity rather than suffer as a burden." He insists that this historic disposition to cultivate the freedom inherent in agency is not to be confused with the mindless "worship of nonconformity" or any sort of romantic doctrine of subjective self-expression. The self here is not something "natural," opposed to history, civilization, and reflective consciousness; it is the "outcome of education." Nor does this disposition have anything to do with so-called "bourgeois morality" or "possessive individualism." In an acerbic footnote, Oakeshott writes that the contraction of the history of the disposition of individuality "into a history of so-called 'bourgeois market society capitalism' is a notorious botch. . . . [A]nyone who believes the Frère Jean des Entommeurs or Parini were 'possessive individualists,' or that it was of such persons that Pico della Mirandola, or Montaigne or Hobbes or Pascal or Kant or Blake or Nietzsche or Kierkegaard wrote is capable of believing anything" (*OHC*, 234–42).[16]

He concludes his account of the disposition to cultivate individuality and value autonomy by asserting that it "has remained the strongest strand in the moral convictions of the inhabitants of modern Europe." He also claims that the understanding of the state that has corresponded to this moral disposition is that of *societas*. "Individuals" are defined by their desire to make choices for themselves, and it is only in a state understood as a *societas* that this freedom to make one's own choices is not compromised. Invoking St Augustine, Oakeshott refers to the state thus understood as a "*civitas peregrinus*: an association, not of pilgrims travelling to a common destination, but of adventurers each responding as best he can to the ordeal of consciousness in a world composed of others of his kind." And he mentions a number of notable writers in whom this understanding of the state can be found. For some of these writers—Machiavelli, Locke, the American Founders, Burke, Paine, Ranke, Tocqueville, and Acton—the understanding of the state as a *societas* appears at the level of an "implicit assumption." In other writers—Montesquieu, for example—there is a more explicit recognition and characterization of this understanding of the state. Finally, there is a select group of political philosophers who not only explicitly identify the state as a *societas* but also seek to theorize this identity in terms of its postulates. Among the most accomplished of these writers Oakeshott names Bodin, Hobbes, Spinoza, Kant, Fichte, and Hegel (*OHC*, 242–52).

Of particular interest are the seven or so pages of discussion he devotes to Hegel's *Philosophy of Right*—the longest discussion to be found anywhere in Oakeshott's writings of the philosopher for whom, apart from Hobbes, he most consistently expresses admiration. Starting with Hegel's understanding of human beings in terms of *der Geist* and *der Wille*, and treating the dialectical transition from "abstract right" to *Sittlichkeit* and from *bürgerliche Gesellschaft* (unfortunately translated as "civil society") to *der Staat*, Oakeshott provides a magisterial reconstruction of Hegel's political philosophy that largely assimilates it to his own conception of nonpurposive civil association (*OHC*, 256–63). Though serving as a useful corrective to excessively metaphysi-cal and communitarian readings of Hegel, Oakeshott's interpretation is ultimately too formalistic, neglecting Hegel's critique of the atomism and narrow self-interest of traditional liberal theory and his attempt to provide the liberal state with a more exalted purpose than mere security of life, liberty, and property.

One point on which Oakeshott decisively breaks with Hegel is the latter's belief that the historic disposition to cultivate the freedom inherent in agency—a disposition traceable to Christianity and postulated by *der Staat*—was coming more and more to characterize European peoples. Like Tocqueville, Kierkegaard, Burckhardt, Nietzsche, and so many other moralists who came after Hegel, Oakeshott discerns another disposition, besides the one to be an individual, at work in the modern world, a disposition evoking an altogether different understanding of the state than that corresponding to *societas*. Where Hegel sees a linear evolution toward a rational state in which the subjective freedom of individuals is developed to its highest degree, Oakeshott sees a tension between *societas* and *universitas*. It is to the intimations of the latter in the modern state that he turns next.

There were several circumstances in early modern Europe that promoted the reading of the state in terms of *universitas*. Oakeshott mentions the emergence of states from landed estates over which kings exercised "lordship," the creation and extension of a central administrative apparatus in modern states, colonial adventure and administration, and finally the experience of war. With respect to the last, he repeats the conviction expressed in a number of his postwar writings: "War in a modern European state is the enemy of civil association" (*OHC*, 266–74).

But the circumstance on which Oakeshott lays the greatest emphasis in his account of the state as *universitas* is the emergence of what he calls the "individual *manqué*." We are familiar with this character from "The

Masses in Representative Democracy," and Oakeshott's description of him here is no less ideologically charged than in his earlier discussion. The individual *manqué* found the freedom resulting from the dissolution of communal life in late medieval Europe burdensome rather than exciting. He "had needs rather than wants" and "sought a patron rather than a ruler, a lord able to make for him the choices he was unable to make for himself rather than a law to protect him in the adventure of choosing." Resentful of his more enterprising counterpart and manipulated by unscrupulous "leaders," the individual *manqué* eventually came to be transformed into the militant "anti-individual," who "united with his fellows in a revulsion against distinctness." The only kind of state that could accommodate such a morally and emotionally impoverished character, Oakeshott maintains, was a *universitas* in which individual choice was removed and a uniform substantive condition imposed on all (*OHC*, 274–78).

Oakeshott goes on to explore several different idioms of teleocratic belief in the history of modern European politics: the state as a cultural and religious *universitas* (e.g. Geneva); as "enlightened" government (e.g. Cameralism); and as a therapeutic enterprise (also explored by Foucault). But by far the most important idiom of teleocratic belief in modern Europe has been the Baconian one in which the state is understood as a corporate enterprise for the exploitation of the resources of the earth. Here the state is recognized not simply to *have* an economy but to *be* an economy. Though this technological vision of the state received its earliest and most audacious expression in Bacon's *New Atlantis*, it remained for Bacon's successors—St Simon, Fourier, Owen, Marx, the Webbs, and Lenin—to develop fully what Oakeshott calls (in yet another Latin expression) a *civitas cupiditatis*. It is clear from everything he has written, both early and late, that Oakeshott regards this technological or economistic understanding of the state as the most serious opponent to civil association in the modern world. All the current versions of the state as a *universitas*, he comments, are "indelibly Baconian" (*OHC*, 279–311; see also *OH*, 153).

Oakeshott does not underestimate the impact the understanding of the state in terms of *universitas* has had on modern politics, writing that it "has bitten deep into the civil institutions of modern Europe," compromising its civil law and corrupting its vocabulary of civil discourse. But his anxiety over this development does not lead him to formulate a one-sidedly pessimistic and monolithic account of modernity of the sort found in thinkers such as Heidegger, Strauss, Voegelin, Marcuse, Foucault, and MacIntyre. As deep as the teleocratic understanding of the state has bitten into the civil tradition of modern Europe, it has never characterized a European state without qualification: "no regime in the five centuries of modern European history has ever 'represented' this understanding of the state entirely without qualification; the voice of civil association has, here and there, sunk to a whisper, but nowhere has it been totally silenced" (*OHC*, 312–13).

In this regard, Oakeshott is particularly concerned to refute the view that there is an inevitable trend toward a teleocratic understanding of the state. This view has taken two forms. In the first, the trend toward teleocracy is seen to be historically inevitable on account of recent, mainly technological, developments. But Oakeshott argues that this belies the real sources of teleocratic belief. The disposition in favor of teleocracy did not emerge in response to recent developments in technology, global economics, or world population; it "has been a feature of the European political consciousness for more than five centuries." The second form of the view that the modern state is evolving toward an unambiguous *universitas* has a romantic, rather than a rationalistic, root. It sees the history of modern Europe as a long, painful effort to recover the warmth and intimacy of communal ties that modern individualism, cold and possessive, reputedly destroyed. But Oakeshott rejects the identification of civil association with "atomized society," "capitalism," "possessive individualism," or "bourgeois morality." These parodies of the individualist tradition have allowed the longing for community to appear respectable and even dominant in our political tradition when in fact it is merely a "relic of the servility of which it is proper for European peoples to be profoundly ashamed." Continuing in this prescriptive vein, Oakeshott adds: "no European alive to his inheritance of moral understanding has ever found it possible to deny the superior desirability of civil association without a profound feeling of guilt" (*OHC*, 320–23; *OH*, 154).

It is clear that Oakeshott prefers civil association or *societas* to the understanding of the state as an enterprise association or *universitas*. The question is whether he has a rational basis for this preference. The one argument he reiterates throughout *On Human Conduct* in defense of his preference is that the state, as a compulsory association, cannot wholly take the form of an enterprise association or *universitas* without affronting the inherent freedom or autonomy of its members (see *OHC*, 115, 119, 157–58, 206, 264, 298, 316–17, 319). But this argument seems to relate only to the extreme or totalitarian case. What about all the in-between cases of states that combine *universitas* and *societas*, enterprise association and civil association, policy purposes and noninstrumental laws, in multifarious ways? What guidance can Oakeshott's distinction provide here?

To be fair, Oakeshott recognizes that modern states must combine elements of both civil association and enterprise association, *societas* and *universitas*. Though *societas* and *universitas* do not have an inherent need of one another, in the modern European state they have had a contingent need of one another. National defense (especially in times of war), for example, has necessarily required that civil association be qualified and the state transformed into at least a partial enterprise association (*OH*, 155, 162–64). The problem of providing for the poor has demanded a similar qualification of civil association. While Oakeshott has little to say about this latter problem, he does invoke Hegel's view that it is necessary to exercise "a judicious 'lordship' for the relief of the destitute," if only to remove the temptation the poor might have to transform the state into an industrial *universitas* with equal rations and assured benefits for all (*OHC*, 304 n3).

But once Oakeshott has opened the door to these sorts of qualifications of civil association, it is not clear why he should not entertain others that might ultimately serve to preserve or strengthen civil association in our current historical circumstances. It is true that we must, as Oakeshott warns, "distinguish between unavoidable qualification and corruption or vacillation" (*OH*, 162), but that would still seem to leave a wide field for inquiry into the contingent enabling conditions of civil association. What, for example, is the effect of radical economic inequality on the fate of civil association? In what way does the individuality that civil association celebrates lead to the malady Tocqueville designated by the term "individualism"—the tendency on the part of individuals in a liberal democracy to retreat into the private circle of their family and friends without connection or a sense of responsibility to the larger community around them? How might the corrosive effects of both capitalism and liberal individualism be counteracted—not in order to create a *solidarité commune*, but simply in order to render the ideal of civil association viable?

While Oakeshott does not necessarily exclude these sorts of considerations of what might be called the social and cultural preconditions of civil association, he nowhere reflects on them very seriously; and he certainly does not allow them to cloud the austere purity of his conception of civil association. This is a real weakness in his political philosophy and sharply differentiates it from that of his mentor, Hegel, who did think deeply about these "sociological" issues and, in the *Philosophy of Right*, delineated a complex network of institutions and associations to mediate between the particular interest of the individual and the universal interest of the state. Oakeshott's refusal to enter on these contingent considerations also differentiates him from American neo-conservatives, who, influenced by Tocqueville, worry about the self-undermining character of liberal individualism and the erosion of the social and cultural preconditions of a free society.

In the end, *On Human Conduct* does not give us much guidance on the practical and contingent question of what the appropriate mixture of civil association and enterprise association, *societas* and *universitas*, should be in a modern state. Nevertheless, it does provide a powerful philosophical statement of what is most important and valuable in our political tradition and thus serves as a necessary prolegomenon to reflection on the difficult practical and contingent issues mentioned above. In one place, Oakeshott states that, in order to defend the "notable invention" of civil association, "we must get to know, not only our opponents, but ourselves more exactly than we do at present; we must defend our position with reasons appropriate to it" (*RP*, 460). *On Human Conduct* makes an important contribution to this task of getting to know ourselves more exactly, distinguishing the liberal ideal of civil association not only from egalitarian misunderstandings of it, but also from conservative misunderstandings of it in terms of a "minimal state" (Nozick), a "free enterprise state" (Milton Friedman), and "the saddest of all misunderstandings" (Hayek's) in which civil association is properly identified as association in terms of noninstrumental rules of conduct, but defended instrumentally "as the mode of association more likely than any other to promote and go on promoting the satisfaction of our diverse and proliferant wants" (*RP*, 456–57). In its freedom from the cant and clichés of both the left and the right, *On Human Conduct* represents a remarkable achievement.

Civil Association and Contemporary Liberal Theory

On Human Conduct appeared fours years after the publication, in 1971, of John Rawls's *A Theory of Justice*, the book that more than any other set the terms for the debate over liberalism for the next 30 years. Apart from a few oblique and isolated references (see *OHC*, 147, 153n.1; *OH*, 156n.13), Oakeshott does not directly engage with Rawls's work or the mountain of commentary and criticism that it spawned.[17] Though he remained remarkably in touch with developments in political philosophy until late in life—at the age of 81 we find him writing excitedly to one of his correspondents that "I have just got a book by a Harvard chap, M. J. Sandel, called *Liberalism and the Limits of Justice*. I saw a review of it which made me think it was the book I have been waiting for"[18]—in many ways his theory of civil association sprang out of earlier political-philosophical debates belonging to postwar, and even interwar, Europe. Nevertheless, the theory speaks profoundly to many of the issues that run through late twentieth-century liberal theory from Rawls to Richard Rorty and deserves to be brought into more explicit dialogue with this later context.

As noted in chapter 1, in his recent *Two Faces of Liberalism*, John Gray usefully distinguishes two different types of liberalism: the first, exemplified by Rawls, is based on rational consensus and animated by the Enlightenment hope for a universal regime; the second, exemplified by Oakeshott and Berlin and referred to by Gray as *modus vivendi* liberalism, views liberal institutions as a means to peaceful coexistence among different ways of life.[19] This classification captures an essential difference between Rawls and Oakeshott, one that is even more fundamental than the obvious difference in their views on distributive justice.

The quest for a consensus on what constitutes justice in a liberal society informs Rawls's political philosophy both early and late. In *A Theory of Justice*, Rawls tried to achieve such consensus by constructing a "neutral" standpoint—the original position—from which individuals could agree on just institutions by abstracting from their own particular interests and conceptions of the good. But critics argued that the design of the original position, far from being neutral, seemed to presuppose a particular conception of the good that was liberal, individualistic, and voluntaristic. Over the next couple of decades, Rawls recast his theory to make it more hospitable to the fact of modern pluralism, formulating a "political" liberalism that no longer rested on any controversial comprehensive doctrine about human nature or the human good. This "political liberalism" was understood to be based, not on a mere Hobbesian *modus vivendi*, but on a genuinely moral, "overlapping consensus" that could be affirmed by a variety of "reasonable" comprehensive moral, religious, and philosophical doctrines. Again, though, critics wondered whether Rawls had succeeded in emancipating his liberalism from dependence on comprehensive moral views. Though more subtly than in *A Theory of Justice*, his political liberalism still seemed to rest implicitly on a comprehensive moral doctrine—encoded in the ambiguous term "reasonable"—that was not as hospitable to moral diversity and pluralism as Rawls supposed.

At one point, Rawls invokes Oakeshott's distinction between civil association and enterprise association to clarify his own distinction between an association governed by a political conception of justice and an association governed by a comprehensive moral, religious, or philosophical doctrine.[20] But there are important differences between Oakeshott's notion of civil association and Rawls's notion of political liberalism. Perhaps the most important one is that civil association, unlike political liberalism, is not directed to achieving moral consensus on justice in conditions of moral pluralism. More than justice, the theory of civil association is concerned with the idea of authority, which does not presuppose agreement on justice or morality. This is the Hobbesian aspect of Oakeshott's thought. As we have seen, though, Oakeshott, unlike Hobbes, does not identify authority with justice and recognizes that *lex* may be considered in terms of *jus*. Unlike Rawls, though, Oakeshott is unwilling to specify *jus* any further than as the "prevailing educated sensibility" of the members of a civil association. Justice is not to be understood as the product of an "overlapping consensus," some sort of neutral consideration that one can affirm regardless of one's comprehensive moral outlook. Oakeshott would no doubt regard such an "overlapping consensus"—not to mention the even more ambitious political consensus sought by Rawls's deliberative democratic progeny[21]—as a piece of rationalistic legerdemain, succeeding only by covertly suppressing certain points of view and characterizing them as "unreasonable."

There is one other important difference between Oakeshott's idea of civil association and Rawls's idea of political liberalism. As part of his effort to emancipate liberalism from comprehensive moral doctrines and prevent it from becoming a sectarian creed, Rawls denies that political liberalism rests on the ideals of autonomy and individuality found in writers such as Kant and Mill. Oakeshott, on the other hand, directly ties the actualization of civil association in the modern European state to the emergence of the historic disposition of individuality, "the appearance of subjects who desire to make choices for themselves, who find happiness in doing so and who are frustrated in having choices imposed upon them" (*MPME*, 84). His heroes in this regard, as we have seen, include not only Kant but also Montaigne, Pascal, Cervantes, Hobbes, Blake, Kierkegaard, and Nietzsche; Mill, on the other hand, he sees as a more equivocal figure with respect to the morality of individuality. The important point, though, is that, unlike Rawls, Oakeshott does not conceive of *societas* as neutral with respect to the good life or independent of the historic ideals of individuality and autonomy.

Given his rejection of Rawlsian neutrality, one might be tempted to place Oakeshott in the camp of communitarian critics of Rawls such as Michael Sandel. But despite his enthusiastic response to *Liberalism and the Limits of Justice*, and despite Sandel's classification of him as a communitarian critic of liberalism,[22] Oakeshott's political philosophy has little in common with Sandelian communitarianism. This can be most easily seen by contrasting Sandel's simplistic account in *Democracy's Discontent* of the steady rise of proceduralism and the steady decline of civic republicanism in American history with Oakeshott's wonderful evocation in *On Human Conduct* of the miscellaneous and fragmentary circumstances of early modern Europe: "The history of modern Europe is the history of Poland only a little more so" (*OHC*, 186). In a way that Sandel does not, Oakeshott appreciates the reasons why civic republicanism is no longer appropriate in modern pluralistic circumstances. He does not deny—nor, it must be said, does Rawls—that civic virtue is necessary in a civil association; only that such civic virtue will be the same in modern liberal democracies as it is in small, homogeneous republics. He mentions moderation, self-restraint, courage, integrity, and even pride as important moral qualities for the denizens of modern liberal democracies to have (see *RPML*, 115; *OHC*, 180).

Of course, it is not only communitarians like Sandel who criticize the aspiration to neutrality in contemporary liberal theory. Perfectionist liberals like Stephen Macedo, Joseph Raz, and William Galston also reject neutrality, but instead of abandoning liberalism they try to show that it rests on its own distinctive conception of the good life. Macedo is interesting in this regard because he refers to Oakeshott at several points in his argument. In the first place, he rejects Oakeshott's critique of rationalism while defending the liberal demand (as epitomized by Jeremy Waldron) that "the social order should in principle be capable of explaining itself at the tribunal of each person's understanding." In this regard, he endorses the Rawlsian attempt to "seek justifications that are widely acceptable to reasonable people with a broad range of moral and philosophical commitments and interests." But unlike Rawls, Macedo does not conceal liberalism's substantive and comprehensive moral commitments. He argues that liberalism postulates and ought to promote the fundamental ideal of autonomy, which he associates with self-conscious, critical reflection on morality and politics. Strangely, he invokes Oakeshott's notion of autonomy, but in fact his moral ideal is far more Millean than Oakeshottian: "The ideal liberal personality is characterized by reflective self-awareness . . . [and] a willingness to engage in self-criticism . . . Liberal politics calls upon every citizen to reason about the law for himself . . . The liberal ideal of autonomy calls upon persons to take up a similar, critically interpretive attitude toward their own characters, commitments, and lives."[23] This is precisely the attitude Oakeshott condemned as rationalistic in his earlier writings and would regard, if adopted as a goal for politics, as destructive of the liberty and individuality that civil association is meant to protect.

The most ambitious and philosophically elaborate statement of perfectionist liberalism is Joseph Raz's *The Morality of Freedom*. Like Macedo, Raz identifies autonomy, which he defines as a life "spent in the pursuit of acceptable and valuable projects and relationships," as the fundamental ideal that liberalism seeks to promote. Against anti-perfectionist thinkers like Rawls, he argues that the pursuit of this substantive and comprehensive ideal by the state is perfectly compatible with moral pluralism. It is doubtful, though, whether it is compatible with Oakeshott's understanding of liberty and individuality. Like many other liberal thinkers, Oakeshott would be worried by Raz's claims that "the goal of all political action [is] to enable individuals to pursue valid conceptions of the good and to discourage evil or empty ones"; that the state is properly concerned with considerations that go beyond "narrow morality" and touch on "the art of life," considerations that instruct "people how to live and what makes for a successful, meaningful, and worthwhile life"; and that the "autonomy principle permits and even requires governments to create morally valuable opportunities and to eliminate repugnant ones."[24] Raz tries valiantly to bring these paternalistic claims into line with more conventional liberal prohibitions, even arguing that they are compatible with a modified "harm principle" that prohibits the use of coercive measures for perfectionist purposes, but his efforts in this regard are ultimately incoherent and unconvincing. In the end, his perfectionist liberalism turns out to be far more perfectionist than liberal.

The opposite might be said of William Galston's perfectionist liberalism in *Liberal Purposes*. The book begins by boldly stating that the "liberal state cannot be understood along Michael Oakeshott's lines as a purposeless civil association structured by adverbial rules. Like every other form of political community, the liberal state is an enterprise association. Its distinctiveness lies not in the absence but, rather, in the content of its public purposes."[25] But Galston's argument for a purposive state turns out to be much more modest than this statement suggests. The theory of the liberal good that he develops is extraordinarily thin, comprising such basic items as life, liberty, and the development of basic capacities. And he further dilutes it by saying that liberalism is distinguished by its "reluctance to move from [its substantive conception of the good] to full-blown public coercion of individuals."[26] Galston's real target in the book is the neutralist liberalism of Rawls, Dworkin, and others that prohibits government from promoting or favoring the virtues of character necessary to maintain a liberal polity—moderation, self-restraint, law-abidingness, tolerance, and so forth. Oakeshott would not necessarily disagree with the claim that liberalism, or civil association, needs certain virtues in order to maintain itself, though (as we have seen) he does not pay sufficient attention to what Galston calls "the cultural preconditions of liberalism." All of this, however, relates more to the prudential means of preserving liberalism than to what defines it as a distinctive form of association. On this latter point, there is more agreement between Oakeshott and Galston than the latter supposes, which is why it is not altogether surprising or inconsistent to find Galston in his next book defending the "diversity state" (rather than the purposive state) and subscribing to the pluralism of Isaiah Berlin.[27]

This brings us to the other side of Gray's classificatory scheme: to the *modus vivendi* liberalism whose chief contemporary exemplars are Berlin and Oakeshott. Gray is right to classify the liberal theories of these two thinkers together, especially in contradistinction to the more rationalistic liberalism of Rawls and his followers (and even some of his critics). Nevertheless, there are important differences between their liberal theories that are worth exploring in some depth, especially since Berlin's brand of liberal pluralism has of late elicited a great deal of interest and become widely influential. Gray himself is not unaware of these differences and ends up criticizing Oakeshott's political philosophy for lacking Berlin's appreciation of radical diversity and conflict.[28] My own interpretation cuts in a different way. Instead of seeing Oakeshott's liberalism as insufficiently pluralistic, I argue that Berlin's pluralism is ultimately incapable of grounding or specifying liberalism in a theoretically satisfying way.

The dominant idea of Berlin's philosophy is, of course, value pluralism. Almost everything he wrote, from "The Hedgehog and the Fox" (1953) to "The Pursuit of the Ideal" (1988), involves an attack on monism—the belief that all human ends are ultimately compatible and fit into a single whole—and a defense of pluralism—the belief that "ends equally ultimate, equally sacred, may contradict each other, that entire systems of value may come into collision without the possibility of rational arbitration."[29] So prevalent is this master dichotomy in Berlin's thought that it can become rather monotonous. And as many commentators have noted, though Berlin identifies with the fox who knows many things, he himself turns out to be something of a hedgehog who knows one big thing: that values are plural, and that rationalistic monism is a mistake.

In his celebrated essay "Two Concepts of Liberty," Berlin argues that his pluralistic conception of value somehow entails the negative liberty that liberalism aims to secure. In a world where ultimate ends collide and there is no "final solution," the freedom to choose takes on supreme importance. The "necessity of choosing between absolute claims" is "what gives value to freedom as . . . an end in itself."[30] As many commentators have noted, however, Berlin's argument from pluralism to liberalism does not really work. It is not clear why, in the face of radical pluralism, one would necessarily opt for satisfying as many goals as possible instead of pursuing a single goal; or why one would give priority to negative liberty over other, equally valuable goods. Gray argues that the ideal of liberalism based on negative liberty cannot simply be inferred from the meta-ethical thesis of pluralism; rather, it rests on the culturally specific value of choice-making. Radical pluralism must include the possibility of ways of life that do not value choice-making; it does not simply underwrite the rather specific values of individuality and autonomous choice that belong to liberalism.[31]

These criticisms of Berlin's attempt to link pluralism and liberalism have not gone unanswered. Several scholars have pointed to those places where Berlin seems to limit the range and scope of value pluralism: places where he suggests that there is "a minimum area of personal freedom" that must be preserved "if we are not to 'degrade our human nature,'" or where he speaks of a common moral horizon, along the lines of H. L. A. Hart's "minimum content of natural law," which serves as a lower bound on our behavior.[32] These scattered references to a common human nature and a common moral horizon, however, remain far too generic and minimal to ground liberalism or justify the priority of negative liberty over other political values. Historically there have been many societies that have fulfilled Berlin's criteria of minimal decency without necessarily elevating negative liberty or the value of choice-making to supreme importance. As Oakeshott brings out so well, it is in the historically specific disposition to value autonomous choice and individuality, not in some generic human nature or universal moral minimum, that the ground of liberal civil association should be sought. This more historicistic argument, occasionally recognized by Berlin but nowhere consistently developed,[33] represents a more coherent response to the question of the basis of liberalism than the attempt to ground it in the nonhistorical fact of pluralism.

Berlin is also less successful than Oakeshott in specifying the nature of liberal society. He characterizes liberal society chiefly in terms of negative liberty, but (as he himself recognizes) no society can simply be based on negative liberty. There must be limits to such liberty, there must be room for state action, and of course there must be limits to state action. Berlin, however, is not very specific about these limits. He indicates that liberty "must be weighed against the claims of many other values, of which equality, or justice, or happiness, or security, or public order are perhaps the most obvious examples." There is no foolproof method by which to adjudicate between these competing claims, so he leaves us with "Burke's plea for the constant need to compensate, to reconcile, to balance."[34] But this would seem to leave the precious negative liberty of liberal society significantly imperiled. Berlin seems to realize this and therefore argues that there "are some absolute barriers to the imposition of one man's will on another." But when it comes to defining what these absolute barriers are based on, he once again becomes vague:

> there must be some frontiers which nobody should be permitted to cross. Different names or natures may be given to the rules that determine these frontiers: they may be called natural rights, or the word of God, or natural law, or the demands of utility or of the "permanent interests of man"; I may believe them to be valid a priori, or assert them to be my own ultimate ends, or the ends of my society or culture. What these rules or commandments will have in common is that they are accepted so widely, and are grounded so deeply in the actual nature of men as they have developed through history, as to be, by now, an essential part of what we mean by being a normal human being. Genuine belief in the inviolability of a minimum extent of individual liberty entails some such absolute stand.[35]

None of this is very satisfying. Most of Berlin's difficulties stem from his understanding of liberalism in terms of the concept of negative liberty. Negative liberty, especially in the implausible Hobbesian-Benthamite form that he sometimes defends it, cannot really distinguish between various types of state action. All state action represents an encroachment on our negative liberty to pursue our wants and desires without obstruction. Thus Berlin is left with the criterionless and tragic balancing of liberty with other competing values. This is not the case with Oakeshott's theory of freedom, which provides both a more perspicuous understanding of the inviolable sphere of human liberty and a way to reconcile this liberty with civil authority, obligation, and law. When properly conceived of in the context of nonpurposive civil association, authority, obligation, and law do not appear as impediments to human liberty but as necessary conditions of it. Oakeshott thus supplies a criterion by which to distinguish different types of state action, depending on whether such action issues in nonpurposive, adverbial rules of conduct or in measures that are instrumental to a substantive purpose. We are not left with a tragic choice between freedom and other values such as equality, justice, security, and happiness; rather, we are given a conception of freedom that specifies just how these values are to be understood if they are to be rendered compatible with liberal life.

A writer who has provided a historicist interpretation of Berlin's liberalism and who has also invoked Oakeshott's ideal of civil association is Richard Rorty. Rorty sees Oakeshott, along with Dewey and Rawls, as a progenitor of the sort of antifoundationalist liberalism he himself espouses, someone who sought "to retain Enlightenment liberalism while dropping Enlightenment rationalism." He also embraces Oakeshott's notion of *societas*, the idea of a society "conceived as a band of eccentrics collaborating for purposes of mutual protection rather than as a band of fellow spirits united by a common goal." Rorty's own ideal of liberal society does indeed sound very Oakeshottian: a society that "has no purpose except freedom, no goal except a willingness to see how such encounters go and to abide by the outcome."[36] And this raises the question—the final one of this chapter—whether Oakeshott's political philosophy can be assimilated to Rortian antifoundationalism and postmodernism.

The short answer is no. Rorty is, of course, famous for his "strong" readings of other philosophers—it is not clear, for example, that either Dewey or Rawls fits his antifoundationalist paradigm—and this is certainly true of his reading of Oakeshott. He interprets Oakeshott's analogy of morality to language, for example, as a rejection of the morality-prudence distinction and as an identification of morality with the interests of the community, a mere matter of "we intentions."[37] It would be hard to find a cruder rendering of Oakeshott's argument in *On Human Conduct*, which in fact is concerned precisely to distinguish a moral practice from a prudential practice and to show that civil association belongs to the former category. Also, Rorty's blithe references to "bourgeois liberalism" and "the practices of rich North Atlantic democracies" blur what Oakeshott is careful to distinguish, namely, the noninstrumental practice of civil association and the instrumental practice of bourgeois capitalism.[38] Finally, there is nothing in Oakeshott to suggest that civil association or liberal society would be better off if "ironism"—the conviction that our central beliefs and deepest desires are merely contingent historical products—became universal and our culture became thoroughly postmetaphysical, "de-divinized," enlightened, and secular.[39] Oakeshott may pay insufficient attention to the moral and cultural preconditions of liberalism, but he is not perverse.

The most important difference between Oakeshott and Rorty lies in their respective conceptions of political philosophy. Oakeshott certainly agrees with Rorty that the task of political philosophy is not to lay "foundations" for liberal democracy. The task of political philosophy is not to *justify* our political institutions but to *articulate* our shared intuitions and beliefs about politics. In this respect, practice is prior to theory, and liberal democracy is prior to philosophy. But Oakeshott does not share Rorty's unproblematic attitude toward the practice they are both theorizing, namely, liberalism. I agree with the critic who says of Rorty that he "simply speaks globally about 'liberal democracy' without ever unpacking what it involves or doing justice to the enormous historical controversy about what liberal democracy is or ought to be."[40] Oakeshott in no way accepts Rorty's implication that "we" all have common intuitions about what liberal democracy means, nor does he assume that there is consensus about the nature of our political tradition. As we have seen, he regards our political tradition as profoundly ambivalent. And he arrives at his theory of civil association only by radically abstracting from the contingency and ambiguity of historical reality.

To state the difference as succinctly as possible: Oakeshott rejects Rorty's pragmatist understanding of philosophy. For Oakeshott, political philosophy is more than the mere expression or justification of current political opinion. While philosophy, owl-of-Minerva-like, comes after and reflects upon liberal democracy, it is not confined simply to mirroring our ordinary practical understanding of this historic practice. Philosophy represents a form of understanding that is radically distinct from, and in certain respects superior to, our ordinary practical self-understanding. For Rorty, on the other hand, there is no such division between theory and practice, and as a consequence political philosophy becomes indistinguishable from political opinion. Thus, when he speaks of liberal democracy, he leaves the term in roughly the same muddle that he found it in the practical realm. And when he later tries to clarify it, he provides a rather banal list of political opinions that currently pass for "social democracy."[41] Ultimately, such pragmatism leads to a historicism in which philosophy becomes indistinguishable from history, "cultural anthropology," "literary criticism," and politics.[42] It is just such historicism, which denies the autonomy of philosophy and reduces it to history and praxis, that Oakeshott avoids. Insofar as he does, his theory of civil association retains more than transitory interest.

Epilogue

Though it is important to situate Oakeshott in the context of contemporary political theory, there is also—it must be admitted—something slightly artificial about it. The sweep of his philosophical vision, the depth of his understanding of history, and his brilliant literary style all make it difficult to fit him comfortably into the narrow confines of contemporary academic political theory. Mark Lilla has recently commented that "what passes for political philosophy or political theory in the university today is almost wholly lacking in the psychological and historical insight [Isaiah] Berlin tried to give readers,"[1] and the same might be said of Oakeshott. Berlin and Oakeshott both belong to that great generation of political thinkers—which also includes Strauss, Arendt, Hayek, and Aron—who came of age between the wars and were formed by the political, intellectual, and philosophical culture of the first half of the twentieth century. In all of these writers, there is a historical and philosophical depth and perspective that is often missing in even the best contemporary political theory.

In the somewhat longer perspective of twentieth-century philosophy and political philosophy, then, what significant or enduring contributions has Oakeshott made that might also serve as inspirations or aids to reflection in the twenty-first century? There are two such contributions that I would highlight.

The first has to do with the theory of civil association that we examined at length in the previous chapter. In this theory, as we have seen, Oakeshott elaborates an essentially liberal political order—characterized by liberty, individuality, and the rule of law—but without recourse to some of the more questionable ethical and metaphysical assumptions that have haunted liberalism since its inception. By conceiving of civil association as a moral, noninstrumental practice, he succeeds in purging liberalism of the materialism or economism that, from Locke to Hayek, has sometimes appeared to constitute its moral ideal. He also manages to free liberalism from its reliance on controversial metaphysical notions such as natural rights and atomism. This latter aspect of Oakeshott's theory of civil association reveals his connection to the Hegelian tradition of political thought and its attempt to overcome the opposition between individual and government, will and law, freedom and authority, that has marked liberal thought from Hobbes to Mill. The nonmetaphysical character of Oakeshott's theory suggests certain affinities to Rawls's political liberalism; but unlike Rawls, Oakeshott offers a rich, historical conception of the self and an imaginative interpretation of the human condition to support his liberal politics. In this respect—and this respect only—Oakeshott resembles John Stuart Mill, who also sought to enrich liberalism with a romantic conception of individuality, albeit (I would argue) less consistently, less imaginatively, and less poetically than Oakeshott.

Oakeshott's second great contribution to twentieth-century thought lies in the area of the theory of knowledge. In *Experience and Its Modes*, Oakeshott was concerned to show that the world of knowledge consisted in a multiplicity of autonomous modes—history, science, and practice—none reducible to or authoritative over any other. It was partly against the claim of science to be the model of knowledge that he wrote, but also (and more distinctively) against the assertion that practice is the primordial or authoritative mode of human activity. Against the two great reductivisms of the twentieth century—positivism and "pragmatism"—Oakeshott defended the autonomy of history, philosophy, and (later) poetry. And he eventually pictured his pluralistic understanding of the world of knowledge in the appealing and oft-invoked image of the "conversation of mankind."

While referring to different realms, Oakeshott's ideas of civil association and the conversation of mankind are nevertheless linked in several ways. First, both ideas reflect Oakeshott's consistent opposition to the reductive and Gnostic tendencies of our age and his profound appreciation of the variety, contingency, diversity, and complexity of human life. Second, the theory of culture embodied in the conversation of mankind in many ways provides the ultimate justification for Oakeshott's ideal of civil association. The gift of civil association—as Oakeshott once remarked in relation to Hobbes—is a negative gift, making possible the more substantial fulfillment of human beings in the realm of culture understood as a conversation (see *HCA*, 79). For Oakeshott, self-realization is to be found in culture—preeminently in a poetized religiosity—not in politics. This idea is nowhere more clearly or beautifully expressed than in his writings on education.

By viewing Oakeshott's idea of civil association in relation to his conception of the conversation of mankind, one sees that he offers us a political philosophy that is more comprehensive and inspiring than, say, the political liberalism of Rawls, and possibly any other liberalism since Mill's. Indeed, it shares something with the older, grander tradition of political philosophy, whose task Oakeshott once defined as "the relation of political life, and the values and purposes pertaining to it, to the entire conception of the world that belongs to a civilization" (*HCA*, 4). This may strike some as too highfalutin' for a skeptic like Oakeshott, but part of the fascination of his philosophy lies precisely in the tension it contains between the grand and the modest, the elevated and the deflationary, idealism and skepticism.

As attractive as Oakeshott's political philosophy is, it is not without its difficulties. Perhaps the most serious of these is Oakeshott's failure to address the crucial, if contingent, question of the social, economic, and cultural conditions necessary for the maintenance and perpetuation of civil association. Though he is careful not to identify civil association with capitalism, it is not clear what he thinks about the corrosive effects on civil life of large inequalities in the distribution of wealth, resources, and opportunities. Nor does he reflect anywhere very deeply on the problem that Tocqueville designated by the term "individualism": the problem of individuals in a liberal democracy retreating into the private circle of their family and friends without connection or a sense of responsibility to the larger community around them; a problem that is exacerbated by the preoccupation with material acquisition and comfort in Western democracies. Also unlike Tocqueville (and Hegel), Oakeshott nowhere brings out the crucial role that the intermediate institutions of civil society play by lifting individuals out of their isolation and identifying them with the political whole. It is not that he is unaware of the pathologies of modern liberal life—one need only recall the devastating portrait he draws in "A Place of Learning" of the shallow and meaningless world in which children now grow up—but his austere conception of philosophy forbids him from considering these contingent "sociological" issues.

This points to one other difficulty with Oakeshott's philosophy that has raised its head at several points in this study: it concerns his hermetic distinction between theory and practice. On the one hand, the sharpness with which Oakeshott draws the distinction between theory and practice allows him to maintain the autonomy of modes of discourse such as philosophy, history, and even poetry and to protect them from the politicization that has posed their greatest danger in the twentieth century. On the other hand, by drawing the distinction so sharply, he deprives these modes of discourse, especially philosophy and poetry, of having any bearing on the way we live our lives. This seems to misdescribe not only philosophy and art in general but Oakeshott's political philosophy in particular. By this I do not mean to make the banal point that Oakeshott covertly slips all sorts of value judgments and normative prescriptions into his supposedly pure theoretical statements. Rather, what I want to underline is that Oakeshott's political philosophy, by deepening our understanding of ourselves and our political tradition, can have a subtle but profound effect on the way we think about and conduct our politics. As he once put it in one of his less hermetic moments, the poet and the philosopher are able "to mitigate a little their society's ignorance of itself" and thereby save it from the "last corruption that can visit a society," namely, the "corruption of its consciousness" (*RPML*, 95–96). Oakeshott's political philosophy surely does this.

Notes

Preface

1. Adam Gopnik, "Man without a Plan," *New Yorker*, 21 October 1996, 194–98.
2. Alan Wolfe, "The Revolution That Never Was," *New Republic*, 7 June 1999, 34–42.
3. David Brooks, "Arguing with Oakeshott," *New York Times*, 27 December 2003, 35.

1 The Oakeshottian Voice

1. I derive this account of Oakeshott's funeral from Josiah Lee Auspitz's wonderful memoir, "Michael Oakeshott: 1901–1990," *American Scholar* 60 (1990–91), 351–52.
2. Noel Annan, *Our Age: English Intellectuals between the World Wars—A Group Portrait* (New York: Random House, 1990), 5.
3. Quoted from a letter in Robert Grant, *Oakeshott* (London: Claridge Press, 1990), 11–12.
4. Oakeshott, "Personal Retrospect: By a Scholar," in *St. George's School, 1907–67: A Portrait of the Founders*, ed. H. W. Howe (Harpendon, 1967), 14–18, excerpts from which can be found in Grant, *Oakeshott*, 119–20. On the cult of games and the stultifying atmosphere of English public schools at this time, see Annan, *Our Age*, ch. 3.
5. There are only two references to Heidegger in Oakeshott's published writings: *OHC*, 26; and *OH*, 20. An undated notebook that seems to come from Oakeshott's LSE days contains notes on *Being and Time*

focusing on Heidegger's view of history as concerned with the "living past" of "present *Dasein*" (BLPES, File 3/5).
6. Sorley wrote a letter to Oakeshott on 24 October 1925 congratulating him on his election to a Fellowship at Caius: "It gives you the chance you need to work out your views and to apply them. I had the privilege of reading your dissertation and I am convinced that you have both the insight and the power of producing a work of genuine value on political philosophy. If you have been ploughing a lonely furrow, you have learned to plough both deep and straight" (BLPES, File 6/1).
7. On Barker's idealism, see Julia Stapleton, *Englishness and the Study of Politics: The Social and Political Thought of Ernest Barker* (Cambridge: Cambridge University Press, 1994).
8. Oakeshott, Review of *The Christian Religion and its Competitors Today*, by A. C. Bouquet, *Journal of Theological Studies* 27 (1926), 440.
9. BLPES, File 1/1/7. The envelope enclosing these lectures has "My First Course of Lectures" written on it and bears the date 1935. Nevertheless, the *Cambridge University Reporter* of 10 January 1928 lists Oakeshott as giving a set of lectures on The Philosophical Approach to Politics in the Lent term of 1928. He repeated the course in the Lent term of 1929.
10. L. Susan Stebbing, Review of *Experience and Its Modes*, in *Mind* 43 (1934): 405.
11. R. G. Collingwood, Review of *Experience and Its Modes*, in *Cambridge Review* 55 (1933–34): 249–50.

12. Found in Shirley Letwin's notes for a projected biography on Oakeshott, BLPES, File 15/8/1.

13. From an interview with Annan, conducted by Shirley Letwin, BLPES, File 15/5/2.

14. Joseph Needham, "A New Civilization?" *Cambridge Review* 57 (1935–36): 325–26.

15. Oakeshott, "Official Philosophy," *Cambridge Review* 56 (1934–35): 108–9.

16. Annan, *Our Age*, 5. Oakeshott taught a course on The Political Theory of Karl Marx in the Easter terms of 1938 and 1939 (*Cambridge University Reporter*, 12 July 1937 and 30 July 1938). This casts some doubt on Eric Hobsbawm's claim in his recent memoir, *Interesting Times: A Twentieth-Century Life* (London: Allen Lane, 2002), that Munia Postan was the only person in the Cambridge history department of the thirties "who knew Marx, Weber, Sombart and the rest of the great central and East Europeans" (203).

17. Lawrence uses the phrase in relation to the industrialist Gerald Crich in *Women In Love*. I owe this reference to Robert Grant, "Michael Oakeshott," in *Cambridge Minds*, ed. Richard Mason (Cambridge: Cambridge University Press, 1994), 236 n2.

18. Peregrine Worsthorne, *Daily Telegraph*, 21 December 1990, 19.

19. Interview with Mark Ramadge, BLPES, File 15/5/1.

20. From an interview with Oakeshott, conducted by Ken Minogue in 1988, BLPES, File 8/4.

21. Annan, *Our Age*, 387.

22. Friedrich Hayek, *The Road to Serfdom* (Chicago: University of Chicago Press, 1944), 216–19.

23. Oakeshott, "The BBC," *Cambridge Journal* 4 (1950–51): 551.

24. R. H. S. Crossman, "The Ultimate Conservative," *New Statesman and Nation*, 21 July 1951, 60.

25. Oakeshott's handwritten introduction can be found in BLPES, File 1/3. Berlin's BBC lectures have recently been published under the title *Freedom and Its Betrayal: Six Enemies of Human Liberty*, ed. Henry Hardy (Princeton: Princeton University Press, 2002).

26. This comment comes from Noel Annan's account of the lecture in *Our Age*, 401. Other accounts of the episode can be found in Michael Ignatieff, *Isaiah Berlin: A Life* (New York: Henry Holt, 1998), 205; Norman Podhoretz, "A Dissent on Isaiah Berlin," *Commentary* 107 (February 1999): 30–31.

27. Berlin writes about this lunch in two letters to Shirley Letwin, one dated 24 November 1991 (in which Berlin refers to Oakeshott's "bitchy introduction"), the other dated 20 April 1993; BLPES, File 15/5/3. In the letter of 20 April 1993, Berlin writes, "I realize that I agree with quite a lot of what [Oakeshott] thought, but I think it violently exaggerated—a curious word to use about so impressionist a writer. . . . I do admit that after I heard him at the Carlyle Club, his views seemed to me a little deranged."

28. Annan, *Our Age*, 401.

29. This change of attitude toward Burke was signaled in a review Oakeshott wrote of Russell Kirk's *The Conservative Mind*, in *Spectator* 193 (1954): 472–74.

30. Irving Kristol, "America's 'Exceptional Conservatism,'" in Kristol, *Neoconservatism* (New York: Free Press, 1995), 373–80.

31. Wolfe, "The Revolution That Never Was."

32. With the exception of "The Study of Politics in a University," these writings on education have been collected by Timothy Fuller in one volume, *The Voice of Liberal Learning: Michael Oakeshott on Education* (London and New Haven: Yale University Press, 1989).

33. Annan, *Our Age*, 395.

34. See Kenneth Minogue, "Michael Oakeshott and the History of Political Thought Seminar," *Cambridge Review* 112 (October 1991): 114–17. I myself was a student in the seminar in 1978–79.

35. Oakeshott's speech at the launch of *Politics and Experience: Essays Presented to Professor Oakeshott on the Occasion of his Retirement*, ed. P. King and B. Parekh (Cambridge: Cambridge University Press, 1968), BLPES, File 1/3.

36. Oakeshott's speech at his retirement dinner at the Garrick Club, June 1969, BLPES, File 1/3.

37. This letter is quoted by Minogue in his memoir, "Michael Oakeshott (1901–1990)," *LSE Magazine* 3 (Summer 1991): 17.

38. One might also want to include here the posthumously published manuscript, *The Politics of Faith and the Politics of Scepticism*, which appears to have been written sometime between 1952 and 1954. Though Oakeshott analyzes the modern European political consciousness in this work as a divided consciousness, the poles of that consciousness are understood in terms of the politics of faith and the politics of passion instead of, as in the later writings, the morality of individuality and the morality of the anti-individual. This is a transitional work—Burke, for example, is positively invoked throughout—which is perhaps why Oakeshott never published it.

39. See Alan Ryan, "Liberalism," in *A Companion to Contemporary Political Philosophy*, ed. Robert E. Goodin and Phillip Pettit (London: Blackwell, 1993), 291–311.

40. John Gray, *The Two Faces of Liberalism* (Cambridge: Polity Press, 2000), 2.

41. Obituary in *The Times*, 22 December 1990.

42. Quoted in several of the obituaries; see *Daily Telegraph*, 21 December 1990; *Guardian*, 22 December 1990.

43. Transcript of "England's Pragmatist," BBC Radio 3 documentary, 23 December 2001, 4.

44. See John Gray's comment in ibid., 8.

45. Letter from Oakeshott to Patrick Riley, quoted in Patrick Riley, "Michael Oakeshott, Philosopher of Individuality," *Review of Politics* 54 (1992): 664.

2 Idealism

1. R. B. Braithwaite, "Philosophy," in *University Studies: Cambridge, 1933*, ed. Harold Wright (London: Ivor Nicholson and Watson, 1933): 1–32.

2. Indeed, Wittgenstein wrote a letter to the editor of *Mind* disclaiming the views Braithwaite attributed to him; see Ludwig Wittgenstein, *Philosophical Occasions, 1912–1951*, ed. James Klagge and Alfred Nordmann (Indianapolis: Hackett, 1993), 156–57.

3. F. H. Bradley, *The Principles of Logic*, 2nd edn. (London: Oxford University Press, 1922), vol. 1, 34.

4. The chapter entitled "The Search for a *Datum*," in Harold Joachim, *Logical Studies* (Oxford: Clarendon, 1948), is perhaps the most thorough of the idealist critiques of the empiri-

cist notion of immediate experience; see also Joachim's inaugural lecture as Wykeham Professor of Logic at Oxford, *Immediate Experience and Mediation* (Oxford: Clarendon Press, 1919).

5. F. H. Bradley, *Essays on Truth and Reality* (Oxford: Clarendon Press, 1914), 209–10. Bosanquet makes a similar criticism of the simile of the foundations of knowledge in *Knowledge and Reality* (London: Kegan Paul, Trench, 1885): "Knowledge is not like a house built on a foundation which is previously laid, and is able to remain after the house has fallen; it is more like a planetary system with no relations to anything outside itself, and determined in the motion and position of every element by the conjoint influence of the whole" (331).

6. See Bradley's essay "On Truth and Coherence," in *Essays on Truth and Reality.*

7. Harold Joachim, *The Nature of Truth* (Oxford: Clarendon Press, 1906), 69–77. On the concrete universal, see Bernard Bosanquet, *The Principle of Individuality and Value* (London: Macmillan, 1927), Lecture 2; also *Implication and Linear Inference* (London: Macmillan, 1920), 4–17.

8. F. H. Bradley, *The Presuppositions of Critical History*, ed. Lionel Rubinoff (Chicago: Quadrangle Books, 1968), 93.

9. Bosanquet, *Knowledge and Reality*, 332 n1.

10. F. H. Bradley, *Appearance and Reality: A Metaphysical Essay*, 2nd edn. (Oxford: Clarendon Press, 1930), 430.

11. Bradley, *Essays on Truth and Reality*, 10.

12. Bradley, *Appearance and Reality*, 236, 250–51.

13. Bradley, *Essays on Truth and Reality*, 12, 15.

14. F. H. Bradley, *Ethical Studies*, 2nd edn. (Oxford: Clarendon Press, 1927), 193.

15. Bradley, *Appearance and Reality*, 482.

16. Ibid., ch. 15.

17. Bradley, *Principles of Logic*, vol. 2, 590–91.

18. See especially Joachim, *Logical Studies*, 11–12, 275–92.

19. Bertrand Russell, *The Problems of Philosophy* (Oxford: Oxford University Press, 1998), 82.

20. See Thomas Baldwin, "Moore's Rejection of Idealism," in *Philosophy in History: Essays on the Historiography of Philosophy*, ed. Richard Rorty, J. B. Schneewind, and Quentin Skinner (Cambridge: Cambridge University Press, 1984): 357–74. Baldwin writes: "Moore's famous paper 'The Refutation of Idealism' contains no argument that an idealist need have been disturbed by" (357).

21. See, for example, Bradley, *Appearance and Reality*, 128–29, ch. 21.

22. Wilfrid Sellars, *Empiricism and the Philosophy of Mind* (Cambridge: Harvard University Press, 1997), 78–79.

23. Richard Rorty, "Knowledge and Acquaintance," *New Republic*, 2 December 1996, 49.

24. For the history of the study of politi-cal science at Cambridge in the late nineteenth and early twentieth centuries, see Stefan Collini, Donald Winch, and John Burrow, *That Noble Science of Politics: A Study in Nineteenth-Century Intellectual History* (Cambridge: Cambridge University Press, 1983), especially chapter 7 on the Comparative Method, chapter 9 on Sidgwick, and chapter 11 on the evolution of the political science curriculum at Cambridge from 1860 to 1930.

25. In an undated manuscript entitled "An Essay on the Relations of Philosophy, Poetry, and Reality" (BLPES, File 1/1/33), Oakeshott takes a different view, arguing that ultimate reality can only be grasped by the intuitive forms of experience of poetry and religion, not by reason or philosophy: "Philosophy may ask 'What is Truth?', and may strive to discover it by the way of pure reason. It is a long and noble struggle, doubt and difficulty beset its way, and even in human matters the probability of error is always greater than that of truth. But amidst all its desire after an intellectual proof, there have been men who have *known* all the time, who have been friends of the truth. These are the poets and mystics, who have desired only a union with Reality, an intuitive knowledge of God for its own sake, caring not at all for proofs and arguments, who claim to have *lived* in the light of that Eternal Day which knows no evening and no dawn" (69–70). This appears to be a very early essay, possibly from Oakeshott's university days.

26. On the D Society, see Tim Fuller's introduction to *RPML*, 4. On theological modernism, especially at Oxford, see James Patrick, *The Magdalen Metaphysicals: Idealism and Orthodoxy at Oxford, 1901–1945* (Macon, Ga.: Mercer University Press, 1985), xviii, xxv–xxix, 18–20. Oakeshott wrote a highly critical review of a book by Bishop Charles Gore, the arch-traditionalist against whom the modernists often defined themselves; see *Journal of Theological Studies* 28 (1927): 314–16.

27. See Bradley, *Ethical Studies*, 155, 233–34, 314.

28. On Needham's theological modernism, see Patrick, *The Magdalen Metaphysicals*, xxvii, 87 n31, 100.

29. Oakeshott, Review of *Science, Religion, and Reality*, edited by Joseph Needham, *Journal of Theological Studies* 27 (1926): 319. In the ensuing years, Webb and Oakeshott conducted a lively exchange on the subject of the historical element in Christianity; see Clement Webb, *The Historical Element in Religion* (London: George Allen and Unwin, 1935), esp. chs 2 and 3, and Oakeshott's review in *Journal of Theological Studies* 37 (1936): 96–98. On Webb's idealism and theological outlook, see Patrick, *The Magdalen Metaphysicals*, ch. 2.

30. Oakeshott studied theology in Marburg in 1923–24 and possibly again in 1925, when Bultmann was a young professor there. Oakeshott's fellow D Society member J. S. Boys-Smith, who is thanked in the preface to *EM*, also studied in Marburg in the 1920s and was influenced by Bultmann's theology. Oakeshott was a great admirer of Schweitzer's *Quest for the Historical Jesus*.

31. Oakeshott amplifies these ideas on the identity of Christianity in a review of *The Making of the Christian Mind*, by G. G. Atkins, *Journal of Theological Studies* 31 (1930): 203–8.

32. Oakeshott, Notebook XIII (date on flyleaf March 1964), BLPES, File 2/1/18, 126.

33. Tim Fuller reports that Pater's *Gaston de la Tour* was one of Oakeshott's favorite books; "The Work of Michael Oakeshott," *Political Theory* (August 1991): 328.

34. Walter Pater, *The Renaissance*, ed. Adam Phillips (Oxford: Oxford University Press, 1986), 152.

35. In *The Principle of Individuality and Value*, Bosanquet, too, uses the notion of a "world" to characterize the concrete universal; and he, too, dis-

tinguishes the unity that belongs to a world from that which belongs to a class (31–41).

36. Bradley, *Appearance and Reality*, 404, 432.

37. T. M. Knox, Review of *Experience and Its Modes*, in *Oxford Magazine* 52 (1934): 552.

38. Bradley, *Appearance and Reality*, ch. 24; also pp. 433–34, 440–41, 492–97.

39. R. G. Collingwood, *Speculum Mentis, or The Map of Knowledge* (Oxford: Clarendon Press, 1924), 15.

40. Collingwood, Review of *Experience and Its Modes*, in *Cambridge Review* 55 (1933–34): 249–50.

41. Collingwood also emphasizes the concrete character of historical fact: "the concrete universal is the daily bread of every historian; and the logic of history is the logic of the concrete universal" (*Speculum Mentis*, 221).

42. Herbert Butterfield, *The Whig Interpretation of History* (London: George Bell, 1931), 10, 11. Both Butterfield and Oakeshott were members of the Cambridge Junior Historians Society in the 1920s and '30s; on this, see Luke O'Sullivan, *Oakeshott on History* (Exeter: Imprint Academic, 2003), 55.

43. Collingwood's description of the breakdown of history in *Speculum Mentis* (231–39, 244–46) parallels Oakeshott's second criticism. For Collingwood, the absolute and concrete whole of historical fact can never be achieved; "all history is fragmentary." This destroys any hope of discovering *was eigentlich geschehen ist* and ultimately leads to historical skepticism.

44. See, for example, Leo Strauss's definition of historicism in *What Is Political Philosophy?* (Glencoe, Ill.: Free Press, 1959): "Historicism is the assertion that the fundamental distinction between philosophical and historical

questions cannot in the last analysis be maintained" (57).

45. T. M. Knox, Preface to *The Idea of History*, by R. G. Collingwood (Oxford: Clarendon Press, 1946), x. This historicistic tendency is most evident in Collingwood's later works, *An Autobiography* (1939) and *An Essay on Metaphysics* (1940).

46. Oakeshott, Review of *The Idea of History*, in *English Historical Review* 62 (1947), 85.

47. Bradley, too, rejected the empiricist understanding of natural science; see *Appearance and Reality*, ch. 22 and pp. 434–40.

48. On the transformation of the world perceived in nature into the mathematical world of the natural sciences, see Edmund Husserl, *The Crisis of the European Sciences and Transcendental Phenomenology*, trans. David Carr (Evanston, Ill.: Northwestern University Press, 1970), 23–59.

49. Oakeshott's account of science as experience *sub specie quantitatis* is similar to the account of physics offered by the eminent Cambridge astronomer, Arthur Eddington, in "The Domain of Physical Science," in *Science, Religion, and Reality*, ed. Joseph Needham.

50. Oakeshott does not mention the science of politics in *EM*, but in a review of G. E. G. Catlin's *The Principles of Politics*, in *Cambridge Review* 51 (1929–30): 400, he discusses the possibility of such a science.

51. See, for example, William Dray, *Philosophy of History* (Englewood Cliffs: Prentice-Hall, 1964), 9–10; "Michael Oakeshott's Theory of History," in *Politics and Experience*, ed. P. King and B. C. Parekh, 24–30.

52. See Bradley, *Ethical Studies*, esp. 231–35, 313–35; *Essays on Truth and Reality*, esp. 6–7, 441–42.

3   Political Philosophy

1. This phrase appears in the post-humously published manuscript, "Political Philosophy," in *RPML*, 138–55. Though the essay bears no date, a reference to J. D. Mabbott's *The State and the Citizen*, which was published in 1948 and reviewed twice by Oakeshott, suggests that it was written somewhere around 1948–49.

2. R. G. Collingwood, *An Autobiography* (Oxford: Clarendon Press, 1939), 167.

3. Perry Anderson, "The Intransigent Right at the End of the Century," *London Review of Books*, 24 September 1992, 7.

4. Bradley, *Ethical Studies*, 193.

5. Cahal B. Daly, *Moral Philosophy in Britain from Bradley to Wittgenstein* (Dublin: Four Courts Press, 1996), 147, 148.

6. Ludwig Wittgenstein, *Philosophical Investigations*, 3rd edn., trans. G. E. M. Anscombe (Oxford: Blackwell, 2001), Part I, 124.

7. Collingwood, *An Autobiography*, 47–49, 147.

8. There has been some controversy over the dating of this manuscript. Fuller suggests 1946 largely on the basis of Oakeshott's reference to having recently "had occasion to consider the writings of Hobbes" (*RPML*, 119). But Oakeshott wrote two lengthy reviews of Hobbes literature in 1935 and 1937. And it doesn't make much sense that he would virtually repeat what he had already published almost a decade before.

9. Oakeshott published two shorter reviews of Strauss's book, one in *Cambridge Review* 58 (1936–37): 150, and the other in *Philosophy* 12 (1937): 239–41.

10. See Leo Strauss, *The Political Philosophy of Hobbes: Its Basis and Its Genesis* (Chicago: University of Chicago Press, 1952), vii–viii, 15–57. Strauss later came to see Machiavelli, and not Hobbes, as the originator of modern political philosophy (see the Preface to the American edition).

11. T. H. Green, "Lecture on 'Liberal Legislation' and Freedom of Contract,'" in Green, *Lectures on the Principles of Political Obligation and Other Writings*, ed. Paul Harris and John Morrow (Cambridge: Cambridge University Press, 1986), 199.

12. Green, *Principles of Political Obligation*, 20.

13. Bernard Bosanquet, *The Philosophical Theory of the State and Related Essays*, ed. Gerald F. Gaus and William Sweet (South Bend: St Augustine's Press, 2001), 2, 258. The quote from Green comes from the essay "On the Different Senses of 'Freedom' as Applied to Will and to the Progress of Man," in *Principles of Political Obligation*, 233.

14. Bosanquet, *Philosophical Theory of the State*, 86.

15. Ibid., 120–21.

16. Ibid., 132–34.

17. Ibid., 156.

18. Ibid.

19. Ibid., ch. 8.

20. Oakeshott, Review of *Bernard Bosanquet's Philosophy of the State: A Historical and Systematical Study*, by B. Pfannenstil, *Philosophy* 11 (1936): 482.

21. Ibid., 482.

22. Oakeshott, Review of *The State and the Citizen*, by J. D. Mabbott, *Mind* 58 (1949): 378–79. Oakeshott also reviewed this book in *Cambridge Journal* 2 (1948–49): 316, 318.

23. J. D. Mabbott, *The State and the Citizen* (London: Hutchinson, 1948), ch. 8.

24. Oakeshott, Review of Mabbott, 386.

25. See Green, *Principles of Political Obligation*, 39–45; Bosanquet, *Philo-*

sophical *Theory of the State*, 122–24. A more positive attitude toward Hobbes is suggested in Collingwood's *New Leviathan* (1942).

26. Anderson, "The Intransigent Right at the End of the Century," 7.

27. Oakeshott, Review of *Natural Law and the Theory of Society*, by Otto Gierke, translated with an Introduction by Ernest Barker, *Cambridge Review* 56 (1934–35): 11.

28. On Barker's love of compromise between contending theoretical perspectives, see Stapleton, *Englishness and the Study of Politics*, 9–10.

29. See Strauss, *Political Philosophy of Hobbes*, ch. 7; C. B. Macpherson, *The Political Theory of Possessive Individualism* (London: Oxford University Press, 1962); "Hobbes's Bourgeois Man," in *Hobbes Studies*, ed. Keith Brown (Cambridge: Harvard University Press, 1965), 169–83.

30. Louis MacNiece, *Autumn Journal* (London: Faber and Faber, 1939), 53.

31. Oakeshott largely repeats this indictment of politics in the original version of his Introduction to *Leviathan* (Blackwell's Political Texts, 1946), deleting it in the revised version in *HCA*: "For politics, we know, is a second-rate form of human activity, neither an art nor a science, at once corrupting to the soul and fatiguing to the mind, the activity either of those who cannot live without the illusion of affairs or those so fearful of being ruled by others that they will pay away their lives to prevent it" (lxiv).

32. R. G. Collingwood, *The Principles of Art* (Oxford: Clarendon Press, 1938), 336. Oakeshott's review appears in *Cambridge Review* 59 (1937–38): 487. On Oakeshott's appropriation of Collingwood's notion of the "corruption of consciousness," see Glenn Worthington, "The Voice of Poetry in Oakeshott's Moral Philosophy," *Review of Politics* 64 (spring 2002): 308–9.

33. See Collingwood, *The Principles of Art*, 292–99, and Oakeshott's review, 487.

4 Rationalism

1. For Ryle, see "Knowing How and Knowing That," *Proceedings of the Aristotelian Society* 46 (1945–46): 1–16; *The Concept of Mind* (London: Hutchinson, 1949), ch. 2. For Polanyi, see *Science, Faith and Society* (Chicago: University of Chicago Press, 1964); *Personal Knowledge* (Chicago: University of Chicago Press, 1958); *The Tacit Dimension* (New York: Doubleday, 1966).

2. Munia Postan makes this mistake in "The Revulsion from Thought," *Cambridge Journal* 1 (1947–48): 395–408. So does Karl Popper in "Towards a Rational Theory of Tradition," in *Conjectures and Refutations: The Growth of Scientific Knowledge* (London: Routledge and Kegan Paul, 1963), 121. In a letter to Popper on 23 January 1948, Oakeshott clarified that "when I argue against rationalism, I do not argue against reason. Rationalism in my sense is thoroughly unreasonable. That reason has a place in politics I do not doubt at all, but what I mean by Rationalism is the doctrine that nothing else has a place in politics" (quoted in O'Sullivan, *Oakeshott on History*, 134).

3. On the Cartesian roots of constructivist rationalism, see the chapter on "Individualism: True and False," in Hayek's *Individualism and Economic Order* (Chicago: University of Chicago Press, 1948). For criticism

of the view that wartime planning should be taken as a model for peacetime society, see Hayek, *The Road to Serfdom*, 2, 206.

4. Hayek, *The Road to Serfdom*, 218–19.

5. Friedrich A. Hayek, *The Constitution of Liberty* (Chicago: University of Chicago Press, 1960), 404.

6. Kristol, "America's 'Exceptional Conservatism,' " 378.

7. G. W. F. Hegel, *Elements of the Philosophy of Right*, ed. Allen Wood, trans. H. B. Nisbet (Cambridge: Cambridge University Press, 1991), 22.

8. See Strauss's characterization of "the crisis of modernity" in "The Three Waves of Modernity," in *An Introduction to Political Philosophy: Ten Essays by Leo Strauss*, ed. Hilail Gildin (Detroit: Wayne State University Press, 1989), 81–82.

9. Peter Winch, *The Idea of a Social Science and Its Relation to Philosophy* (London: Routledge and Kegan Paul, 1958), 54–65.

10. Michael Walzer makes this criticism in *Interpretation and Social Criticism* (Cambridge: Harvard University Press, 1987), 28–29.

11. Hanna Pitkin, "The Roots of Conservatism: Michael Oakeshott and the Denial of Politics," *Dissent* 20 (1973): 518.

12. Crossman, "The Ultimate Conservative," 60–61. Gray, in *Two Faces of Liberalism*, 32–33, 53, provides a recent version of the second criticism.

13. Hayek, *Constitution of Liberty*, 398.

14. Gertrude Himmelfarb, "The Conservative Imagination: Michael Oakeshott," *American Scholar* (summer 1975): 417–18. In a letter to Noel O'Sullivan on 28 July 1975, Oakeshott remarked about this article that "when [Himmelfarb] starts talking of the 50's and 60's [her

article] relapses into a peculiar kind of American fantasy."

15. From a personal letter Gadamer wrote to Richard Bernstein, reprinted in Bernstein's *Beyond Objectivism and Relativism: Science, Hermeneutics, and Praxis* (Philadelphia: University of Pennsylvania Press, 1985), 263–64.

16. J. W. N. Watkins, "Political Tradition and Political Theory," *Philosophical Quarterly* 2 (1952): 336.

17. Oakeshott, "*Rationalism in Politics*: A Reply to Professor Raphael," *Political Studies* 13 (1965): 90.

18. "Political Discourse" not only echoes the ideas of Oakeshott's 1965 "Reply to Professor Raphael" but also follows closely the argument made in his article "Political Laws and Captive Audiences," in *Scaling the Wall: Talking to Eastern Europe*, ed. G. R. Urban (London: Spottiswoode, 1964), 291–302, all of which argues for a composition date in the mid-1960s.

19. Oakeshott wrote a highly critical review of Kirk's *The Conservative Mind*, in *Spectator* 193 (1954): 472, 474. The review encapsulates the basic point of view of "On Being Conservative."

20. On American conservatism, see George H. Nash, *The Conservative Intellectual Movement in America since 1945* (New York: Basic Books, 1976), esp. chs 2, 3, 6, 8, and 11.

21. Oakeshott, Review of *The New Science of Politics*, by Eric Voegelin, *Times Literary Supplement*, 7 August 1953, 504.

22. See Hayek, "Individualism: True and False," 25–27.

23. Alfred Cobban, "The Decline of Political Theory," *Political Science Quarterly* 68 (September 1953): 321–37; J. W. N. Watkins, "Is Political Philosophy Dead?" *Encounter* 10

(June 1958): 57–67; Isaiah Berlin, "Does Political Theory Still Exist?" in *Philosophy, Politics and Society (Second Series)*, ed. Peter Laslett and W. G. Runciman (Oxford: Basil Blackwell, 1962), 1–33.

24. *Philosophy, Politics and Society*, ed. Peter Laslett (Oxford: Basil Blackwell, 1956), vii.

25. T. D. Weldon, *The Vocabulary of Politics* (Harmondsworth: Penguin, 1953), 9.

26. Irving Kristol, "A Philosophy for Little England," *Encounter* 7 (July 1956): 85, 86.

27. Ernest Gellner, *Words and Things: A Critical Account of Linguistic Philosophy and a Study in Ideology* (London: Victor Gollancz, 1959). Ved Mehta provides a lively journalistic account of the controversy raised by Gellner's book in *Fly and the Fly-Bottle: Encounters with British Intellectuals* (Boston: Little, Brown and Company, 1962), chs 1–2.

28. T. D. Weldon, "Political Principles," in *Philosophy, Politics and Society*, ed. Laslett, 22.

29. Oakeshott, Review of *The Vocabulary of Politics*, by T. D. Weldon, *Spectator*, 9 October 1953, 405–406; Review of *The Concept of Mind*, by Gilbert Ryle, *Spectator*, 6 January 1950, 21–22.

30. Winch, *The Idea of a Social Science*, 3.

31. Oakeshott, Review of *Dominations and Powers*, by George Santayana, *Spectator*, 2 November 1951, 578.

5   The Conversation of Mankind

1. Hobbes, *Leviathan*, ch. 15.

2. F. R. Leavis, "The Idea of a University," in Leavis, *Education and the University: A Sketch for an 'English School'*, New Edition (London: Chatto and Windus, 1948). See also an early version of this essay, "Why Universities?" *Scrutiny* 3 (1934–35): 117–32.

3. Walter Moberly, "The Universities," *Cambridge Journal* 3 (1949–50): 195–213.

4. F. R. Leavis, "Two Cultures? The Significance of Lord Snow," reprinted in Leavis, *Nor Shall My Sword: Discourses on Pluralism, Compassion and Social Hope* (London: Chatto and Windus, 1972): 41–74.

5. See quote from the Robbins Report in Leavis's essay "Luddites? Or There Is Only One Culture," in *Nor Shall My Sword*, 99.

6. See Leavis, "The Idea of a University" and "Why Universities?"

7. Annan, *Our Age*, 397.

8. This passage, quoted on p. 297 of *EM*, can be found in Rainier Maria Rilke, *Erzählungen und Skizzen aus der Frühzeit* (Leipzig: Insel-Verlag, 1928), 280.

9. Pater, *The Renaissance*, 153.

10. Oakeshott's linking of poetry with religion goes all the way back to the early "Essay on the Relations of Philosophy, Poetry, and Reality" (BLPES, File 1/1/33), though there these two "intuitive" forms of experience are seen as providing not merely intense practical satisfaction but access to ultimate reality.

11. Walter Pater, *Appreciations* (Oxford: Basil Blackwell, 1967), 61–62.

12. Collingwood, *Principles of Art*, 29.

13. Ibid., 336.

14. Pater, *Appreciations*, 61–62.

15. Edward Bullough, "'Psychical Distance' as a Factor in Art and an Aesthetic Principle," in *Aesthetics: Lectures and Essays*, ed. Elizabeth M. Wilkinson (London: Bowes and Bowes, 1957). This essay was first published in 1912. This volume also contains the lectures on "The Modern Conception of Aesthetics"

that Bullough delivered annually at Cambridge from 1907 until his death in 1934. Oakeshott's obituary for Bullough can be found in *The Caian* 43 (Michaelmas term, 1934): 1–11.

16. Bullough, " 'Psychical Distance,' " 93–94.

17. Grant, *Oakeshott*, 107–8.

18. John Keats, "The Fall of Hyperion," Canto I, lines 187–90.

19. R. G. Collingwood, *The Idea of History* (Oxford: Clarendon Press, 1946), 213–15; on the doctrine of historical reenactment, see 282–302.

20. Oakeshott, Review of *The Idea of History*, 84–85.

21. Oakeshott, "Mr. Carr's First Volume," *Cambridge Journal* 4 (1950–51): 350; see also Oakeshott's review of *An Introduction to Philosophy of History*, by W. H. Walsh, *Philosophical Quarterly* 2 (1952): 277. Marc Bloch, in *The Historian's Craft*, trans. Peter Putnam (New York: Alfred E. Knopf, 1953), makes similar claims about the superiority of the historian's understanding of the past to that of any participant in it (see, e.g., 50). This view of Bloch's has recently been invoked by John Lewis Gaddis, who uses Caspar David Friedrich's painting of *The Wanderer above the Sea of Clouds* to capture the wider perspective of the historian; see *The Landscape of History: How Historians Map the Past* (Oxford: Oxford University Press, 2002), 4–5.

22. Leo Strauss, "On Collingwood's Philosophy of History," *Review of Metaphysics* 5 (1952): 573–85.

23. Ibid., 561–64, 566–74.

24. See Karl Popper, *The Open Society and Its Enemies* (London: Routledge, 1945), ch. 25 and *The Poverty of Historicism* (Boston:

Beacon, 1957). In both the former work (vol. 2, 342 n7) and the latter work (144 n), Popper claimed authorship of the covering law model of explanation.

25. Carl Hempel, "The Function of General Laws in History," *Journal of Philosophy* 39 (1942): 35–48.

26. See Morton White, "Historical Explanation," *Mind* 52 (1943): 212–29; Patrick Gardiner, *The Nature of Historical Explanation* (Oxford: Oxford University Press, 1952); William Dray, *Laws and Explanation in History* (London: Oxford University Press, 1957); Maurice Mandelbaum, "Historical Explanation: The Problem of 'Covering Laws,' " *History and Theory* 1 (1961): 229–42; W. B. Gallie, *Philosophy and the Historical Understanding* (London: Chatto and Windus, 1964); Arthur Danto, *Analytical Philosophy of History* (Cambridge: Cambridge University Press, 1965). *Theories of History*, ed. Patrick Gardiner (Glencoe: Free Press, 1959) is an anthology that contains a number of essays relevant to this issue.

27. Isaiah Berlin, "Historical Inevitability," in Berlin, *The Proper Study of Mankind* (New York: Farrar, Strauss and Giroux, 1997), 121–45.

28. Ibid., 145–49, 156–70; see also Berlin, "The Concept of Scientific History," in *The Proper Study of Mankind*, 41–58.

29. On the debate between Berlin and Carr, see Mehta, *Fly and the Fly-Bottle*, 123–30; Jonathan Haslam, *The Vices of Integrity: E. H. Carr, 1892–1982* (London: Verso, 1999), 196–203.

30. E. H. Carr, *What Is History?* (New York: Vintage, 1961), 10–11, 23–26, 42, 54, 113–43, 158–76.

31. Isaiah Berlin, "Mr. Carr's Big Battalions," *New Statesman*, 5 January 1962, 15–16.

32. Oakeshott, "Mr. Carr's First Volume," 345–46.
33. Ibid., 346–50. Oakeshott refers explicitly to Collingwood's doctrine of reenactment in a review written one year later, arguing that "the main difficulty of this view [is] that an historical account of the past at least purports to present something which was never in the mind of anybody at the time; the historian at least appears to have a way of thinking about the past which would have been impossible for anyone who lived in that past" (Review of Walsh, 277).
34. Oakeshott, Review of *The Origins of Modern Science, 1300–1800*, by Herbert Butterfield, *Times Literary Supplement*, 25 November 1949, 761–63.
35. Oakeshott, Review of *George III and the Historians*, by Herbert Butterfield, *Spectator*, 22 November 1957, 718.

6   Civil Association

1. Quoted in Minogue, "Michael Oakeshott (1901–1990)."
2. He actually expressed his disappointment in two letters to Noel O'Sullivan, of 26 June 1975 and 28 July 1975. In the second letter, he complained that *OHC* had been misunderstood by many reviewers, especially the one who claimed "there was not much argument" in the book.
3. Alan Ryan, Review of *On Human Conduct*, in *The Listener*, 17 April 1975, 517–18.
4. Hanna Pitkin, "Inhuman Conduct and Unpolitical Theory: Michael Oakeshott's *On Human Conduct*," *Political Theory* 4 (August 1976): 302.
5. G. J. Warnock, "The Minefields of Moral Philosophy: Oakeshott,

Hampshire, Kenny," *Encounter* 46 (April 1976): 84–85. Warnock's wife, the philosopher Mary Warnock, wrote an equally negative and uncomprehending review of *OHC*, in *New Society*, 1 May 1975, 288. She too complained that the reader of the book "will be disappointed if he hopes for arguments."
6. See Winch's criticisms of Oakeshott's notions of habit and tradition in *The Idea of a Social Science*, 54–65. In "On Misunderstanding Human Conduct," *Political Theory* 4 (August 1976): 364, Oakeshott remarks that in *OHC* he has "abandoned 'tradition' as inadequate to express what I want to express."
7. See Oakeshott, "On Misunderstanding Human Conduct," 363.
8. This passage echoes Iris Murdoch's critique, in *The Sovereignty of Good* (London: Routledge and Kegan Paul, 1970), of the picture of the self as an isolated and empty choosing will found in existentialism and much analytic philosophy (e.g. Stuart Hampshire). It also anticipates Michael Sandel's critique of the "unencumbered self."
9. Oakeshott, "On Misunderstanding Human Conduct," 366.
10. Lon Fuller, "Positivism and Fidelity to Law," *Harvard Law Review* 71 (1958): 644–48; *The Morality of Law* (New Haven: Yale University Press, 1969), esp. ch. 2.
11. For Kant's distinction between law and morality, see the Introduction to the *Metaphysics of Morals*. H. L. A. Hart draws the distinction between laws and morals in a similar fashion to Oakeshott, see *The Concept of Law* (Oxford: Clarendon Press, 1961), 163–76.
12. I borrow the phrase "standards of civility" from Shirley Letwin's essay "Morality and Law," *Encounter* 35

(November 1974): 35–43, which provides a plausibly Oakeshottian treatment of this theme.

13. Judith Shklar, "Purposes and Procedures," *Times Literary Supplement*, 12 September 1975, 1018.

14. John Liddington, "Oakeshott: Freedom in a Modern European State," in *Conceptions of Liberty in Political Philosophy*, ed. Z. Pelczynski and John Gray (New York: St Martin's Press, 1984), 313. See also John Gray, "Oakeshott on Law, Liberty, and Civil Association," in Gray, *Liberalisms: Essays in Political Philosophy* (London: Routledge, 1989), 210–11.

15. See Richard Friedman's helpful essay "What Is a Non-Instrumental Law?" *Political Science Reviewer* 21 (Spring 1992), esp. 96–98.

16. The obvious reference in the final passage is to C. B. Macpherson's *The Political Theory of Possessive Individualism* (1962). But Oakeshott's criticism also applies to Leo Strauss, who saw Hobbes as the author of a new, bourgeois morality and interpreted the liberal tradition largely in this light. See Strauss, *The Political Philosophy of Hobbes*, ch. 7; *Natural Right and History* (Chicago: University of Chicago Press, 1953), 189; *What Is Political Philosophy?*, 48.

17. In a review of *Philosophy, Politics and Society (Second Series)*, edited by Peter Laslett and W. G. Runciman, Oakeshott actually spent several paragraphs discussing Rawls's early article "Justice as Fairness," calling it possibly "the most brilliant essay in the book"; *Philosophical Quarterly* 15 (1965): 281–82.

18. Letter to Noel O'Sullivan, 6 March 1982. The letter continues: "I have not yet got far into it, but it begins with the best criticism I have seen of Rawls and Dworkin, and in spite of its *isms* I don't think I am going to

be altogether disappointed. I could have done without the 'Liberalism' part, but no American writer can avoid it."

19. Gray, *Two Faces of Liberalism*, 2.

20. John Rawls, *Political Liberalism* (New York: Columbia University Press, 1993), 42 n44.

21. See, for example, Amy Guttman and Dennis Thompson, *Democracy and Disagreement* (Cambridge: Harvard University Press, 1996).

22. In *Liberalism and Its Critics*, ed. Michael Sandel (New York: New York University Press, 1984).

23. Stephen Macedo, *Liberal Virtues: Citizenship, Virtue, and Community in Liberal Constitutionalism* (Oxford: Oxford University Press, 1990), 22–25, 40–59, 215–27, 251, 269–70, 282–83. See also what Macedo says about "liberalism with a spine" in his more recent *Diversity and Distrust: Civic Education in a Multicultural Democracy* (Cambridge: Harvard University Press, 2000).

24. Joseph Raz, *The Morality of Freedom* (Oxford: Clarendon Press, 1986), 133, 213–14, 417.

25. William Galston, *Liberal Purposes: Goods, Virtues, and Diversity in the Liberal State* (Cambridge: Cambridge University Press, 1991), 3.

26. Ibid., 89 and ch. 8 in general.

27. William Galston, *Liberal Pluralism: The Implications of Value Pluralism for Political Theory and Practice* (Cambridge: Cambridge University Press, 2002).

28. Gray, *Two Faces of Liberalism*, 32–33, 53; see also "Berlin, Oakeshott and Enlightenment," in Gray, *Endgames: Questions in Late Modern Political Thought* (Cambridge: Polity Press, 1997), 86–91.

29. Isaiah Berlin, "The Originality of Machiavelli," in *The Proper Study of Mankind*, 320.

30. Isaiah Berlin, "Two Concepts of Liberty," in *The Proper Study of Mankind,* 239.

31. John Gray, *Isaiah Berlin* (Princeton: Princeton University Press, 1996), 159–61.

32. Berlin, "Two Concepts of Liberty," 198; "The Pursuit of the Ideal," in *The Proper Study of Mankind,* 15.

33. See, for example, the famous concluding paragraph of "Two Concepts of Liberty," where Berlin remarks that "it may be that the ideal of freedom to choose ends without claiming eternal validity for them, and the pluralism of values connected with this, is only the late fruit of our declining capitalist civilization: an ideal which remote ages and primitive societies have not recognized," etc. (242; see also 201).

34. Berlin, "Two Concepts of Liberty," 240.

35. Ibid., 235–37.

36. Richard Rorty, *Contingency, Irony, and Solidarity* (Cambridge: Cambridge University Press, 1989), 45–51, 57, 60.

37. Ibid., 58–60.

38. See Richard Rorty, "Postmodernist Bourgeois Liberalism," *Journal of Philosophy* 80 (1983): 583–89.

39. Rorty, *Contingency, Irony, and Solidarity,* xv, 45.

40. Richard Bernstein, "One Step Forward, Two Steps Backward: Richard Rorty on Liberal Democracy and Philosophy," *Political Theory* 15 (November 1987), 545–46.

41. Richard Rorty, "Thugs and Theorists: A Reply to Bernstein," *Political Theory* 15 (November 1987): 564–80.

42. Richard Rorty, *Philosophy and the Mirror of Nature* (Princeton: Princeton University Press, 1979), 381; *Consequences of Pragmatism* (Minneapolis: University of Minnesota Press, 1982), xxxvii–xliv. For a particularly egregious example of Rorty's pragmatist understanding of philosophical truth, see "Thugs and Theorists," 577 n20, where he claims "that the only argument for a theory of the self that I can offer is that it suits the political purposes of us social democrats." He then goes on to endorse Roberto Unger's slogan—anathema to Oakeshott—that "everything is politics."

Epilogue

1. Mark Lilla, "Inside the Clockwork," *New York Review of Books,* 25 April 2002, 43.

Further Reading

The most comprehensive bibliography of writings both by and about Oakeshott has been compiled by John Liddington in *The Achievement of Michael Oakeshott*, ed. Jesse Norman (London: Duckworth, 1992). An updated version of this bibliography can be found at the Michael Oakeshott Association website (www.michael-oakeshott-association.org). At this same website, there is a link to the online catalog of the collection of Oakeshott materials at the archive of the British Library of Political and Economic Science at the London School of Economics and Political Science. A list of Oakeshott's most important writings can be found in the Abbreviations at the head of this book. I have listed below only a very select bibliography of secondary writings on Oakeshott to serve as a guide for further reading.

Books

Coats, Jr., Wendell John, *Oakeshott and His Contemporaries: Montaigne, St. Augustine, Hegel, et al.* (Selinsgrove: Susquehanna University Press, 2000).

Devigne, Robert, *Recasting Conservatism: Oakeshott, Strauss, and the Response to Postmodernism* (New Haven and London: Yale University Press, 1994).

Franco, Paul, *The Political Philosophy of Michael Oakeshott* (New Haven and London: Yale University Press, 1990).

Gerencser, Steven, *The Skeptic's Oakeshott* (New York: St Martin's Press, 2000).

Grant, Robert, *Oakeshott* (London: Claridge Press, 1990).

Greenleaf, W. H., *Oakeshott's Philosophical Politics* (London: Longmans, 1966).

Nardin, Terry, *The Philosophy of Michael Oakeshott* (University Park: Pennsylvania State Press, 2001).

Imprint Academic has begun to publish a series of revised dissertations on Oakeshott, of which the following titles have appeared already or are about to appear:

O'Sullivan, Luke, *Oakeshott on History* (2003).

Podoksik, Efraim, *In Defence of Modernity: Vision and Philosophy in Michael Oakeshott* (2003).

Sullivan, Andrew, *Intimations Pursued: The Voice of Practice in the Conversation of Michael Oakeshott* (forthcoming).

Tregenza, Ian, *Michael Oakeshott on Hobbes* (2003).

Tseng, Roy, *The Sceptical Idealist: Michael Oakeshott as a Critic of the Enlightenment* (2003).

Worthington, Glenn, *Religious and Poetic Experience in the Thought of Michael Oakeshott* (forthcoming).

Collections

The Achievement of Michael Oakeshott, ed. Jesse Norman (London: Duckworth, 1993).

"In Memoriam: Michael Oakeshott, 1901–1990," *Political Theory* 19 (August 1991): 323–35.

Michael Oakeshott, Philosopher: A Commemoration of the Centenary of Oakeshott's Birth, ed. Leslie Marsh (London: Michael Oakeshott Association, 2001).

"Morality, Politics, and Law in the Thought of Michael Oakeshott," ed. Timothy Fuller, *Political Science Reviewer* 21 (Spring 1992): 1–147.

Politics and Experience: Essays Presented to Professor Oakeshott on the Occasion of his

Retirement, ed. Preston King and Bhikhu Parekh (Cambridge: Cambridge University Press, 1968).

"Remembering Michael Oakeshott," *Cambridge Review* 112 (October 1991): 99–124.

"A Symposium on Michael Oakeshott," *Political Theory* 4 (August 1976): 261–367.

Articles and Book Chapters

Annan, Noel, "The Deviants—Michael Oakeshott," in *Our Age: English Intellectuals Between the Wars—A Group Portrait* (London: Weidenfeld and Nicolson, 1990), 387–401.

Auspitz, J. L., "Individuality, Civility, and Theory: The Philosophical Imagination of Michael Oakeshott," *Political Theory* 4 (August 1976): 261–94.

—— "Michael Oakeshott: 1901–1990," *American Scholar* 60 (1990–91): 351–70.

Coats, Jr., Wendell John, "Michael Oakeshott as Liberal Theorist," *Canadian Journal of Political Science* 18 (December 1985): 773–87.

Covell, Charles, *The Redefinition of Conservatism: Politics and Doctrine* (New York: St Martin's Press, 1986), 93–143.

Cowling, Maurice, *Religion and Public Doctrine in Modern England* (Cambridge: Cambridge University Press, 1980), 251–82.

Cranston, Maurice, "Michael Oakeshott's Politics," *Encounter* 28 (January 1967): 82–86.

Crick, Bernard, "The World of Michael Oakeshott: Or the Lonely Nihilist," *Encounter* 20 (June 1963): 65–74.

Flathman, Richard, *The Practice of Political Authority* (Chicago: University of Chicago Press, 1980), esp. chs 2–4.

Franco, Paul, "Michael Oakeshott as Liberal Theorist," *Political Theory* 18 (August 1990): 411–36.

—— "Oakeshott's Critique of Rationalism Revisited," *Political Science Reviewer* 21 (Spring 1992): 15–43.

—— "Oakeshott, Berlin, and Liberalism," *Political Theory* 31 (August 2003): 484–507.

Friedman, Richard, "Oakeshott on the Authority of the Law," *Ratio Juris* 2 (1989): 27–40.

—— "What Is a Non-Instrumental Law?" *Political Science Reviewer* 21 (Spring 1992): 81–98.

Fuller, Timothy, "Authority and the Individual in Civil Association: Oakeshott, Flathman, and Yves Simon," in *Authority Revisited* (Nomos 29), ed. J. R. Pennock and J. W. Chapman (New York: New York University Press, 1987), 131–51.

Grant, Robert, "Michael Oakeshott," in *Cambridge Minds*, ed. Richard Mason (Cambridge: Cambridge University Press, 1994), 218–37.

Gray, John, "Oakeshott on Law, Liberty and Civil Association," in *Liberalisms: Essays in Political Philosophy* (London: Routledge, 1989), 199–216.

—— "Berlin, Oakeshott and Enlightenment," in *Endgames: Questions in Late Modern Political Thought* (Cambridge: Polity Press, 1997), 84–96.

Himmelfarb, Gertrude, "The Conservative Imagination: Michael Oakeshott," *American Scholar* 44 (Summer 1975): 405–20.

Johnson, Nevil, "Michael Joseph Oakeshott, 1901–1990," *Proceedings of the British Academy* 80 (1993): 403–23.

Letwin, Shirley, "Morality and Law," *Encounter* 43 (November 1974): 35–43.

Liddington, John, "Oakeshott: Freedom in a Modern European State," in *Conceptions of Liberty in Political Philosophy*, ed. Z. Pelczynski and John Gray (New York: St Martin's Press, 1984), 289–320.

Minogue, Kenneth, "Michael Oakeshott: The Boundless Sea of Politics," in *Contemporary Political Philosophers*, ed.

Anthony de Crespigny and Kenneth Minogue (New York: Dodd Mead, 1975), 120–46.

Modood, Tariq, "Oakeshott's Conceptions of Philosophy," *History of Political Thought* 1 (1980): 315–22.

O'Sullivan, Luke, "Michael Oakeshott on European History," *History of Political Thought* 21 (Spring 2000): 132–51.

O'Sullivan, Noel, Obituary for Michael Oakeshott, *Independent*, 22 December 1990, 10.

Parekh, Bhikhu, "Michael Oakeshott," in *Contemporary Political Thinkers* (Baltimore: Johns Hopkins University Press, 1982), 96–123.

——"Oakeshott's Theory of Civil Association," *Ethics* 106 (October 1995): 158–86.

Pitkin, Hanna, "The Roots of Conservatism: Michael Oakeshott and the Denial of Politics," *Dissent* 20 (1973): 496–525.

Postan, Munia, "The Revulsion from Thought," *Cambridge Journal* (1948–49): 395–408.

Rayner, Jeremy, "The Legend of Oakeshott's Conservatism: Skeptical Philosophy and Limited Politics," *Canadian Journal of Political Science* 18 (June 1985): 313–38.

Watkins, J. W. N., "Political Tradition and Political Theory," *Philosophical Quarterly* 2 (1952): 323–37.

Worthington, Glenn, "The Voice of Poetry in Oakeshott's Moral Philosophy," *Review of Politics* 64 (Spring 2002): 285–310.

Index